Praise for *The World Is Curved*

"David Smick understands, as few do, that international finance depends on politics and passions as much as on policies. Agree or disagree, his sense of where we have been and where we are going deserves close attention. He writes in a way that makes giving close attention a pleasure."

—**Lawrence H. Summers,** director, National Economic Council

"*The World Is Curved* is an essential read for those who wish to understand the workings, politics, and distresses of the global financial system. David Smick has done an outstanding job in drawing on his interactions with many of the key players in international finance to produce an insightful and entertaining book."

—**Alan Greenspan,** former chairman of the Federal Reserve Board; author of *The Age of Turbulence*

"Smick is a world-class thinker. Any serious investor must read what he has to say."

—**Barton M. Biggs,** Traxis Partners; author of *Hedgehogging* and *Wealth, War, and Wisdom*

"*The World Is Curved* makes transparent all the challenges facing today's new global economy. Read along while Smick exposes the hidden global economic dangers and what steps must be taken to correct an imperfect system."

—**Bill Bradley,** former U.S. senator

"*The World Is Curved* affords an engrossing look at the edifice upon which global finance has been built. It's a vision we ignore at our peril."

—**George P. Shultz,** former U.S. secretary of state

"This is a very inspiring and intellectually stimulating book that makes remarkably transparent a number of factors behind the booms and busts of today's global finance."

—**Jean-Claude Trichet,** president, European Central Bank

"*The World Is Curved* is a brilliant, if disturbing, exposé of today's global financial minefields and an equally compelling description of possible remedies. The next president would do well to read this book."

—**Lawrence Eagleburger,** former U.S. secretary of state

"David Smick's probing insights in *The World Is Curved* stem from an extraordinary vantage point few observers can match."

—**George Soros,** Soros Fund Management

"*The World Is Curved* presents a brilliant picture. It is a must-read for investors, policymakers, and anyone worried about the challenges facing today's global financial system."

—**Stan Druckenmiller,** Duquesne Capital Management

"David Smick, who founded *The International Economy* and made it into a highly respected magazine on world economic affairs, now offers us a trenchant and timely analysis of the downside of financial globalization. Capital flows are the soft underbelly of globalization, and no one who values the enormous benefits of globalization of trade and multinational direct investments can afford to miss out on reading this important book."

—**Jagdish Bhagwati**, Columbia University; author of *In Defense of Globalization*

"There are at least three reasons to read this book. First, it is an incredibly thoughtful insight into the workings of global finance, written by the ultimate insider in a highly engaging way that any reader of the *New York Times* could easily digest. Second, its central theme about the extreme fragility of the world economy will keep you up at night and force you to think hard about issues that are not yet out in public. And third, it provides a realistic road map out of the horrendous mess we are in, one that should capture the attention of policymakers, financiers, and yes, even the next American president."

—**Jeffrey E. Garten**, Yale School of Management; former U.S. undersecretary of commerce for international trade; former managing director, Blackstone Group

"Lively, well written, and insightful, *The World Is Curved* by David Smick probes and thoughtfully examines the strains and imbalances in the global economy and international financial markets. Smick also presents a series of innovative recommendations and observations designed to address the problems he describes, and challenges us to come to grips with them before they worsen."

—**Robert Hormats**, vice chairman, Goldman Sachs International

"This book is excellent. It is hard to read *The World Is Curved* without being concerned by recent trends. David Smick offers a thoughtful and readable analysis of globalization's flaws and benefits. This is an important book."

—**Frank C. Carlucci**, former U.S. secretary of defense

"David Smick knows as much about world financial markets as any man alive today. In his fascinating (or maybe terrifying) book, *The World Is Curved*, he lays out the potential for disaster in this new, intricate, global financial marketplace. This book is an easy read even though it deals with unbelievably complicated (i.e., 'curved') subjects."

—**William Seidman**, chief financial commentator, CNBC; former chairman, Federal Deposit Insurance Corporation

"David Smick has identified a dangerous gap that separates the policy world and the financial world. *The World Is Curved* will go a long way toward bridging that gap, which is essential to ensure stability and prosperity in the global economy."

—**Lee H. Hamilton**, president and director, Woodrow Wilson International Center for Scholars

"David Smick's *The World Is Curved* couldn't have come at a better moment. I couldn't lay the book down. It offers an unusually knowledgeable insight into the world of international finance. *The World Is Curved* is highly relevant to today's situation."

—**Karl Otto Pöhl**, former president, Deutsche Bundesbank

"Smick's dos and don'ts for future economic policymakers are so readable, they can be easily understood by those without economic degrees."

—**Carla Hills**, co-chair, Council on Foreign Relations; former U.S. trade representative

"David Smick is a fascinating tour guide to the construction of our present financial system over the last three decades. He takes us from the financial salons of Europe to the Asian bureaucratic ministries of unfathomable wealth to the back rooms of the Washington power elites to the chaotic trading rooms of Wall Street. It is a great read."

—**Louis Bacon**, Moore Capital Management

"David Smick turned *The International Economy* magazine into the must-read magazine on world economic affairs. He does the same with globalization in *The World Is Curved*. Globalization is the game changer of our time, and David Smick's insights on global capital flows are significant. Anyone who wants to understand financial globalization and its policy implications will want to read this book."

—**R. Glenn Hubbard**, dean, Columbia University Graduate School of Business

"David Smick has written a first-class book on 'possible dangers' of globalization. I found it difficult to put it down."

—**A. W. Clausen**, former president, World Bank

"A timely and important analysis, *The World Is Curved* offers a whirlwind tour of the dynamics across the globe that are driving the gears of the world's financial markets. Accessible and instructive for layperson and policymaker alike."

—**Yoichi Funabashi**, editor in chief, *Asahi Shimbun*

"*The World Is Curved* examines the fragile international financial system and finds it rather treacherous and not easy to fix. Rather than being flat, our new globalized world is rather bumpy."

—**James Schlesinger**, former U.S. secretary of energy, secretary of defense, and director of central intelligence

"David Smick takes the reader into the inner sanctum of the global financial system as no one else can. With riveting stories, Smick leaves no doubt that this complex system has created huge benefits but has left us facing grave risks. And he offers a solution."

—**John B. Taylor**, Stanford University

"David Smick is right: The global world *is* curved. We cannot foresee the precise future, especially not in crisis situations."

—**Hans Tietmeyer**, former president, Deutsche Bundesbank

"A worthy successor to Tom Friedman's *The World Is Flat*. *The World Is Curved* takes up where Friedman left off, lucidly explaining the vital but poorly understood role of the financial system that provides the essential underpinnings of the world economy."

—**Murray Weidenbaum**, Washington University

"The world *is* curved. Even a high-flying satellite can see no more than half of it at a time. But David Smick takes us to both sides—from Washington to Beijing and beyond."

—**Peter B. Kenen**, Princeton University

"*The World Is Curved* makes for fascinating reading, showing how politics and economics are inseparably intermingled. A bright analysis of risk, success, and failure in today's global financial markets."

—**Otmar Issing**, former member of the executive board, European Central Bank

"*The World Is Curved* is thoughtful, balanced, and provocative—a must-read."

—**Pedro Pablo Kuczynski**, former prime minister, Peru

"A lucid, informed, and insightful interpretation of the global financial system. Readers . . . are guaranteed to be entertained and provoked."

—**Edwin (Ted) M. Truman**, former director, International Finance Division, Federal Reserve

"The consummate insider's account of global capital markets. Truly informative and most entertaining. *The World Is Curved* reveals . . . why the next thirty years will be just as perilous as the past."

—**Gary Clyde Hufbauer**, Peterson Institute for International Economics

"An insightful insider's tour of the global economy and financial system. Readers will have a big head start in diagnosing the problem and devising sensible solutions."

—**Michael J. Boskin**, Stanford University

"In *The World Is Curved*, David Smick treats us to a vision of the uncertainties in financial markets as the American Century drifts to its end."

—**Allan Meltzer**, Carnegie Mellon University

"Both insightful and provocative in discussing a dominant contemporary question— where do we go from here?"

—**Michael Steinhardt**, Steinhardt Management

"Over the last thirty years, David Smick has had a unique front-row seat at the revolution in global finance. If you want a clear explanation of what's going on in the revolution in global finance, read *The World Is Curved*."

—**Peter R. Fisher**, former vice president, Federal Reserve Bank of New York

"*The World Is Curved* is by far the nearest thing to a consummate insider's guide to today's financial world as can be found outside of a central bank."

—**John Williamson**, Peterson Institute for International Economics

"I always look forward to conversations with David Smick. He never repeats the conventional wisdom, and he always has a new and provocative take on what's going on in our political economy. Now he's distilled his thoughts into an important book. You'll enjoy reading *The World Is Curved*, you'll learn from it—and most important, it really will make you think."

—**William Kristol**, *The Weekly Standard*

"Financial innovations, including those that new electronic technology makes possible, enable both firms and individuals to carry out their ordinary business more effectively and to protect themselves better from the risks to which they are inevitably exposed. But these innovations also make it possible for both firms and individuals to take on new risks to which they never would have been exposed in the first place. What are meant to be improvements, therefore, sometimes make people worse off, and when the risks involved are sufficiently intertwined, those supposed improvements can make people worse off who never even sought to take advantage of them. In *The World Is Curved*, David Smick deftly offers example after example of how just this process of unintended consequences has recently unsettled the world's financial markets, and how the process may not be over yet."

—**Benjamin M. Friedman**, Harvard University; author of *The Moral Consequences of Economic Growth*

"The world is indeed curved, and I can think of no better guide to the global capital markets of the twenty-first century than David Smick. The book takes you through Smick's personal journey over the past thirty years as an adviser to investors, hedge funds, central bankers, and policymakers. After reading this book, you will appreciate as perhaps never before the sweep of recent financial history and the risks that lie ahead."

—**Richard H. Clarida**, Columbia University; PIMCO; former U.S. assistant secretary of the Treasury

"*The World Is Curved* intonates today's global financial issues in a dramatic, quasi-Beethoven style."

—**Norbert Walter**, Deutsche Bank Group

"David Smick is a pioneer in the globalization of real-time information. Who better to present us with the most recent and relevant information on globalization?"

—**Ron Insana**, Insana Capital Partners; CNBC senior analyst

THE WORLD IS CURVED

David M. Smick advises some of the world's most successful money managers through his investment and strategic consulting firm, Johnson Smick International, Inc. He is also the founder, editor, and publisher of *The International Economy*, an acclaimed quarterly. He has served as an adviser to presidential candidates and has written for such publications as *The Wall Street Journal*, *The Washington Post*, and *The New York Times*.

THE WORLD
IS CURVED

---

*Hidden Dangers to
the Global Economy*

DAVID M. SMICK

PORTFOLIO

PORTFOLIO

Published by the Penguin Group

Penguin Group (USA) Inc., 375 Hudson Street, New York, New York 10014, U.S.A.
Penguin Group (Canada), 90 Eglinton Avenue East, Suite 700, Toronto, Ontario,
Canada M4P 2Y3 (a division of Pearson Penguin Canada Inc.)
Penguin Books Ltd, 80 Strand, London WC2R 0RL, England
Penguin Ireland, 25 St Stephen's Green, Dublin 2, Ireland (a division of Penguin Books Ltd)
Penguin Group (Australia), 250 Camberwell Road, Camberwell, Victoria 3124, Australia
(a division of Pearson Australia Group Pty Ltd)
Penguin Books India Pvt Ltd, 11 Community Centre, Panchsheel Park,
New Delhi – 110 017, India
Penguin Group (NZ), 67 Apollo Drive, Rosedale, North Shore 0632, New Zealand
(a division of Pearson New Zealand Ltd)
Penguin Books (South Africa) (Pty) Ltd, 24 Sturdee Avenue, Rosebank,
Johannesburg 2196, South Africa

Penguin Books Ltd, Registered Offices: 80 Strand, London WC2R 0RL, England

First published in the United States of America by Portfolio, a member of
Penguin Group (USA) Inc. 2008

This edition with a new epilogue published 2009

5 7 9 10 8 6 4

Copyright © David M. Smick, 2008, 2009
All rights reserved

THE LIBRARY OF CONGRESS HAS CATALOGED THE HARDCOVER EDITION AS FOLLOWS:
Smick, David M.
The world is curved : hidden dangers to the global economy / David M. Smick.
p. cm.
Includes bibliographical references and index.
ISBN 978-1-59184-218-7 (hc.)
ISBN 978-1-59184-290-3 (pbk.)
1. International finance.   2. Financial crises.   3. Globalization—Economic aspects.
4. International economic relations.   I. Title.
HG3881.S5397 2008
337—dc22   2008019435

Printed in the United States of America
Set in Janson Text
Designed by Victoria Hartman

To my wife, Vickie,
and to Peter, Sarah, and DJ

Contents

Prologue

I t was not without enormous frustration that I approached writing a book about today's new global economy. After all, what do we make of a world financial system that one minute appeared to be performing beautifully, and the next acted as if the world is coming to an end? One minute the cybernetic (computer) revolution has transformed the economy into a veritable global wealth machine, as stock markets around the world soared to new highs. The next moment, markets plummeted. People then read newspaper stories suggesting the value of their home was less than their mortgage. They discover that their family's life savings—even their cash left in supposedly ultra-safe money market funds—could soon go poof in the night.

In trying to fully grasp the significance of the new global system, I began by rereading the seminal book on the subject of globalization, Tom Friedman's bestseller *The World Is Flat: A Brief History of the Twenty-first Century*. Friedman compellingly describes globalization *as it is*, with concentration on the global supply chain for goods and services. The stories are mesmerizing—taking the reader from India's Silicon Valley in Bangalore to villages in northeastern China. Friedman's book describes how digital technology shortened the distances between countries and revolutionized the global supply chain. This permitted people to engage in business with one another across the globe, with each nation bringing its comparative advantage to the table of world commerce. An award-winning columnist for the *New York Times*, Friedman wisely warns that the U.S. economy must adapt to this new and changing environment or retrench economically. The book stands as a historic achievement in introducing a broad audience to the new world of opportunity and challenges beyond national borders.

After rereading *The World Is Flat*, I had lunch one day at the Hay-Adams Hotel in Washington, D.C., just across from the White House, with an old friend, John Despres, who had been Democratic U.S. senator Bill Bradley's longtime foreign policy guru. "John," I said as we were being seated, "I am trying with great frustration to get my arms around globalization. Frankly speaking, from the perspective of the financial markets, the world is *not* flat. Unlike the world that produces goods and services, in the financial world nothing happens in a straight line. Instead, there is a continual series of unforeseen discontinuities— twists and turns of uncertainty that often require millions of market participants to stand conventional wisdom on its head. In the financial world, John, nothing much seems to happen in a straight line."

A pensive man in his sixties who chooses his words carefully, Despres sat there thoughtfully. He stroked his chin, pondering as he gazed off into the distance past Lafayette Park to the front columns of the White House. "So what you're saying," he slowly began, pausing for several more seconds, "is that the world is not flat; the world is curved."

"Yes," I responded, "for the financial markets, the world is curved. We can't see over the horizon. As a result, our sight lines are limited. It is as if we are forced to travel down an endless, dangerously twisting and turning road with abrupt steep valleys and risky mountainous climbs. We can't see ahead. We are always being surprised, and that is why the world has become such a dangerous place."

By way of background, financial markets have always been plagued by uncertain and incomplete information—a lack of transparency. There have always been things that investors and traders didn't and couldn't know. But in the new global economy, this crazy ocean of global liquidity has not only increased the number of unknowns but also rearranged their relationships and relative importance.

There were new players with new perspectives. All of a sudden, a huge pool of leveraged funds was competing around the world for investment opportunities. Bankers, businesspeople, and governments in industrialized economies competed with entrepreneurs, start-ups, and old state-controlled companies in emerging economies to attract those funds. With new kinds of securitized debt, mezzanine investing, and outrageously complicated financing instruments, it became almost impossible to figure out what is going on at any given time. Investors needed new kinds of information to make good decisions. But exactly what kind of information is that? And where do they get it?

Financial markets have always operated on inequalities of information and analysis. You think or know A. I think or know B. But in recent years policymakers and market traders were forced to depend more than ever on their gut instincts. The playing field became bigger, the stakes higher, and the system, because of its leveraged size and complexity, turned unbelievably fragile. It became a house of cards that came tumbling down for a number of reasons. Today's collapse of those highly leveraged global financial markets followed by plummeting worldwide demand have taken us from an era of excess financial risk-taking to a situation that may be even more dangerous—no financial risk-taking. The future appears uncertain. We have experienced the deleveraging of the global financial system in which the value of virtually every asset in the world has been reappraised downward.

As the global financial system collapsed, suffocated by a lack of financial oxygen, economic chaos spread. Economies, particularly the emerging markets, found they had become dangerously dependent on exporting to a gluttonous, debt-ridden American consumer who, suddenly, had gone into hiding. A globally interconnected banking system went into cardiac arrest. All of these ugly developments left real questions about the future of the global economy itself.

After all, what do we really know about what is about to unfold in China, which has an economy that even its own leadership cannot fully understand? To what extent is China a social bubble in danger of further bursting? What do we know about the mind-set of the Japanese housewife who, as strange as it sounds, plays a huge part in the direction of the future flow of the world's savings? What about the political future of Europe's monetary union, burdened by a toxic-ridden banking system representing more than 300 percent of Europe's GDP? What do we still know about the accuracy of the accounting ledgers of even our largest, most trusted financial institutions or whether the sophisticated financial instruments these firms deploy should continue to exist? What do we know about the long-term strategic implications of today's enormous debt and the fact that excess savings are still being controlled by nondemocratic governments? And what are the social and political implications of global wealth continuing to be so unevenly distributed?

In addition, the markets lack information about what may be the most critical issue of all—whether the trend of globalization itself will be allowed to continue. The politics of globalization have exploded as the anxiety produced by the power of free-flowing capital and goods have skyrocketed. Amazingly, a recent *Wall Street Journal*/NBC poll revealed that in the United States, by a two-to-one majority, even Republicans believe free trade is hurting America. The troubling turbulence of the subprime-initiated Great Credit Crisis has created doubt about the viability of today's model of liberalized financial markets. Large segments of society distrust the financial sector and prefer more government say over the allocation of capital. Around the world, leaders flirt with beggar-thy-neighbor trade and currency policies as domestic constituencies react angrily to today's new austerity.

"Perhaps most troubling," I said as our lunch concluded, "is that most people today lack a historical perspective. The boom period was taken for granted. Median-age American voters today were born in the mid-1960s. They have no recollection of the stagflation and long gas lines of the 1970s, the period before today's globalized economy. Nor do they understand the fundamentals of the period that led to the Great Depression. They have never known anything but a highly productive economy, with impressive stock markets and ample jobs. Many key constituencies of globalization have been lulled into complacency. Therefore, the period ahead will be one of potentially imprudent, overly reactive policy change in a world potentially gone mad.

"To top it all off," I stressed to Despres, "policymakers don't appreciate the fragile nature of today's global financial system and how even our remaining prosperity can stealthily slip away through the unintended consequences of well-intentioned policy actions that attempt to legislate or regulate economic security. Today, we find ourselves in a situation in which the globalized financial system both enables and threatens our national well-being."

I concluded by suggesting that Friedman's book brilliantly presents the first installment of the globalization story, but there is a second installment as well—the financial side of the story. That's the subprime side where, for example, a small village in Arctic Norway can see its entire financial future destroyed because its financial managers invested heavily in a Citigroup product called a collateralized debt obligation. When the housing markets an ocean away in Florida and California collapsed, the debt obligations soured, and the Norwegian village had to shut down kindergartens and health care services for the elderly.

At the end of our conversation we turned to history, agreeing that nothing about the world's current political, economic, and financial predicament is new. Indeed, today's world economy bears a striking resemblance to the integrated markets and overwhelming prosperity of the period from 1870 to 1914, which noted economist John Maynard Keynes described as "an extraordinary episode in the economic progress of man." That, too, was a period punctuated by continual financial crises—and also of great prosperity. Ironically, today we ask the same questions as they did in 1914: What does it take to sustain this new, successful global economic system? What policymaking perils could reverse this wealth creation? Stagflation? Deflation? Protectionism? What unexpected financial explosion or implosion could create further waves—curves—that the world remains unprepared to handle except through trade wars, strict capital controls, and other beggar-thy-neighbor policies—all policy blunders resulting from human error?

Today's industrialized world wants the Chinese to better manage their currency but remains unsure of the precise policy prescription or even of the capabilities of the conflicted Chinese leadership. The world hates America's twin budget and current account deficits, but no one has yet figured a safe way out of them in today's climate of economic and financial collapse. Nor does it seem like an answer will come any time soon. Much of the world's excess savings sits in the hands of non-democratic regimes, led by China, but what this portends for the future, nobody knows. The industrialized world's debt is soaring while those excess savings are shrinking. The European and U.S. banking systems' toxic assets continue as a stranglehold on future economic growth. The Federal Reserve, in coming to the rescue of the financial sector, appears to have provided a de facto government guarantee of the investments of the entire financial sector, while offering unprecedented amounts of monetary stimulus. The long-term implications for regulatory oversight, and the level of lending and future inflation under this new policy are anybody's guess. We live in a globalized world where the economic model under which we have operated for more than two decades—the emerging market export model—is crash landing. But nobody has yet figured out the new model for prosperity.

In his book, Friedman warns American policymakers of the need for tax credits, improved teachers' salaries, and novel approaches to creating, attracting, and retaining the new creators of value—the engineers. Yet retaining the free flow of capital to keep globalization's bloodstream pumping may also require the most sophisticated team of global financial brain surgeons. That is because the world today lacks a financial doctrine, or even much in the way of a set of informal understandings, for establishing order in a financial crisis. Instead, we

have to grope and manage incrementally, like trying to perform delicate brain surgery with one hand tied behind our back and the other
wearing an ill-fitting boxing glove. The financial markets have simply
become too big, and at times too threatening, for our governmental
institutions to be fully effective in maintaining stability.

The 1870–1914 period, eerily similar to what we face today, met a
bitter new reality with the opening shots of World War I. Within a
decade and a half, capital and trade flows collapsed, which helped set
the stage for the Great Depression. Today one of the world's promi-
nent global monetary policy theorists, and a former governor of the
Federal Reserve, Frederic Mishkin, argues ominously that "the possibility of another Great Reversal is very real." Martin Wolf of the
Financial Times writes that "the breakdown of the early twentieth century occurred, in part, because of the pressures to accommodate rising
powers in the global economic and political order." He suggests that
today's rise of China and India will create comparable pressures—"a
spiral of mutual hostility that undermines the commitment to a liberal
international economic order."

Of course, the world won't necessarily cast some dramatic veto to
end the current system as we know it. Reversals seldom come in one
cruel, visible, planned policy blow. Instead, like death from a thousand
cuts, they come from a series of small, seemingly benign, but dangerously destabilizing changes that reach a terrifying tipping point of
market uncertainty and fear. Today we have reached that tipping point
and moved beyond. We are still at risk of further financial calamities
that threaten a vicious spiral of destruction and heartache.

I undertook the task of writing about this complicated system we
call the new global economy because I have had a front row seat, and
probably played some modest role in its creation. Over my thirty-year
career, I have watched the forces that created financial globalization
unfold, and I have consulted regularly with some of the major players
in the field of global finance. I feel obliged to share what I have learned
with those who have not been afforded such access.

Over the years, I first served as the chief of staff to a senior member of the U.S. congressional leadership, and then as an adviser on economic issues to both Democratic and Republican presidential candidates. For the last twenty years, I have worked with some of the world's most successful money managers, including George Soros, Michael Steinhardt, Louis Bacon, Stan Druckenmiller, and Julian Robertson, through my global macroeconomic advisory firm Johnson Smick International. We serve as specialized quasi journalists—like a paid cable TV service compared with free network television.

In addition, I founded and continue to edit *The International Economy*, a magazine geared to the global central bank and finance ministry community. I also conceived and organized the U.S. Congressional Summits on the Dollar and Trade, a series of important conferences in the late 1980s and 1990s involving the world's finance ministers, central bankers, and the U.S. congressional leadership.

For two decades I have interacted daily with the most senior economists and most visible market traders on the front lines of financial globalization. They have all been grappling with the same issue: how to survive and prosper in this troubling new system.

In January 2007, more than six months before the outbreak of the subprime crisis, I commented one evening to the other guests at a Washington dinner party that "the average person today would be shocked to know how much the global financial system, though robust, faces a potential risk to its own survival. It is vulnerable to a psychological herd effect that could wreak havoc with the industrialized world economies." On the drive home from the dinner party, my wife, Vickie, remarked, "You should write a book on the subject. If the central bankers and Wall Street know what's behind the curtain, why shouldn't everyone else? Why don't you say what all the big money players already know about how these uncertainties could affect all of us?"

I therefore credit my smarter half for recognizing the need for such a book, and for providing the needed spark that motivated me to take on this project.

1

The End of the World

There is nothing quite like the potential for the world economy's coming to an end to focus the mind and shake up a quiet summer. It was the morning of August 10, 2007, and I was chugging away on an exercise bike at the Westmoor Club on Nantucket, a vacation island off the coast of Massachusetts. Improbably piped overhead was Paul Simon singing "Slip Slidin' Away." On the wall, a soundless flat-screen television showed a gaggle of high-cheeked Victoria's Secret underwear models strangely giggling as they "opened" the New York Stock Exchange. The day before, the Dow Jones Industrial Average had crashed a whopping 387 points, nearly 3 percent. The previous night the Asian markets had plummeted, and by morning European markets were sinking by an even greater magnitude. The excited commentators on CNBC, the cable business channel, had reached a state of apoplexy.

The industrialized world was facing a full-fledged liquidity crisis, the Great Credit Crisis beginning in 2007–2008. In a flash, the world's banks and other financial institutions had stopped making loans. Across the globe, financial deals screeched to a halt. In the United

States, potential home buyers couldn't close on their purchases. The global financial system was slip sliding away. It was as if the body's blood had stopped pumping, and the patient, who had seemed healthy only a few days earlier, was slipping into a coma.

Financial market crises are not new to me. As a macroeconomic adviser to many of the big hedge funds and to the proprietary trading desks of some of the world's largest financial institutions, I remember vividly the tense, through-the-night telephone calls during the 1987 stock market crash.

Even the self-assured billionaire financier George Soros had, I recall, a slight tremor in his voice as we both realized that the bottom might be falling out of the world financial system. A decade later, in the fall of 1998, New York Federal Reserve president Bill McDonough nervously explained to a small audience (including me) that the collapse and subsequent market rescue of the trading firm Long-Term Capital Management had brought the world economy closer to the edge than anyone had realized.

As I sat on that exercise bike, leafing through some paperwork that had just been sent from my Washington, D.C., office, I focused on Paul Simon as he sang, "You know the nearer your destination, the more you're slip slidin' away." One of the papers offered a jarring quote. U.S. Treasury secretary Hank Paulson had recently declared: "This is far and away the strongest global economy I've seen in my business lifetime." Yet just that morning *New York Times* columnist Paul Krugman had suggested that the current credit crisis could cause a nightmare "chain reaction of debt defaults." Even worse, he said, policymakers were powerless to respond.

None of this makes sense, I thought. The markets had become hysterical over losses in the so-called subprime market, the relatively small market of mortgages and mortgage-related financial instruments tied to borrowers with no credit histories or abysmal ones. But why a near-global stock market meltdown and a collapse of lending simply because of some mortgage foreclosures? After all, the problem loans amounted to, at worst, $200 billion in exposure in a global market worth hundreds of trillions.

True, the global economy was in the process of de-leveraging—gradually reducing risk while a housing bubble deflated—but the markets had known that for months. The situation was perplexing. Why would the stock of the world's largest blue-chip companies, which can easily finance their own expansion internally without bank loans, be hit so hard initially by the subprime foreclosures? All of this was a development that should have represented a mere sideshow in the overall scheme of things.

Without a doubt, this would be an interesting day. Already the markets had been spooked earlier in the week when a spokesman for the French bank fund BNP Paribas announced confidently that it had no subprime exposure, then soon thereafter was forced to admit to an uncertain amount of unpriceable mortgages. This mysterious admission pounded both European and U.S. stock markets. It had raised the question: Why didn't the stock of BNP alone take the hit—why the massive losses throughout the industrialized world markets?

Within days the crisis had spread to the commercial paper market, long considered one of the safest bases of investment for money market mutual funds. That meant that middle America was now in trouble. Suddenly, the one market considered the safest, most liquid (non-government-related) investment in the world became suspect. The very foundation of the financial system faced a crisis of confidence. The lifeblood of the global system was suddenly at risk as investors poured their funds into the one short-term investment deemed trustworthy—three-month U.S. Treasury bills. Why is that dangerous? It means that the financial market's liquidity is drying up. When panicked in a similar way during the Great Depression, investors and savers stuffed their money into mattresses. Big corporations had parked their cash reserves in the commercial paper market.

Throughout that Friday in August, the craziness continued. The Federal Reserve responded by injecting $19 billion into the banking system to keep it afloat and allowed short-term interest rates to float down. This followed the previous day's Fed injection of $24 billion. A fearful European Central Bank injected a whopping 240 billion euros during the first stage of the crisis, believing the European banks were at serious risk. Yet by Tuesday of the following week, despite these infusions of emergency cash, the Dow continued to plummet—first by 207 points, then 167 the next day, then by 280 less than a week later. On Friday, August 17, a spooked Japanese stock market dropped by 874 points, more than 5 percent. Most world markets seemed in a state of free fall. Bond markets were in turmoil as money, distrustful of the private sector, poured further into Treasury bills.

Nobody trusted anybody, so suddenly nobody lent to anybody. The world's credit markets seized up as nobody was sure of their contingent liabilities. That's dangerous because if the private credit markets stop functioning, the entire economy is at risk—people lose jobs, their pensions dissolve, the net worth of average families immediately collapses as the price of their homes plummets below the price of their mortgage. Already the interest rate on consumer loans—automobiles, credit cards, and everything else—was soaring, meaning sooner or later the economy would take a hit.

As I began to reflect on this situation, I realized that, in essence, what really had happened was that American financial institutions had previously placed a large part of their bad subprime loans—their toxic waste—into separate holding facilities, divided the total sum into many smaller portions, and sold these pieces to financial institutions throughout Europe and Asia. Soon the toxic waste was sprinkled throughout the entire industrialized world's financial system, but nobody knew where. Now there was a reason for the rest of the world to hate America.

It is important to remember that the issue here was not the size of the subprime mess; the financial markets could figure that out. The issue was where the toxic waste was located. Who had the cancer and who was healthy? Ultimately, the issue was information, or the lack of it. And soon a skeptical global financial market would look beyond the subprime mortgage problem and begin to question the credibility of one of the main arteries of the global credit system, the asset-backed securities market.

The following Friday, the Federal Reserve took further action, cutting its discount rate while making available generous loans to the banking system. The goal: to place an emergency ring of safety around the U.S. banking sector based on the belief that if the banks collapsed, so would the U.S. economy. Small businesses would first feel the hit, but soon the entire real economy and the base of American employment would take a real hit. The Fed, still uncertain about which financial institutions held the most toxic waste, needed to stabilize the situation in order to buy time.

By the end of that week, I reflected further on the unexpected turn of events. A relatively minor development had mushroomed into something more, causing the U.S. stock market's value to decline by nearly 10 percent (before eventually recovering after the Federal Reserve cut interest rates). That amounts to a sudden, instant, nearly $2 trillion loss equal to nearly one-sixth the size of U.S. GDP (gross domestic product).

To add to this bizarre climate, in the middle of the crisis Ben Stein, the comedic actor (who is also an economist), wrote a much-talked-about article in the *New York Times* arguing that for most of the world the subprime exposure is so minuscule, the global reaction made no sense. "How are the risks in Thailand or Brazil or Indonesia intrinsically related to problems in a housing tract in Las Vegas? . . . Why should a mortgage company in Long Island have anything to do with them?" the actor/economist asked.

Part of the answer is that we live in an era of globalization where financial markets have been internationalized through an intricate web of financial engineering called securitization, a subject I will discuss in the next chapter. As Eric Jacobson of the Chicago research firm Morningstar put it, "There are so many interconnections today between different parts of the market that otherwise seem so disparate." But globalization fails to explain why, seemingly overnight, the financial markets appeared to split from reality, and what the ensuing chaos means for our future.

In the weeks after the outbreak of the crisis, I began to ponder what had happened. How could financial markets reflect a robust economy one moment (the best the U.S. Treasury secretary has experienced in his lifetime) before turning to panic the next? How could apparent calm turn to a genuine threat to the entire economic system virtually overnight?

The best metaphor I can summon is that global financial markets are a bit like a rich, generous, but occasionally deeply paranoid great-uncle. Normally, this benevolent great-uncle sprinkles money calmly and wisely throughout the family, taking a careful reading of risk and the potential investment reward relating to each family member's scenario. But, every so often, a deep, sudden feeling of paranoia overtakes him. Suddenly wary of the landscape, a panicked great-uncle cuts off the spigot of money. What precipitates the sudden paranoia? Nothing more and nothing less than the lack of clear, unambiguous, and reliable information about what is happening. The great-uncle thinks his relatives are not telling him everything he needs to know; they are holding back on him.

During the Great Credit Crisis, the benevolent great-uncle panicked, not because of the subprime mortgage default, or a U.S. housing bubble that was spreading beyond its shores. The world's financial markets were fully aware of these developments. The panic unfolded precisely because suddenly nobody could say which financial institutions held the subprime toxic waste, and at what price. The situation was exacerbated by the sudden complexity of the financial system as a result of securitization, which resulted in a lack of transparency. There was also the discovery of the market's massive, irresponsible leverage of these securitized assets. When the benevolent great-uncle becomes paranoid as a result of poor transparency, bad things happen. Panic sets in. In this case, the great-uncle suddenly began to doubt the value of the financial markets' complex new debt investment instruments. For these "paper" securities, the only measure of risk and value came from the credit rating agencies, which measured risk based merely on sophisticated mathematical models.

In some cases, lack of transparency can lead to euphoria that fuels financial bubbles because of lack of factual information. In this case, however, lack of reliable information caused global lending to screech dangerously to a halt. But there is a broader point of this discussion. The dramatic rise in financial panics is the direct result of the last quarter-century's economic globalization of the world economy. Globalization led to greater worldwide wealth, which created a volatile ocean of capital that roamed the world in search of investment opportunities. This ocean of capital became our policymakers' greatest nightmare.

Many months before this great crisis, I began pulling together my thoughts for this book. The subject would be the imperfect good we call globalization. My thesis: that the integration of the world's financial markets during the past quarter-century led to a golden age of wealth creation and poverty reduction never before seen in the history of mankind. That's the good news. With the introduction of China and India to the global capitalist system, the industrialized world during this remarkable period accomplished the near miraculous. In little more than two decades, the global free market experienced an unprecedented doubling of its labor force—from 2.7 billion to 6 billion, with no revolution, no serious riots in the streets, not even a threatened, across-the-board shutdown of the trading system.

This phenomenal success stemmed from a global paradigm shift, accelerated by the collapse of the Berlin Wall, which led to the broad-based belief that economic success results, not from government or even from the large corporate sector, but from the ongoing innovations by a risk-taking global entrepreneurial class. It was this class that allowed economies to continually reinvent themselves. Most important, this innovation and economic reinvention was fueled by a modernized, global financial system of capital allocation, risk assessment, and cross-border investment within a climate of open trade.

The result, financial crises notwithstanding, was an unprecedented wave of prosperity—forty million new jobs in the United States alone, under both Republican and Democratic presidents, which was more than was created by the rest of the industrialized world combined.

During this quarter-century, the Dow Jones Industrial Average climbed from 800 to 14,000, before the financial crisis hit. To match that stock market success in percentage terms over the next twenty-five years, the Dow would have to exceed 170,000. In 1982, at the beginning of this period of global financial market integration, the net worth of U.S. households equaled $11 trillion; just before the crisis hit, it had exceeded $56 trillion, according to the Federal Reserve. Even when adjusted for inflation, this represented an amazing feat of wealth creation, at least on paper.

From 1980 to the crisis, the value of all global financial assets had jumped from $12 trillion to $140 trillion, a 1,166 percent increase. Global financial assets had jumped from roughly 100 percent of worldwide GDP in 1980 to 325 percent just before the crisis.

The bad news is that this spectacular global economy was both unstable and unsettling. As jobs and investment moved around the world, people lost incomes and pensions. And as these enormous shifts occurred, the economic benefits of the system were often unfairly distributed. As *Fortune*'s Nina Easton wrote, "There's not a lot of security in a fast-paced global economy where workers get ahead by chasing opportunities (not obediently following official rules), by constantly reinventing their careers (not relying on seniority), and by self-investing their savings (not counting on company pensions)."

Despite enormous wealth creation, this new era of free-flowing global capital and abundance was accompanied by an era of financial crises. Charles Kindleberger, in his book *Manias, Panics, and Crashes*, catalogs a full history of financial crises. Yet, according to the World Bank, the last quarter-century of prosperity has been the high point for systemic banking crises, far more, for instance, than during the pre-globalization quarter-century. Yet at the same time, the world benefited from reduced volatility in inflation and jobless rates.

How to confront these opposing economic factors is the most critical issue facing worldwide policymakers today. If they overreact to the uncertainty of today's crisis liquidity and credit situations, they risk a continued financial and economic reversal that will affect us all. Ironically, the best intentions can lead to greater joblessness, continued deterioration in equity markets, less charitable giving, and a devastatingly bitter rise in the levels of global poverty. However, financial collapse does not have to be permanent if policymakers recognize the fragility of the capital markets and adopt new, carefully targeted strategic approaches to this brave new world.

Make no mistake, financial instability has all but destroyed the credibility of the last quarter-century of liberated global financial markets and free trade, which appeared to have produced the proverbial goose that laid the golden eggs, in terms of political freedom, wealth creation, and poverty reduction. In 1975, for example, only 25 percent of the 147 countries of the world were considered democracies; after a quarter-century of globalized markets, that figure had jumped to 58 percent. As Kofi Annan, former secretary general of the United Nations, has said: "The main losers in today's very unequal world are not those who are too much exposed to globalization. They are those who have been left out."

Gary Hufbauer of the nonpartisan Peterson Institute for International Economics still argues that the United States is more than "one trillion dollars richer each year because of globalized trade." That amounts to nearly 10 percent of GDP, or an incredible $10,000 per household. In their book *World Capital Markets: Challenge to the G-10*, Hufbauer and Canadian economist Wendy Dobson assert that the economic gains from liberalized capital flows now equal or exceed those from liberalized trade.

Robert Bartley, the late editor of the editorial page of the *Wall Street Journal*, wrote a book about the Reagan economy called *The Seven Fat Years* (November 1982–July 1990). If someone writes a sequel, it should be called *The Twenty-five Fat Years*, including the amazing time of peace and prosperity under President Bill Clinton, who was a champion of the new global financial system.

Before the outbreak of the financial crisis, the last quarter-century represented the most successful period of mass poverty reduction in the history of mankind. In 2006, I commissioned an article for my magazine, *The International Economy*, to try to measure the globalized financial market's performance at poverty reduction since 1980. The writer, I reasoned, should come from neither any government agency nor any think tank dependent on a relationship with the World Bank; nor any private poverty agency, many of which were almost psychotically distrustful of markets. Nor should the writer be on an ideological mission on the right. Adam Posen of the Peterson Institute, and an executive editor of our magazine, recommended Surjit Bhalla, a former World Bank official and Goldman Sachs partner who now is a private investor. Known for highly independent thinking and research, Bhalla accepted the task.

He concluded that we were witnessing something historic. The last quarter-century had represented a golden age of poverty reduction, all occurring during the shift toward globalized financial markets. With poverty defined by the traditional dollar-a-day measure (the standard used by the international agencies), about a billion people had been moved out of poverty since 1980. Put another way, during the period 1950–1980, when the World Bank and other international agencies, flush with money, were in their heyday, there was actually a significant *increase* in global poverty. And this was the period of big government spending, including major loans and grants to the developing world. These well-intentioned efforts suffered because without efficient and honest institutions in recipient countries, the results of government-to-government transfers will always disappoint.

The golden age of poverty reduction came in the post-1980 period of globalized markets, with the level of poverty declining an astonishing 20 percent. Large turnarounds, not surprisingly, appeared in India and China after both embraced entrepreneurial capitalism and lowered tariffs. But even Latin America and Africa, the big holdouts, began to see poverty decline starting in the year 2000. With the collapse in global demand and trade, of course, this miracle period has come to an end.

To be sure, the world still contains much pain and suffering. Greater public and private efforts are needed to confront, in particular, the rampant AIDS crisis that exerts a choke hold on the African continent. One dollar per day may also be too low a measure for the poverty line, even though it remains the industry standard based on a 1994 dollar baseline valuation. But in the end, simply looking at bottom-line results, it appears that entrepreneurial capitalism within a financially integrated global system is still the only model that has even come close to delivering full-throated, out-and-out poverty reduction. Witness the billion people who were lifted out of poverty in the past quarter-century.

To reiterate, none of this is to suggest that efforts to alleviate health and medical problems are not essential, particularly now with the col lapse of the global economy. High-profile philanthropists such as Bill and Melinda Gates deserve enormous credit for their efforts. Rock star Bono performs an important and commendable service by snapping at the heels of the World Bank and the international drug companies to offer support. But these efforts will remain a sideshow relative to the potential power inherent in market capitalism. Bono himself recognized this point. In March 2007 he told the *New York Times*, "One of the things that I have learned in Africa is the crucial role that commerce will play in taking its people out of extreme poverty."

Although flawed, sometimes disappointing, and often unpredictable and at times too dangerously dependent on leverage, globalization has been a wealth-creating machine. But, after twenty-five years of dramatic economic performance, we still do not know all the implications—good and bad—of globalization. We do know that despite several decades of a rapidly globalizing system, government policymakers and politicians for the most part understand little about the unique nature of today's economy.

For many, the economy remains a static entity to be fought over by competing political forces in an emerging era of class warfare. Actually, the global economy is more like a highly dynamic, living organism heavily dependent on risk-taking and failure as the ironic ingredients for success. *Newsweek*'s Robert Samuelson notes a remarkable statistic: "Every three months, seven to eight million U.S. jobs disappear and roughly an equal or greater number are created."

Most of all, this new global economy is vastly different from the old system in which corporations and their elite handlers worked a global system of controls to maintain relative stability. Now, just the opposite is the case. More than ever before, large corporations are forever threatened with obsolescence by a risk-taking, extraordinarily venturesome entrepreneurial class of individuals, who themselves constantly face the possibility of failure. Just as IBM was once threatened by Microsoft, now Microsoft is threatened by upstart Internet-enabled companies, such as Google or the open-source operating system Linux.

The situation may be further complicated by the reality that we are entering a new interactive age where a mass collaboration via the Internet is transforming the way businesses create and add value. This is a populist-style process of international business reform in which a bottom-up dynamic may gradually be taking over the global economy. In a later chapter, I will discuss what this means for China, where the government now has implemented a strange new policy to try to police Internet content. Ultimately, however, we have no other choice in this increasingly volatile world but to embrace and reform the globalized market and to subtly direct it to a greater good with the least number of negative, unintended consequences. As President Bill Clinton said in his 2000 State of the Union address, "There's no turning back. And our open, creative society stands to benefit more than any other."

As a result of globalization's wealth creation, the world has been awash in money, and much of it in the buildup to the financial crisis sought haven in the United States. Dino Kos, the former head of the New York Federal Reserve's foreign exchange desk, watched tides of large capital come in every day. Here is how he summed up the situation before the outbreak of the credit crisis: There was "an ocean of liquidity out there. The productivity revolution had gone global. The entire world had gotten a lot richer a lot faster than any of us realized."

Indeed, there was for a while a shortage of global investment opportunities with too much of the world's capital dependent on investment in U.S. and other industrialized world financial assets. Since 1995, for example, $6.5 trillion in net foreign capital has flowed into the United States, which is $1.7 trillion more than the trade deficit for this period. The international system became out of balance, which is why Federal Reserve chairman Ben Bernanke has argued for a long-term policy of global rebalancing. The United States, he argues, needs to undergo "a shifting of resources out of sectors producing non-traded goods and services to those producing tradables." Translation: America needs to reduce its budget deficits and dependence on foreign oil while expanding its exports of goods and services. Other countries need to stimulate domestic demand so they can purchase more imports and rely less on exports. This shift, however, will take time and, in the meantime, the U.S. economy will depend on foreign investment. Indeed, this dependence is accelerating as American budget deficits explode.

Furthermore, some in the U.S. political community have taken the posture that foreign investment, like some mad monster, threatens the core of America's existence. The situation is not that simple. In reality the threat to that existence, in the short run, is the widespread perception that America no longer welcomes foreign capital. For decades, global investors have regarded the U.S. economy as a safe haven for international capital. Studies show that U.S. companies financed by direct foreign investment issue big paychecks, 32 percent above the average for the rest of the private sector, according the the *Wall Street Journal*. America has been a highly attractive investment target for the global financial system. Only a fool would do anything to alter that perception until the global system is rebalanced, with the United States putting its fiscal house in order and other parts of the world restructuring economically to become less dependent on exports. But for now, populist political rhetoric against foreign capital has triggered global financial market trader and investor nervousness. They ask: Do the American economic populists understand the extent to which they are playing with fire? If foreign investment in the U.S. Treasury market dried up, U.S. interest rates would skyrocket.

In the end, the future of the globalized world economy rests on these fundamental questions: What is the definition of liquidity? And why does liquidity (and its cousin, credit availability) one minute seem to be in overwhelming abundance and the next minute appear to have completely vanished? To what extent does liquidity reflect true growing value in an expanding global economy?

Perhaps the best metaphor to illustrate liquidity is the oil in an automobile engine. If the oil just collects in the bottom of the engine pan, even if there is plenty of oil, the engine seizes up. The oil needs to move freely throughout the engine.

Today's central bankers struggle with the issue of liquidity. At times, in a financial panic, liquidity (oil) can suddenly move quickly to one location (down to the engine pan), which in today's economy means purchasing only short-term government debt. When that happens, credit contracts and the entire economic and financial system is at risk. The engine's pistons could soon stop pumping.

During the Asian and Russian financial crises in 1997–1998, for instance, global liquidity instantly dried up. After a period of abundant liquidity, credit was nowhere to be found. The Great Credit Crisis of 2007–2009 was accompanied by a similar development. The situation was frightening in both cases, but why did the liquidity dry up so quickly? And, indeed, what drives this thing we call liquidity?

When it is pared down to its essence, it may be that liquidity, when all is said and done, is not much more than confidence. Federal Reserve governor Kevin Warsh makes this case, arguing: "Powerful liquidity in the U.S. capital markets is evidenced when the economic outcomes are believed to be benign. When the [highly negative] outcomes are either highly improbable or, at the very least, subject to reasonably precise measurement, the conditions are ripe for liquidity to be plentiful." Alan Greenspan as Federal Reserve chairman also argued that liquidity is just another word for confidence. In a later chapter, I'll discuss how the former chairman and I have had a number of discussions about how the job of central banking, because of this need to bolster confidence, has become an elaborate form of "theater," with the financial markets acting as the audience. Liquidity, therefore, to a significant degree depends on the market's confidence that policymakers in the near future won't make a series of huge blunders. During the subprime crisis, the world's central banks from the start flooded the world with injections of available "liquidity." Yet the credit crisis continued because of the global market's lack of confidence in the financial architecture, including the financial system's ability to truly measure risk.

In essence, the survival of the world financial system depends on an elaborate global game of confidence. The size of the financial markets, relative to the governments, has become so monstrously huge, there is no other means of maintaining stability than to establish a psychology of confidence. The governments themselves cannot by edict restore order. They cannot demand risk-taking occur. They can only project to the markets a sense that they know what they're doing. They can create a climate conducive to risk taking.

Consider the example of UBS, Switzerland's largest bank and one of the largest financial institutions in the world. During the 2007–2008 subprime crisis, the Swiss central bankers discovered, to their utter dismay, that the total financial exposure of just one of their banks, UBS, amounted to more than 2 trillion Swiss francs, according to the Swiss National Bank. Yet Switzerland's entire GDP is only 475 billion Swiss francs. In the event of a panic and serious capital outflows, the liabilities of one bank alone are more than four times the size of the entire economy. Translation: The Swiss government in a time of crisis could not afford to bail out its financial system even if officials wanted to. Projecting confidence therefore is essential. Policymakers in the rest of the industrialized world find themselves in a similar situation, particularly when considering the fact that financial institutions engage in a considerable amount of leveraging (borrowing against current investment assets to make new investments).

For today's policymakers, financial market panics represent the ultimate enigma. Whenever the psychology of human paranoia comes into play, uncertainty rules the day. Experts still debate the factor, or set of factors, that led to the 1987 crash of the U.S. stock market, a market correction that in today's terms would amount to a one-day 3,500-point drop in the Dow Jones Industrial Average. At first, conventional theory blamed the crash simply on the role of computerized portfolio insurance in worsening an initial market slide. Yet what is now clear is that a series of seemingly benign developments, when piled together, seriously undermined confidence, which led to the sudden breakdown of the international financial order.

Market participants came to believe that policymakers were disrupting the global system, a development that led to broad investor panic and a loss of confidence. In the lead-up to this period, policymakers made some seemingly minor blunders that, as they snowballed, turned out to have devastating consequences as millions of market participants lost confidence in the future. The comparison to today is not without merit.

For example, in the fall of 1987 a public dispute emerged between U.S. Treasury secretary James Baker and his German counterpart, Gerhard Stoltenberg, over the dollar and interest rates. This created the perception of the loss of international financial order and certainty. The Reagan administration had also levied trade sanctions against Japan, creating uncertainty about the future of free trade. A week before the crash, the House Ways and Means Committee announced plans to raise taxes on debt associated with corporate takeovers, which many market participants interpreted as a highly bearish development for financial markets. Around that time, a U.S. House of Representatives subcommittee passed the amendment of 1988 Democratic presidential candidate Richard Gephardt (an adviser to Hillary Clinton in the 2008 presidential election) that would slap nasty sanctions on countries running "excessive and unwarranted" trade surpluses against the United States. All of these developments left markets fearful that global capital flows were at risk of disruption.

The bottom line is that in 1987 a deadly combination of seemingly minor technical missteps and less-than-careful political posturing nearly sank world stock markets—and the global economy to boot. In the world of policy and markets, people matter. Financial markets were jittery and suddenly perceived an unwillingness of the big powers to cooperate. Almost overnight, stock price declines fed on themselves, creating a financial horror show of historic proportions. True, the stock market bounced back, helped by the sense among financial participants that the G7 industrialized-nation policymakers (from France, Germany, Japan, the United States, Canada, Italy, and the United Kingdom) coordinated their actions when the crisis erupted. Given today's key players—which include China, India, Russia, and the other oil-producing, excess-savings economies—such coordination and single-mindedness are far less likely to happen in the event of a major market meltdown.

What is clear is that financial instability is here to stay. In a study of the history of financial turbulence, noted economists Barry Eichengreen of the University of California at Berkeley and Michael Bordo of Rutgers make the case that financial crises today "are twice as prevalent" as they were a century ago.

The Great Credit Crisis is the ultimate case in point. But could today's new independent ocean of liquidity further dry up, causing the global wealth machine to shut down? Unfortunately, the picture is not reassuring. That's because the rest of the world's politicians are likely to follow in America's missteps, especially on the issues of protectionism and clumsy financial market overregulation.

There are a number of key unknowns, but one of the most vexing is political uncertainty. Globalization's opponents include both Republicans and Democrats in the U.S. Congress. Backed by powerful interest groups worried about the uncertainties of international competition, they already are labeling the process "the world's race to the bottom." Early on in the 2008 U.S. presidential race, both Democrats (led by former senator John Edwards) and Republicans (led by former governor Mike Huckabee) uttered strikingly similar antiglobalization themes, with most of the other candidates refusing to defend the system. That is because globalization, while creating enormous wealth, has produced widespread anxiety. Job outsourcing, once limited to relatively unskilled labor, now poses the appearance of a real threat to middle-class jobs. The truth is that America so far has been a massive net "insourcer," not an outsourcer, of jobs. Foreigners invest a half trillion dollars more in the United States than Americans invest abroad, which is one reason the United States in the past regularly created a net two million new jobs every year.

A study by economists Gordon Hanson and Robert Feenstra argues that outsourcing has actually raised the real wages of unskilled workers. Economists William Dickens and Stephen Rose argue that the outsourcing criticism is exaggerated: "Modern market economies regularly destroy and create tens of millions of jobs just from their own internal dynamics. Trade plays a very small role in this job churning. The largest source by far of job loss remains *domestic* competition." McKinsey's Martin Baily and Harvard's Robert Lawrence agree, arguing that 90 percent of jobs lost in manufacturing are the result of domestic forces, mostly technological advancements that force companies to eliminate workers.

Still, the global system is changing, with a potential economic shift in coming years from manufacturing to services. China, India, and the other Asian economies could soon reach a state of huge excess capacity in manufacturing. To maintain their economies, these nations will turn to services, the mainstay of the U.S. and U.K. economies (in the United States, more than 80 percent of jobs are in the services industry). Even if America remains a huge net-jobs insourcer, the anxiety felt by those in the service sector will remain and intensify. Accountants, lawyers, radiologists, and others already fear that their livelihoods could be at risk, given the new breed of competitors from abroad. Even though some experts feel that the fear regarding service jobs is somewhat overblown, the fears themselves are a threat.

Economists such as Columbia University's Jagdish Bhagwati, for example, counter that in the services industry, "proximity of personnel is often indispensable" as many services jobs "cannot be done long distance." I agree that the threat is exaggerated, but the *feelings* of anxiety are very real, and they are likely to trigger a very real U.S. political counterresponse that could prove highly unsettling to global markets. Indeed, in America, the cauldron of populist discontent against the so-called big corporate interests is boiling faster by the day.

The worrisome question is whether politicians realize how little they can control this global system with legislative or regulatory intervention without producing unintended negative consequences. This situation evokes memories of what the British government did in the 1960s when they tinkered with their financial system by prohibiting people from taking money out of the country. What was, in effect, an elaborate, seemingly benign policy experiment intended to keep the currency from weakening (despite running questionable expansionary policies during a period of rising inflation) proved disastrous. The market tinkering backfired, nearly destroying the savings of the British middle class. That is why policymakers, with today's raging ocean of capital, should approach policy tinkering with a strong dose of humility. The global markets can be an angry, unpredictable beast, easily provoked.

Today we are living in strange new times where, with the exception of nations that export commodities (Russia and the other oil producers), the global economy is becoming increasingly beyond the positive control of the governments. Even China cannot easily be controlled by its central government, which errs in trying to micromanage when the market could better allocate resources.

In this new world, governments are struggling to manage the economy without killing it. Not that long ago, the picture was much clearer. For example, government institutions such as the World Bank, the International Monetary Fund, and the Paris Club of Third World debtors were instrumental in helping to coordinate capital flows. With the emerging markets having paid off debt, these governmental institutions are working to develop a new international role.

They haven't a moment to lose. The Chinese and Indian governments are already moving throughout the emerging markets handing out cheap (subsidized) loans tied to agreements involving the exchange of commodities, led by oil. But these actions have already raised the levels of tension and resentment throughout the global economy. A perception is growing that while China benefits from the global system of trade in goods and commodities, it does little to enhance the stability of that system and, at times, undermines its stability.

Essentially, the Chinese and others are underbidding the World Bank—and, unlike the World Bank, their loans involve no environmental or human rights standards. For evidence that China, India, and others are marginalizing the World Bank, IMF, and other agencies, consider what happened in Washington the weekend of April 14, 2007. The industrialized nations held an important IMF–World Bank meeting of finance ministers and central bankers. The Chinese didn't bother to show up. At the next meeting in early October 2007, the Chinese sent a relatively powerless central bank deputy instead of the most senior officials. The reason cited for their absence: They were preoccupied with more pressing domestic concerns. Since then, Beijing officials use these international gatherings as stages to stoke up nationalistic sentiment back home.

In chapter 4, I will show the potentially unsettling nature of China's relationship with the world in coming years. Greg Mastel, the former chief trade adviser to the U.S. Senate Finance Committee (2000–2003), suggests that there are many examples of future turmoil, including coming disagreements over environmental policy. Argues Mastel: "If China were to exempt its steel or chemical industry from greenhouse gas emission controls or pay them large subsidies, competing industries in the United States and Europe would be at a devastating disadvantage." This is because the bylaws of the World Trade Organization (WTO) make the United States and Europe relatively powerless to respond with effective tariffs on Chinese imported products. The WTO allows trade restrictions only for "the conservation of exhaustible natural resources." The rules regarding trade actions in response to national environmental policies are murky at best. Mastel foresees a situation in which the United States and Europe could see core industries unfairly hollowed out, with little they can do legally in response.

Yet in this globalized world, where capital flows have made up for America's budget and current account imbalances, one assumption has remained constant—that global capital must continue to flow freely. If these capital flows cease, whether because of government intervention, heavy-handed partisan politics, or the complete breakdown of the international order as a spin-off of a trade war with China, the potential for a negative global herd effect is enormous. Global money managers talk to each other. In a new world of dominant global markets ruled by sentiment and psychology, just the whiff of a protectionist economy or an economic turf war between countries will have disastrous consequences.

We may not like the interdependent nature of this system, but it is the reality of the day. And in this new interconnected world, pessimism can be highly contagious. Market theorists are already speculating that environmental forces and the forces behind free trade are on a collision course. Should it become apparent that America is going the way of trade protectionism, there is a real risk that the remaining confidence in the global entrepreneurial model of free-flowing capital could dry up overnight. The danger to the global economy is enormous because today's protectionist tweaking can easily become tomorrow's trade and commodity war—resulting in a new, frightening era of even scarcer liquidity.

Over the last quarter-century, America has championed the bipartisan concept that open markets, a turbocharged entrepreneurial capitalism, and freely flowing international capital markets represent a magic formula for economic success. Wealth stems from imagination, discovery, and innovation. In recent decades, America has proved to be a veritable hotbed for technological breakthroughs—from the iPod to Google to YouTube, although the situation is now changing.

Geopolitical complications in the Middle East, the collapse of confidence in the credit markets and our financial architecture, and global uncertainty in general have already cast a gray cloud over the innovation process in the United States. It is not surprising that American corporate CEOs, even before the subprime-related crisis, were beginning to pull back, preferring stock buy-backs and mergers and acquisitions over the risk of investment in new ventures. A dispirited U.S. Congress, with record low approval numbers, was already losing confidence in America's global economic future. That governing body is clearly mulling over the possibility of placing the economy in hibernation in an attempt to achieve some false sense of economic security by offsetting risk.

The Law of Unintended Consequences is about to take over because policymakers worldwide still believe they can control the global economy. We are about to discover the implications of this misconception as millions of market decision makers—the stewards of this new ocean of capital—weigh their options.

Several years ago, someone asked me to name specific examples of how the new global economy could further unravel. There are hundreds of possibilities. After all, who would have predicted the global devastation as a result of the U.S. subprime mortgage collapse? Imagine, I said, that Washington policymakers become even more involved in setting America's accounting standards so there develops a clear division between the United States and the rest of the world to America's disadvantage. This move would isolate the United States in such a way as to further discourage foreign investment.

Or imagine the U.S. Congress setting up investment barriers to foreign ownership of U.S. companies. The rest of the world responds with tax hikes and/or regulatory assaults on U.S.-owned company assets overseas. Think such a nationalistic scenario is far-fetched? In 2005, fifteen Democrats in the U.S. House of Representatives crossed the aisle to support the Central American Free Trade Agreement, or CAFTA. Since then the so-called CAFTA 15 have nearly been run out of the party for their free-trade transgressions.

Imagine a populist political tide rising up to replace the alternative minimum tax in the U.S. tax code with, say, a 70 percent or 80 percent tax on personal income above $2 million. As a result, a significant part of the American entrepreneurial and financial services sector moves offshore, which produces the unintended consequence of severely crunching the U.S. charity sector. Or imagine that the Doha Trade Round collapses for good and the global free-trade consensus vanishes. It is hanging by a thread now. Suddenly, emerging market political leaders tell the world to hell with patents or guaranteed payments on loans on anything considered a "public good" (pharmaceuticals, water treatment facilities, etc.). The United States retaliates by putting up barriers. Global commerce drops like a stone while the world's financial markets melt down.

Imagine that Washington decides to restrict cross-border movement of intellectual property, and foreign graduate students are banned from U.S. universities. Within several years, the United States becomes like Europe—far less innovative.

Imagine some well-intentioned administrative tax or minor regulatory change on the U.S. Treasury market causing a swift decline in the value on T-bills. Then a group of enterprising bond traders in Japan, or, more likely, France, takes advantage of this change in circumstances, driving the U.S. bond market into broad-based chaos and collapse. Or imagine that the United States and Europe band together to heavily regulate energy efficiency. They produce environmental standards in the form of a tax on imported goods from economies producing high carbon emissions, with China being the major culprit. China retaliates with a tariff on the American agricultural and banking sectors, causing a further Wall Street meltdown.

With pension funds pressured to increase yield, imagine a bumbling U.S. congressional effort to reduce risk-taking by financial traders, which over time produces the unintended consequence of a pension fund crisis, not dissimilar to the commercial paper crisis of 2007. Imagine a continuation of the post–Sarbanes-Oxley climate of caution that slowly eats away at American corporate competitiveness. Think of the unintended consequences of Americans feeling that they are no longer number one. Less competitive, they become peeved. Congress reacts, matters escalate, and the thing most essential to the survival of the new global economy—liquidity—further dries up. Interest rates soar and the cycle of economic terror begins. And for average investors, there is no place to hide.

The global system is becoming more vulnerable with each passing month. Recently, efforts were launched to give the U.S. Congress greater political influence over CFIUS, the Committee on Foreign Investment in the United States, a government agency with the power to void foreign investment in the United States based on national security concerns. CFIUS, which performs a vital public policy function, is aimed at the roughly dozen foreign state-owned investment funds (known as SWFs, or sovereign wealth funds) owned by the commodity-monopoly-dependent states (Saudi Arabia, United Arab Emirates, Dubai, Russia, etc.) that control roughly $2.5 trillion.

But the question is whether these necessary efforts at greater oversight of the state-owned investment funds reach beyond their stated mission of monitoring for national security concerns. The early signs are not encouraging. Already the European Commission is in the process of implementing rules significantly more restrictive than those the U.S. plans. The suspicion is that the European bureaucrats are using this situation as an invitation to increase regulatory control over financial markets in general. One of their goals is to protect domestic firms from the traditionally highly competitive U.S. financial services sector.

Yet the Western political anxiety associated with these state-owned funds cannot be dismissed. After all, China, India, and the oil-producing economies control large amounts of the world's excess savings. In the end, are Americans going to be comfortable allowing, say, a KGB-controlled Russian government or the Chinese government to buy 10 or 15 percent stakes in Microsoft, Google . . . or Boeing, potentially with seats on the boards of directors and access to proprietary information? And if not, how will the Russian, Chinese, and Saudi governments respond given the enormous Western investment in their economies? Where do we draw the line between free enterprise within the global marketplace and strategically oriented decisions by government-controlled investment vehicles with political agendas?

On a recent trip through Europe, I spoke with the head of a major European central bank who told me of his recent visit to Shanghai. The Chinese government, in providing a tour of the city, took him by car on a thirty-five-minute drive outside Shanghai to a small "city" of large, spanking new, completely empty office buildings. The European official responded to his host: "These buildings are spectacular, but they are all empty. Why is that?" The Chinese host responded: "The office buildings won't be empty for long. Soon they will house the employees of our government's new overseas investment agency." Said the European: "I can see the government is redefining the concept of central bank reserves. They're not reserves any longer; they're your government's investment capital ready to go on a global buying spree." The Chinese host's response: "Something like that," which brings up the question: Do the world's industrialized economies have an effective strategy for understanding the nature of these proposed investment flows?

Yet to add to the confusion, most sovereign wealth funds, ironically, so far tend to be interested largely in passive, nonleveraged, long-term investments in Western enterprises. In other words, to date they, thankfully, are likely to be the last to sell in a market downturn. In the next chapter, I will discuss today's roving bands of international investors called hedge funds. It may be that in the event of widespread global economic weakness the following scenario unfolds: The hedge funds short, or bet against, the global economy while the large sovereign wealth funds working side by side with the industrialized world central banks fight to counter the pessimism with major investments in the industrialized world markets. Some small, more independent sovereign wealth funds, to confuse matters even more, may short the market through private hedge fund investments made through international trading collectives called funds of funds.

What this all adds up to is that the world today appears to be moving away from the model of globalization and unfettered free markets of recent decades toward something more reminiscent of the nineteenth-century model of globalization—a new, more mercantilist era of backroom rivalries, deal-making, and tensions based on ambitious national political agendas and capital shifts controlled by governments. The innocent, well-meaning G7 policy coordination by democratically oriented industrialized nations of recent decades, what little there was, is fading fast. The so-called Anglo-Saxon world of free capital markets is under siege. The upshot is that the potential for disruption in the entire global financial market is growing exponentially.

Not convinced? One of the things contributing to today's soaring oil prices is hoarding by sovereign governments. China, India, and other major consumers are distorting the world market by increasing energy reserves with the expectation of higher prices. As analyst Harald Malmgren notes, "The expectation of rising prices is also reducing the incentive [of the oil producers] to increase production as oil in the ground looks like an asset with rising value." Other global entities currently hoarding oil include military services, farmers, trucking companies, producers of fertilizers and plastics, power plants, and other large-scale users. Note too that if energy prices spike further, the impact on world food prices will be huge, as the costs of fertilizers and farming transportation skyrocket.

Today, the world is undergoing a kind of tectonic change in the area of finance. The United States, once a bastion of trust for its transparency, rule of law, benign political environment, and overall conditions that nurtured increases in economic productivity, is being viewed with skepticism around the world. America finds itself in a precarious position at the precise moment that other countries have emulated America's productivity-enhancing practices and have started to become relatively attractive targets for global investment. As a result, the global center of financial activity has begun to shift away from the reality that placed the United States at the epicenter of all things financial—not unlike the situation the British found themselves in during the period after World War I.

Still not convinced? A few years ago, a Swiss banker described to me the process by which a Chinese company's initial public offering was financed with the modest help of its Swiss bank. In conducting the transaction, the Chinese took the unusual move of simply bypassing the New York and London financial centers, traditionally the intersection of global financial intermediation, and appealed directly to Dubai financial sources—something that would have been unheard of a decade ago. Because of the uncertainty now surrounding the U.S. financial system, particularly in the wake of the subprime disaster, America is at risk of losing its perceived uniqueness as a trusted repository for global investment.

That is why the world capital markets have become a veritable house of cards. The world is at risk of losing its anchor, its admittedly flawed, yet reliable voice consistently in favor of free trade and open capital markets—the United States. But to truly understand the risks out ahead, it is essential to know how we arrived at our current predicament. In other words, how did globalization come about and what are the terrifying dangers lurking just around the corner?

2

A Dangerous Ocean of Money

One steamy day in August 1987 I received a call in my Washington consulting office that was to vividly define for me personally how radically the new ocean of money in the global economy was changing the rules of the game. Before the phone call, I already had the sense that the increasingly interconnected global system was, for better or worse, unleashing extremely powerful market forces. But, as a result of that call, I would quickly discover how confusing financial globalization was making the world, even for the most financially astute.

The call came from Singapore's ambassador to the United States, Tommy Koh. It was one of those late summer days in Washington, D.C., where a thick blanket of humidity covers the city while most of the residents are away at the beach. "Do you ever travel to Singapore?" the ambassador asked. "Only Tokyo and Hong Kong," I responded. The ambassador suggested that if on one of my trips I also made my way down to Singapore, I might find a major consulting contract with the central bank, the Monetary Authority, in the offing. We set a date for my visit in the fall, which turned out to be less than one week after the world stock markets crashed.

Singapore, the small city-state of the Pacific Rim economies, was the successful brainchild of Lee Kuan Yew. He ran the country as a benevolent dictator. I knew of his reputation as a brilliant global strategist, and wondered whether, during this trip, I would hear stories of Lee Kuan Yew's insights into the changing nature of the global economy. I was not prepared for what was about to unfold.

My plane touched down in Singapore in the early evening. As my government handler and I sped in our limo through the small city-state, we passed row after row of beautiful hotels, with bright landscape lighting and striking, sparkling fountains. But when we arrived at the hotel that had been selected for me by my Singapore government hosts, it turned out to be a strip mall hotel. My room reeked of stale cigarette smoke with a slight tinge of urine covered up by a disinfectant. I disappointedly described it to my wife, Vickie, back in Washington over the phone. "After a long flight," I said, "I was ready for something more comfortable—and better smelling."

The next morning, my government handler met me in the hotel lobby. "So sorry to hear you did not find your room comfortable," he said. My jaw dropped, as I racked my memory with some annoyance for whatever else I might have said inadvertently over the phone. Riding in the car to the central bank, I began to wonder, "Why am I here?" I thought of the signs in the airport warning of the death sentence for drug dealers, stories about the physical caning of American college students for misdemeanors, and the ban on chewing gum. Yet my intuitive sense told me this might become a new business opportunity, or at least a fascinating experience, so I kept going.

For years, the Singapore government had employed Richard Helms, the former head of the Central Intelligence Agency, as its consultant. But Helms, a close friend of the "father" of Singapore, Lee Kuan Yew, was oriented toward national security issues. Now the central bank wanted less analysis about the Russians and more about what was likely to happen as the G7 industrialized nations sought to survive and prosper in a rapidly globalizing international system. The economists at the central bank were professional: They could see globalization coming. Similar to other central banks in the region, the Monetary Authority was like one giant financial trading operation, sort of a government-sponsored Goldman Sachs.

"Your meetings have gone well," Finance Minister Richard Hu told me midway through the second day of my visit. "All you need now," he said, "is a simple handshake with the Leader, a five-minute meeting." The Leader, of course, was Lee Kuan Yew, the man whom Richard Nixon thought to be the smartest person he ever met. Surprised by my predicament, I braced myself to be impressed. When I arrived at a colonial-style building, surrounded by cricket fields, a receptionist led me into a medium-sized conference room.

After a few moments, the Leader entered, dressed in a white, collarless, stiffly starched shirt with a facial expression that suggested, "I don't suffer fools easily." He sat at the far end of the conference table. For two or three minutes we sat in silence, his gaze focused toward the ceiling fans spinning above us. Then he looked at me with a deep scowl. I immediately knew why the central bank folks, who were in attendance every moment up until then, had peeled off. "They bring me a child as an adviser," the Leader moaned with deep disappointment. "You've been in Tokyo," he barked. "With the stock market crash, they must be ready to bail out of America, given your irresponsible fiscal policies."

My sweaty palms gripped the seat. The Leader's scowl intensified. I thought, This is not a good sign. He's boring in, getting ready for the kill to save the economic future of his friend Helms. One of the central bank officials had earlier suggested that if my firm was hired, Helms would likely lose his consulting contract.

Mustering the courage for a counterpunch, I responded that, in fact, I had just met with all the Japanese insurance companies and the Ministry of Finance, and there was no sense of panic. Tokyo seemed to be planning massive purchases of the U.S. market. Translation: The stock market crisis was likely over and the climate would stabilize relatively quickly because of the new, interconnected nature of the global system.

"That's the stupidest thing I've ever heard," the Leader bellowed in an Oxford accent, looking for an assistant as if he was about to declare the meeting over. "Our people in New York just spoke with our people here. They know the market and they say just the opposite. This is a waste of a conversation."

At that point, I realized I had nothing to lose. With the contract spiraling down the drain, I shoved back—and hard. "With all due respect, sir," I began, "I firmly believe my analysis is correct." I felt adrenaline flowing. I went on. I couldn't be stopped. "Your New York advisers may be smart, but they didn't just come from several days with all the big money players in Tokyo. And I can assure you the Japanese will be buyers of the U.S. market big time over the next week or so. They have too much to lose if the American economy goes down. Plus, they see the world increasingly in global terms, and they have long-term confidence in the United States as a destination for investment."

The Singapore economists, I was convinced, had based their analysis on the old financial model, which held that the United States was still a closed economic and financial system. The large U.S. budget deficit at the time would turn the stock market collapse into more than a financial event. The collapse would lead to broader-based economic calamity. The pool of available domestic savings needed to finance the deficit, the model maintained, would leave inadequate financial resources to revive the stock market.

My intelligence, based on listening to the Japanese, convinced me that the global economy was undergoing a fundamental change. Shifts in savings across borders were making the old financial models obsolete. That is why I predicted the U.S. stock market would bounce back from collapse, fueled in part by foreign purchases and also by American investors now more easily able to borrow in the foreign markets to purchase U.S. stocks. It turned out this new globalized financial system prevented an international fire sale of U.S. equity assets. Financial globalization helped save the day.

What was to have been a quick handshake, however, turned into a bruising, hour-long exchange. Everything I said, Lee Kuan Yew disputed. My prediction about the Japanese buying spree was an educated guess, based on the nature and tone of the questions the Japanese had asked several days earlier. That intuition, that educated guess, turned out to be correct even earlier than I had predicted. The U.S. economy survived the crash and went on to prosper precisely because of the globalized nature of this new financial system.

The Japanese, regardless of conventional wisdom and the politicized climate back in the United States, felt in their collective gut a confidence that America was an exceptional destination for investment. America was committed to free markets, the free flow of capital, and an entrepreneurial capitalist future. I left Singapore telling the folks at the central bank, however, that my chat with the Leader was a fiasco, one of the worst interviews I had ever experienced. Nixon was right—the man was brilliant and the conversation riveting and fast-paced, but I was relieved just to get on the plane.

About a month later, after the dreadful interview had largely vanished from my mind, Ambassador Koh called my office: "Your contract is signed and ready to be picked up." Apparently, the Leader relented because virtually everything I had predicted in Singapore had turned out to be correct. The central bank went on to become a client, always posing first-rate questions about the global economic system. But I shall never forget Lee Kuan Yew's sense of shocked disbelief at the suggestion that the United States could survive, even prosper, under a scenario of both budget and current account deficits. Indeed, in that meeting I offered an analogy that the U.S. debt during the late nineteenth century, piled up by a newly industrializing America to build the western railways, failed to prevent the United States from overtaking Great Britain, its largest creditor, in both national income and stock market capitalization. But the Leader was to have none of it, no doubt because my optimistic analysis ran completely counter to conventional thought. Then again, he also may have been merely testing me to see if I could handle a tough verbal assault.

Why the United States, despite its deficits, went on to survive and prosper can be stated in one word: globalization. One minute, the United States was a closed system; the next it was part of an interconnected global network. Global transfers of savings, for better or worse, were redefining and reshaping the world economic landscape.

When most people picture globalization, they don't immediately picture financial market traders or trillions of dollars moving around the globe. They think of a Kentucky Fried Chicken franchise plopped down in the middle of downtown Beijing, or Dell or Gateway computers being assembled at rock-bottom prices using parts constructed in Asia, with each separate economy bringing to the table its individual comparative advantage. They think of making a telephone call for technical help on a product bought in Toledo, Ohio, and speaking to a service technician in New Delhi. The image is of the arrival of the computer chip that globally has made everyday life more efficient, often creating more with less. But how did all of these amazing developments come about? What started it all?

The answer, I believe, lies in looking at the way financial markets became internationalized. Discussing capital flows may not be as exciting as new computer wizardry developed by specialists living on separate continents, but the financial markets are what got globalization started. Before the 1980s, the United States was a relatively closed system, except for some global trade, largely in goods. Other than recycled oil money from the oil producers, passing through the U.S. banks into investments in Latin America, capital tended to remain at home (except when necessary to finance trade). It was as if each country owned its own private pool of capital from which it financed economic expansion. The financial markets were simple, sleepy, inefficient, and relatively predictable for policymakers. Unfortunately, this system enjoyed relatively limited means of financing entrepreneurial initiative and assessing new investment risk. Banks preferred investments in established entities, the larger the better. Small entrepreneurial ventures were mostly left to their own devices. There was little thinking about how to gear up to finance unborn enterprises, the major source of new employment.

But in 1979, the U.S. Labor Department under President Carter modified its rule on how pension funds could invest their assets. Once restricted to conservative, blue-chip stocks, the pension funds were allowed under the new rule to invest in smaller, less-established companies. This was a boon to the venture-capital industry, which received 44 percent of its capital from pension funds between 1980 and 2002. Billions of dollars of America's sleeping capital were mobilized for more productive purposes.

Conventional wisdom holds that in the last quarter-century, the capital of the rich alone rejuvenated the U.S. economy—the so-called trickle-down theory of prosperity. Actually, the entire nation, unwittingly or not, contributed to the rejuvenation as private and public pensions and other formerly staid financial vehicles were unleashed into the markets. Congress terminated the regulations capping the interest rate paid on savings accounts. Authorities also lessened the amount of capital that banks were required to keep in reserve and began to reduce the restrictions on bank investments put in place in the 1930s after the Great Depression. In 1978, the Democratic Congress cut the capital gains rate. Next came the establishment of the 401(k) account, an extraordinary development in the freeing up and deploying of financial capital.

By the mid-1980s, liberalized U.S. financial markets were feeding capital to the once-ignored small- and medium-sized ventures through a modernized, multilayered financial system that featured a diverse range of financial tools: private equity funds, private debt placements, hedge funds, high-yield bonds, venture capital funds, turnaround funds, and private mezzanine investing. Eventually, on a global scale, new cross-border transfers of savings would contribute to broad-based global investment in new start-ups and economic rejuvenation (the breakdown of the Bretton Woods fixed exchange rate system in 1971 and the move to an international regime of floating exchange rates also contributed to the opening up of capital flows).

Banks and investment houses in New York, London, Tokyo, Paris, and Frankfurt were being internationalized for one other reason:

Advances in communications and computer technology allowed money and international securities transfers to be accomplished instantaneously. You simply pushed a button and money flew across the world. American hedge funds were among the first to take advantage of these changes, sensing that capital was no longer confined to separate lakes or pools but had combined into a massive, borderless ocean of money. At the same time, the world's major individual financial markets, which had begun to be liberalized, saw the pace of that deregulation accelerated.

In Europe, Germany liberalized capital flows (meaning authorities allowed money to freely leave the country) earlier than France, yet the French unwittingly played a major role in spreading financial liberalization throughout Europe. Starting in 1981, France began a disastrous experiment with capital controls, trying to keep capital from leaving the country. The controls were so stringent that French tourists could not take more than the equivalent of $427 with them and were prohibited from using credit cards when out of the country. The French economy stagnated. Within a few years, then president François Mitterrand, to save his political hide, reversed course and implemented a sweeping liberalization of capital flows.

Mitterrand's policy reversal became contagious. Soon the European Commission pressed for all European economies to support a directive lifting capital controls, allowing money free international movement. At that point, a new international competition was on, with countries scrambling to become the strongest global magnet to attract the newly released capital as it swirled around the global ocean. The race was on to see which country could free up its financial markets and restructure its economy the fastest, to show itself as the leanest and meanest to attract more capital investment from abroad.

Soon capital was flowing from country to country, followed by a massive surge in the global trade of goods and services. As an economist would put it, in the past, trade normally came first—it always "drove" capital flows. Now it was the reverse. The desire to attract capital was driving free trade. Within two decades, there would be more than two hundred country-to-country free trade agreements, as countries attempted to impress world capital markets with their free and open markets for not only capital, but also goods and services. Global capital was particularly attracted to the United States by Ronald Reagan's commitment to the entrepreneurial capitalist model for growth, as well as to Bill Clinton's advocacy of free trade and liberalized financial markets.

The free-trade, entrepreneurial shift marked the birth of globalization. The effort to deregulate financial markets had forced the gates of the global trading system wide open. Computers and emerging technologies now had free access to transform manufacturing and service industries around the world. The growth of container shipping also dramatically increased the efficiency of international trade by eliminating the need for repeated packing and unpacking of merchandise and permitting fast, computer-directed distribution.

At first the new global investments, through venture capital firms and other forms of financial intermediation, targeted the financing of new entrepreneurial sectors mostly in the United States, the European countries, the United Kingdom, and Canada. But eventually China, India, Korea, Israel, and the Nordic countries became a significant part of the new, globalized investment environment.

Since the 1980s, the international financial system has developed new risk management techniques and a host of new financial wizardry with the goal of making capital less expensive and more available to the entrepreneur. In many ways, the effort has been a success. Securitization, a sophisticated process of financial engineering that allows global investment to be spread out and separated into multiple income streams to reduce risk (unless the entire global financial system comes under stress, as during the Great Credit Crisis of 2007–2009), has made the financing of the global entrepreneurial revolution far more ample. Small, promising ventures, once ignored by the big banks, could easily obtain financing. That's the good news. Most of the time, securitization has been like the yeast that allows the loaves of bread to rise. Senior financial executives lump their investment assets (which are sometimes mortgages) into a pile, divide them into multiple income streams, and, for a fee, sell each diversified piece as an asset-backed security. But this financial bundling process, called securitization, itself created a new set of problems that proved disastrous for the world financial system.

The bad news is that while securitization has revolutionized the financing of the economy's economic risk-takers and allowed for a more broad-based financing of the economy, it has come at a cost. During periods of panic, the public is right to be terrified because the intricate web of financial connections created by securitization becomes impenetrable. Witness the dispersal of the anonymous packets of "toxic waste" in the subprime debacle.

Also, securitization, even though it is essential to wealth creation, is so arcane that few people can understand its workings, especially during periods of financial market volatility. The reality is that the industrialized world has surrendered control of its financial system to a tiny group of five thousand or so technical market specialists spread throughout investment banks, hedge funds, and other financial institutions. These insiders are the rare few who know how the securitization process works, particularly during times of crisis. And even they at times are dubious that the securitized assets reflect the value stated. But want an even scarier thought? Picture the U.S. Congress trying to effectively legislate the regulation of something as complicated as the securitization process.

Securitization contributes one other huge weakness to today's financial system: The bankers who engage in lending are no longer tied to the risk of the borrower. The lender no longer has the incentive to avoid dangerous risk at all costs because the risk, when cut up into pieces, is quickly shoved out the lender's door to be packaged with pieces of other risk and to be sold as investment to the unknowing global financial community. In the final chapter, I'll explain further how the world credit system nearly collapsed as the subprime meltdown triggered a crisis of confidence by global investors in these new financial instruments.

Yet nothing about securitization is black and white. One of the prime reasons China will face serious problems ahead is that the system there needs some means like securitization to better manage financial risk and distribute capital. Instead, the Chinese system is still dominated by large, inefficient, often corrupt state-run banks that lack the necessary means for distributing capital effectively down to the entrepreneurial level. The paradox is that the system that allocates capital so successfully for the industrial world—securitization—is a risky, frustrating phenomenon we find hard to live with or without. If, for example, the U.S. Congress today in a financial reform effort were to outlaw securitization, it is likely the economy would dramatically contract from a severely reduced rate of overall lending. The emerging market economies, a major destination for U.S. exports, might never recover.

The key point, however, is that since the 1980s, a powerful global capital surge has occurred. This was due to the perception that the world had largely reached a consensus in favor of entrepreneurial capitalism within a climate of free trade and unimpeded financial flows. This international exchange of goods and capital—or, put another way, this foreign investment—has been of significant benefit to America. In the United States, more than five million people today work for companies that are headquartered overseas. According to the U.S. Treasury, although these jobs account for only 4 percent of the American workforce, they account for 10 percent of capital investment, 15 percent of yearly research and development (R & D), and 20 percent of American exports. Moreover, more than 30 percent of these foreign direct-investment-related American jobs are in manufacturing (compared to 10 percent in manufacturing for the overall U.S. economy).

The new workings of the world financial markets were apparent in some cross-border developments of the 1980s. During the Reagan era of budget deficits, the world experienced a perfect storm of savings shifts. With capital moving freely, suddenly large savings imbalances emerged among the major industrial nations. By the mid-1980s, the United States had run up significant deficits at the same time Japan found itself with a huge savings surplus, largely as a result of a drop in the yen price of commodities and a boom in exports to the United States. The upshot was that Japan, in addition to other global investments, bought U.S. Treasury debt. This prevented U.S. interest rates from exploding upward, as many conventional economists had forecast. That enabled the U.S. economy to go into overdrive. Nobody would have planned this sequence of developments, but it allowed for an extensive period of strong economic growth, albeit with mixed long-term consequences.

I mention all of this because the financial markets, as I started my consulting business in the mid-1980s, had become a global cauldron of uncertainty. Under globalization, many of the tried-and-true rules of economics and financial trading suddenly no longer applied. No econometric model—no magical black box of economic formulas— was useful anymore in predicting the future. Financial liberalization had created an ocean of liquidity that was sloshing all over the economic and financial rulebooks. Success required, more than ever, operating creatively from gut instinct.

The existence of a huge global pool of savings that can flow around the world in a second doesn't mean that budget or current account imbalances—the so-called twin deficits—are good policy. They are not, and there needs to be an internationally coordinated effort to reduce these imbalances. As I'll show in chapter 5 using the example of the Japanese financial system, there are limits to the amount of debt an economy can finance without the central bank's monetary policy losing its flexibility and effectiveness to influence the broader economy. But the effort to deal with today's imbalances will be complicated by the fact that some of Washington's most sophisticated political opinion leaders don't know the difference between a budget deficit and a current account deficit. Both are economic measurements, but they measure different things. A budget deficit or surplus represents the difference between how much tax money a government takes in and how much public spending goes out. A current account deficit or surplus shows the difference between the amount of money and goods coming into a country from abroad and the money and goods pouring out.

The current account deficit is tougher to understand and lately more abused by partisan politicians. Theoretically, an economy can run a current account deficit simply because it offers the global capital markets extraordinary investment opportunities. If huge amounts of investment capital rush in, the economy's current account deficit goes up, all other things being equal. At other times, however, a deficit can be a sign that an economy is not globally competitive and that consumers prefer imports over domestic products. Or, because domestic saving is insufficient to finance domestic investment, the budget deficit constitutes negative saving. It eats up domestic saving that would otherwise finance investment. To avoid reducing domestic investment, and thus reducing the standard of living, deficit-ridden economies import capital from the global financial markets.

For the United States, the current account deficit is high as a percentage of GDP because foreign capital finances America's debt, but capital also rushes in because the American economy historically has offered attractive investment opportunities. Today investors controlling the world's savings roam the globe in search of investment opportunities in new entrepreneurial ventures as well as in physical assets such as real estate and established companies.

For American policymakers, understanding the significance of budget and current account deficits is key to avoiding a further financial meltdown. The deficits desperately need to be reduced, but the policy prescription for doing so requires extraordinary sensitivity and understanding from our policymakers. It seems as if one half of our political leaders treat the deficits as merely a political football while the other half operates as if the deficits don't exist. Policymakers should begin with the fact that in the last quarter-century the so-called twin deficits have been an unreliable predictor of economic performance. Therefore, gearing policy to the twin deficits alone, as if deficits are all that matter, may in the end yield disappointing results for the broader macroeconomic economy. But in the long run, so would acting as if the deficits are irrelevant.

In recent decades, a cottage industry has formed offering predictions that America's twin deficits would spark high inflation, high interest rates, a dollar crisis, and economic collapse. Such predictions made sense when you had to consider only the resources generally available in the domestic economy. But globalization has muddied the picture.

The United States has experienced current account deficits since the 1980s, which, until roughly the year 2000, produced higher real U.S. interest rates. Since 2000, however, the U.S. current account deficit jumped from 4 percent of GDP to over 6 percent, yet real interest rates declined. Most economists attribute this outcome to the sudden glut in global savings (the lower real interest rates encouraged the beginning of an overinvestment in housing) as a result of the worldwide productivity increases and output growth associated with globalization.

But here's the problem. Just because America successfully dodged the twin-deficits bullet in the past, there is no guarantee of success or safety in the future, particularly as America's deficits rise to levels once thought unimaginable. U.S. imbalances have been financed increasingly by foreign central bank reserves, not private capital markets. The situation will become even more complicated if other economies, including those of Europe, become more attractive destinations for global investment—and the U.S. economy less attractive, as appears to be happening in the aftermath of the subprime crisis with the lessening of U.S. financial transparency and the rise in political resistance to international capital flows, and general class warfare.

Yet consider how the data can run counter to conventional thinking. For example, U.S. interest rates (the ten-year Treasury bond yield) did not drop below 5.25 percent during the entire eight years of the Clinton administration, which for a while produced a domestic budgetary surplus. However, at one point during the deficit-ridden George W. Bush administration, Treasuries dropped to nearly the 3 percent level—and did so at a time when the economy was prospering. Federal

Reserve chairman Alan Greenspan has called this situation "a conundrum." In traditional economics, government budget deficits are supposed to crowd out private investment and cause interest rates to skyrocket, particularly during high-growth periods. But this didn't happen, in part because of U.S. monetary policy but largely because of a large influx of global capital.

It is just as curious that during the period of 1998–2001, when the budget was in surplus, private savings in the United States reached 18 percent of GDP. During the period 1981–1989, with deficits averaging 4 percent of GDP, private savings also amounted to the same 18 percent of GDP.

Clearly the conventional relationships between data points are not fully reliable. By the same token, if this sounds like budget and current account deficits are irrelevant, think again. In today's world of unpredictable financial markets, the past is certainly no guarantee of success in the future. This is true particularly because of changing political attitudes in America, not to mention the decline in credibility of the U.S. financial system in the aftermath of the subprime debacle.

In a perfect world, it would be best to balance the budget and limit current account imbalances. But that requires the world's economic systems to be in balance, which almost never occurs. Some analysts argue theoretically that as long as current account deficits are the result of private, market-related decisions, the global financial system is safely stable. In other words, to a certain extent current account imbalances are inevitable; without them the concept of liberalized capital flows would be meaningless because global economies are never equally efficient. Seldom do economies offer equally attractive investment opportunities for global capital. But there are limits to the definition of a normal, healthy imbalance. Moreover, predicting the edge of those limits—the tipping point where market participants become concerned—is difficult and may be impossible.

Make no mistake, the United States consumes too much, saves too little, and relies too much on foreign oil. The downsides of this dependence are not to be ignored. Robert Hormats, a leading expert on international finance, notes that "for more than two hundred years, the [American] government has mobilized massive amounts of capital for national security; during the new war on terrorism, it must mobilize a massive public effort to reduce oil use and dependence." But it must also be understood that simply restricting imports entails dealing only with the consequence, not the cause, of the current account problem. To reduce its imbalances, the United States must increase domestic saving. At the same time, many other economies consume too little and offer too little in the way of safe and credible investment opportunities for global capital. Many of these countries have excess saving because they limit domestic investment opportunities through taxation, regulation, a lack of financial transparency, and the rule of law. It is important to note that it is investment, not saving, that improves living standards. Saving without investment is impotent. The old Soviet Union had tons of saving because there was nothing to buy.

Never before has the United States run such large twin deficits. Never has the U.S. financial system faced such a lack of transparency and credibility as it has in the aftermath of the subprime debacle. Never has the price of oil hovered at these record levels for so long a period. Some experts have argued that America's destiny is dangerously in the hands of foreigners, and that the United States faces the potential for a dollar free fall that could send the U.S. economy into complete collapse.

A few years ago, investor Warren Buffett bet big on a dollar free fall. He predicted that foreign investors would flee the United States in droves, sending the dollar down in a vicious spiral. He called the trade a "slam dunk," yet he lost a reported billion dollars on the bet because the dollar failed to experience any free fall at all. (The dollar has, however, trended downward against the euro and British pound since 2000, with a period of appreciation in the middle of the decade, and dropped significantly after the Federal Reserve slashed short-term interest rates in early 2008 in the midst of the subprime-related credit crisis.)

The proponents of the earlier free-fall theory blew the call because they underestimated the ability of the U.S. economy, despite America's policy blunders, to import capital. Ignoring the historic dynamism of the U.S. economy and its role as an international safe haven, skeptics at the time fixated only on the size of the current account deficit. The prudent alternative, however, would have been to weigh the imbalances but also to pay attention to the performance of asset markets (stocks, bonds, real estate, etc.), which at the time were reflecting reasonably strong economic fundamentals.

Economist David Hale argues that the reason the dollar, while weakening with the softening of the U.S. economy, back then failed to crash is that the current account deficit, while high relative to GDP, is only 1 percent of the total value of all American private assets. Hale argues that "the dollar, as the world's reserve currency, will always be volatile because investor perceptions of the outlook for asset returns in global markets continue to change."

By the same token, Hale insists, the dollar skeptics failed to appreciate that "America's asset markets are too large and flexible for there to be a sustained interruption of capital inflows and an enduring decline in the dollar"—that is, unless one development unfolds: Policymakers foolishly do something that impedes capital flows by abruptly making the United States a less attractive destination for investment, or by outright restricting foreign capital. Given the breakdown of the U.S. bank regulatory structure during the subprime crisis, the recent rise in trade protectionist and class warfare rhetoric in America, and the growing hostility toward international capital flows, including populist attempts to delude holders of U.S. bonds, such foolishness appears to be quickly setting in.

Let me put the debt situation into perspective. In 2008, foreigners owned $2.2 trillion of U.S. Treasury notes and bonds. That sounds like a huge number, but not when compared to the net worth of American households, which exceeds $45 trillion. Many analysts, playing the fear-of-foreigners political card, fixate on America's national debt as if the United States is some isolated renegade—a debtor nation without peer—within the international system.

Too much debt is never a good thing, and in many respects Americans may be living on borrowed time. Normally the dollar's weakening would produce higher import prices. But to date, those price hikes instead have eaten away at the profit margins of foreign producers, a situation that won't last forever. But it is important to keep things in perspective: America's gross national debt (65.7 percent of GDP) is less than Germany's (66.8 percent), while Japan's debt is roughly three times as large as America's (176.2 percent). During the much-praised Clinton growth years of the 1990s, gross national debt was actually slightly higher than it was in 2007 (68.9 percent of GDP in 1996). U.S. federal debt held by the public, 38 percent of GDP in 2007, was 48.5 percent, or 25 percent higher, in 1996.

The critical point is this: Whether the U.S. financial system avoids catastrophe depends on more than merely correcting financial imbalances, as important as that goal remains. After all, a big story of late 2007 was the decline (though hardly a free fall) in the U.S. dollar against the euro, a development that materialized ironically *after* a yearlong period in which both the U.S. budget and current account deficits actually declined as a percentage of GDP (the dollar strengthened significantly against the euro). Clearly, the dollar bears were influenced by something else. Most likely it was the dual fears of the lack of financial transparency caused by the U.S. subprime mess and the effect that the housing crisis would have on consumer demand (and the likelihood of significant short-term interest rate cuts by the Federal Reserve, which would mean European and other country bonds would yield more to an investor than U.S. bonds, thus drawing more capital flows into the euro-zone economy).

In the end, apart from these interest differentials (the differences in the bond yields of various economies), the fate of the dollar rests in large part on the attractiveness of the American economy as a global investment target. The past record has been impressive. A survey issued by the World Economic Forum concluded that despite its high levels of debt and low rate of savings, the United States still ranks first in the global competitiveness race. In recent years, the United States has remained a prime target for global investment because of its labor market flexibility, higher education, benign political environment, innovative strategies, and quality of corporate management. In the same survey, China ranked thirty-fourth.

But the question remains: Is the attractiveness of America fading as a global investment destination? Is America living the illusion that its past success is a guarantee for the future? In the final analysis, the future success of the American economic and financial system depends on politics—the politics of globalization and whether capital is allowed to flow freely. Ultimately, success depends again on whether America's asset markets can remain a big, fat, juicy—and transparent—target for global investment. Clearly, on this question the jury is still out.

Still, nothing about today's environment is simple or predictable. The Asian economies led by China continue to pile up large current account and trade surpluses, much of it against the United States. That almost certainly has to matter, although we aren't sure exactly how, or how much. We are witnessing a new world financial scenario playing out before our eyes, and none of it is by design.

The new world, as we now know it, developed, to a significant degree, after the 1997–1998 Asian financial crisis. During that period, the Asian economies (known for running a system called "crony capitalism," involving less than transparent banking and accounting standards but with surprisingly good economic fundamentals) faced a classic financial panic. Global "hot money" investors headed for the doors as Asian bank failures piled up and the Asian currencies plummeted almost across the board, creating economic and financial chaos.

In the aftermath of this destructive period, as a kind of insurance policy against another crisis unfolding, most Asian policymakers tied their currencies more or less to the U.S. dollar, the currency of the largest consuming country in the world. Their intent was to become a giant global export machine and their ultimate target was the American consumer. The initial goal was to accumulate a large stockpile of cash on hand in dollars to defend against future speculative attacks (rather than do what they should have done in the first place—reform their financial systems, including creating greater levels of transparency).

Today U.S. and European officials are scrambling to convince Asian policymakers that this heavy reliance on exports and undervalued currencies, with restrained domestic consumption, is not a healthy policy for anyone. But the situation is not about to reverse itself anytime soon. In large part, this is because the Asian societies are also aging rapidly, and these older people will tend to save more than consume, regardless of government policy. Therefore, the world will have to cope.

Indeed, the issue for global policymakers today is not whether this system devised by China and the other Pacific Rim economies has worked; the problem is that it has worked too well. Their giant export machine is piling up excess savings by amounts almost beyond imagination, a development I will explore further in chapter 4 on China. At the same time, the demand for commodities, including oil, by this huge and growing export machine had raised the world price of commodities dramatically. Suddenly the commodity-rich countries, led by the oil producers, including Saudi Arabia and Russia, had also begun piling up excess savings. In fact, China and India had accounted for 70 percent of the jump in global oil consumption. The result: Parts of the world today are still sitting on significant supplies of excess savings, earning low interest rates that will be recycled back to the rest of the world to allow for global economic expansion. At issue is the nature in which these savings will be recycled.

Historically, the United States, with its extraordinarily deep and flexible financial markets backed by a predictable legal and political system, has been the primary magnet for these excess savings. Some savings have gone into the U.S. stock and corporate bond markets, but a lot of the world's excess savings have purchased ultrasafe U.S. Treasury bonds, the securities used to finance America's debt.

The notion that the American economy is dependent on foreign capital may sound threatening, and certainly it would be better if the United States were financially self-sufficient, but the situation has not been as grave as many pessimists have suggested. The reason is that the world's excess savings, still largely denominated in U.S.

dollars, are so huge there are only two practical global targets large enough to handle that much capital—dollar assets and euro assets. The gold market is simply too small to handle such a supply of savings without forming a dangerous market bubble, which may already be happening. But as I'll demonstrate shortly, the last thing European policymakers want is for the world's excess savings to pour in and drive the value of the euro ever higher, because this would put the European export sector, Europe's one consistently reliable economic engine in recent decades, at a global competitive disadvantage. Europe's Mediterranean economies—Greece, Spain, Portugal, and Italy (plus Ireland) are already suffering from the strong euro and their lack of global competitiveness.

True, the dollar's positioning as the global reserve currency has probably peaked. Some diversification into the euro is inevitable. But the key point is that the dollar's role will likely remain essential because it is the primary currency vehicle for the world's commodity, currency, and derivatives markets. Economists Jeffrey Frankel and Menzie Chinn make the compelling argument that unless the United Kingdom joins the euro zone, making London Europe's new financial center, the dollar, not the euro, will remain the dominant currency.

Economist Martin Feldstein adds to the debate the audacious argument that the dollar hasn't really declined very much at all: "The real, inflation-adjusted value of the dollar against a broad basket of currencies has declined only 7 percent over the last 20 years (i.e. less than 0.5 percent per year)." Whether Feldstein is correct is open to discussion, but one thing seems certain: The dollar's strength, after accounting for inflation, against the yen and most of the Asian currencies has been unrealistically strong. Fred Bergsten, who heads the Peterson Institute for International Economics, in the spring 2008 edition of *The International Economy* argued for an "Asian Plaza Accord," an orderly, organized effort by American, Japanese, and Asian governments to fix these currency mismatches, with the goal of correcting trade imbalances. In the end, however, if Washington fails to restore the credibility of the U.S. financial system or the Federal Reserve loses its fight in tamping down inflationary expectations, this debate will be over: The dollar will collapse in an environment of chaos.

Meanwhile, the Japanese, Chinese, and others continue to buy U.S. Treasury bonds, and the question is whether that is making America vulnerable, in case they should decide to pull out. It is important first not to exaggerate the potential ramifications of the U.S. predicament. Several years ago, I asked a senior official at the New York Federal Reserve what would happen if China decided no longer to recycle its dollars by purchasing U.S. Treasury securities. "U.S. interest rates would skyrocket," the official quickly responded. I assumed he meant that U.S. interest rates would shoot up by 300 to 400 basis points (3 or 4 percentage points) when the official stunned me by adding: "The ten-year [Treasury bond] could go up thirty-five basis points—in a worst case scenario by even fifty basis points!" I was underwhelmed, as obviously the bond market and the potential pool of investors in U.S. bonds are far deeper than I had anticipated.

A 2007 study by the Wachovia Economics Group adds to this debate, arguing that no single nation holds anywhere near enough American debt to cause a major disruption. The study states: "Contrary to the popular perception that central banks in Asia, especially in China, are financing the entire U.S. current account deficit via massive purchases of U.S. Treasury securities, foreign holdings of U.S. securities are rather well diversified   There is no single country or central bank that the United States relies on to finance its current account deficit." Let me add that, by definition, a current account deficit is always financed. The question is at what price. The key is the exchange rate.

If, for example, the Chinese chose instead to switch to buying only European government bonds (again, because of the size of their reserves, the only other practical alternative for their savings recycling), the entire European policy community would revolt. Such a move, the Europeans would fear, would cause the euro to skyrocket more than it already has, potentially making European goods less globally competitive, particularly in Asian markets where the euro has already soared in strength against the yen and the Chinese yuan. The

European political and industrial world already perceives the euro as too strong at its current valuation level. Finance ministers in the euro zone, for example, regularly attack European Central Bank president Jean-Claude Trichet for allowing, in their view, the currency to strengthen as a direct result of a monetary policy that has kept short-term interest rates high relative to other interest rates.

Some strategists suggest a significantly higher euro could threaten the very independence of the central bank itself. That's because European politicians believe they have a legal right to choose the foreign exchange regime (fixed, floating, etc.) and to force the central bank to manage that regime. If the politicians mandated a regime calling for a weaker euro in the event of a huge influx of foreign capital, the European Central Bank would have its hands full. If it complied with this demand during an environment with inflation above the central bank's target, the institution's credibility could be seriously damaged.

In the end, the Asian central banks will do nothing intentionally to hurt the value of the U.S. dollar, including selling their U.S. Treasury holdings. The reason for this? Doing so would only undermine the value of their own massive dollar holdings, so it would be like shooting themselves in the foot. If China dumped its U.S. bond holdings, China would suffer a huge financial loss on its bond portfolio as prices fell. According to the International Monetary Fund, the dollar today still makes up 65 percent of the world's stockpiles of currencies, about where it has been historically. Indeed, if you add in the amount of U.S. currency hoarded by Middle Eastern and Chinese private concerns, the dollar today is still widely used, an amazing fact given the chaotic developments of recent years with the decline in credibility of the U.S. financial system.

In the long run, Americans may not always feel comfortable about this new world financial system of shifting savings pools. The United States should work quickly to bring about an international effort to correct global imbalances and negotiate a more uniform global financial regulatory structure with greater transparency. The long-term viability of the global system depends on those goals being met. But can the United States continue to thrive economically in the meantime under such a complicated arrangement? The answer is that it can unless U.S. policymakers, because of political pressure, are panicked into making serious blunders, including trade protectionism, caps on incoming foreign capital, overregulation, legal impediments and/or higher taxes on capital and entrepreneurial initiative, as well as allowing a continuation of inadequate financial market transparency. These are all developments that could serve as a tipping point for a complete breakdown of global confidence in the American system.

After all, the three largest buyers of U.S. Treasury debt are Britain (often investing developing-world capital, including central bank reserves), Japan, and China. They are buying not out of charity but because they believe U.S. policymakers will continue to allow the American wealth machine to create healthy growth, low rates of inflation and unemployment, and entrepreneurial initiative with the avoidance of class warfare or other economically destructive actions. These actions include deliberate efforts to destroy the value of the dollar for trade purposes. Because investors believe that the entrepreneurial capitalist model in America is intact, they are willing to buy a wide variety of non-Treasury security assets as well.

It is hard to overestimate how closely the world watches the American political, economic, and financial situation. When President Clinton took office, for instance, foreigners owned 19 percent of U.S. Treasury debt. Attracted to Clinton's approach to the economy, foreigners had raised that percentage to 35 percent by the time the president left office. Today, in part because of the relative shortage of global investment opportunities and heightened geopolitical risk, foreigners own 52 percent of U.S. Treasury debt.

At the beginning of the credit crisis some analysts suggested that the rest of the economic world would soon decouple from the United States. In other words, places like China would soon enjoy thriving consumer economies with less dependence on exports to the West. But this argument was highly suspect given the ugly demographic problems of China's aging society. These demographics have already produced a significant headwind to strong domestic consumption that will only worsen in coming years. In China, personal consumption over the last decade or so has actually declined significantly. According to Nicholas Lardy of the Peterson Institute for International Economics, "personal consumption in China in 2005 was 30 percent less than the level that would have been achieved if the household consumption share of GDP had remained at the level of 1990 rather than falling by more than ten percentage points."

Many friends of mine in the European central banking community initially bought into the decoupling theory. After all, European trade with the United States is less than 10 percent of European trade. Yet today, the same individuals acknowledge that while trade relationships are one thing, the degree of *financial* integration, as the subprime crisis revealed, is another. The policy world had underestimated how much the United States and Europe are inseparably entwined financially, and the same is true for the United States and most of the world.

Ultimately, what the decoupling theory's eager proponents under-appreciated, to a dangerous degree, was the role the United States has played for the past quarter-century as linchpin for the current system of open capital and trade markets. This was a role critical to the foundation of globalization. With the U.S. economy decoupled from the rest of the world, assuming that such a separation were possible, a new world comprising competing national interests and growing trade friction would not be pretty. Who, if not America, would defend the globalization model? Who would establish even the broad outlines of a financial order? Japan? France? Mexico? Russia? Would Canada set the policy pace for the global economic and financial system? The reality is that any decoupling is likely to be short lived.

Looking to the future, today's financial system is fragile precisely because the countries that have experienced the largest amounts of excess savings—again, the oil producers, China, and the rest of Asia— will likely accumulate even greater amounts of surplus savings over the next decade. Why? Because the low consumption/high export–dependent model is simply too much for those countries to resist.

A country like China has no Social Security or welfare system, a fact that creates a huge incentive for people to save more than to consume. Moreover, compared to the model of broad-based consumption and individual entrepreneurial initiative that exists in the West, the mercantilist export model is far more easily controlled by government bureaucrats—and more open to corruption.

A 2007 report by the McKinsey Global Institute describes the parameters of today's global financial landscape and the new shift in financial power. Notwithstanding the drop in commodity prices in particular and the global slowdown in general, the study describes the four new "power brokers" of the global economy: (1) investors from oil-exporting nations; (2) Asian central bankers and their sovereign wealth funds; (3) hedge funds; and (4) private equity firms. The Big Four new power brokers increasingly control and shape the global financial system, with assets that have more than doubled since 2000. Incredibly, this amounts to more than 40 percent of the capital controlled by global pension funds. Pension funds traditionally have been the big kahuna as a fund-raising source for global investment.

Of the Big Four power brokers, the Asian central banks control more than $3 trillion, with the Chinese controlling more than half of that amount. The private equity firms still control more than $2 trillion in global capital. And, you ain't seen nothin' yet. The McKinsey Global Institute estimates that the Big Four's collective assets will continue to grow significantly, reaching an amount comparable to more than 75 percent of the assets held by global pension funds.

One does not need to be a rocket scientist to see the picture emerging ahead. As the McKinsey Global report puts it: "Financial wealth and power, for so long concentrated in developed economies of the United States, Europe and Japan, is dispersing." The question is how much of their industrial base will Americans and Europeans allow to be sold to foreign-controlled governmental units. How will the U.S. Congress react, for instance, when a Chinese or Indian government-controlled investment unit attempts to purchase stakes in the American semiconductor and high-tech industries? As mentioned before, what if China attempts to purchase large stakes in Microsoft or IBM, and then demands seats on the boards of directors for Chinese government officials? What if the Chinese government begins accumulating the stock of Boeing? How will foreign investors respond to increasing limits on U.S. investment opportunities?

Laura Badian and Gregory Harrington of Arnold and Porter LLP in a recent issue of *The International Economy* cataloged the sovereign wealth fund activity for 2007 alone. Things began early in 2007 when China shifted $200 billion of its then $1.2 trillion in central bank currency revenues into riskier sovereign wealth fund investments. Immediately, the Chinese took a $3 billion investment in the private equity firm Blackstone Group LP. In July 2007, China Development Bank bought 3.6 percent of the British bank Barclays (as part of its bid for ABN AMRO). In October 2007, the Industrial and Commercial Bank of China made a $5.5 billion investment in Standard Bank Group Ltd., meaning the Chinese now own more than 20 percent of Africa's largest bank.

In November 2007, China's largest securities corporation signed on to an alliance with the U.S. investment bank Bear Stearns, a relationship that is now complicated by the U.S. firm's demise. In December 2007, China Investment Corporation bought a 9.9 percent equity participation in Morgan Stanley.

Of course, China is not the only player in this arena. In October 2007, Dubai International Capital purchased a 9.9 percent piece of Och-Ziff Capital Management, the large New York hedge fund. That came a month after Bourse Dubai bought roughly a 20 percent stake in the stock market NASDAQ. Bourse Dubai also bought NASDAQ's nearly 30 percent ownership of the London Stock Exchange. Badian and Harrington add that in late November 2007, Dubai International Capital placed a large investment in Sony. Not long thereafter, the Abu Dhabi Investment Authority announced it had become Citigroup's largest shareholder, not the smartest investment in the history of mankind.

Despite the funding needs of the industrialized economies, an international push-back to these purchases is just beginning. German chancellor Angela Merkel is already making noises about stopping international attempts to purchase German companies. Indeed, on the issue of sovereign wealth fund investment in Europe, the best bet is that European policymakers will demand total reciprocity, something most developing economies will never provide, which at some point in the next few years could create a global confrontation. Note that this is not just a large-country phenomenon. Even in Thailand, intense political heat recently developed overnight when a Singapore governmental investment unit attempted to purchase the Thai telecommunications conglomerate Shin.

For the West, the question is how China, India, and the others respond to existing American and European investment in their own industrial infrastructure. Will there be some form of irrational retaliation in the event their investment plans in the United States and Europe are stymied? Such an outcome seems hardly out of the question, particularly if access to Western technology is severely restricted on the basis of national security, meaning that global capital flows could well face new obstructions in the near future.

Jeffrey Garten, professor of international trade at Yale University, makes the case that European and U.S. policymakers have no choice but to better coordinate policies in light of the sovereign wealth fund activities. Garten argues that without coordination, these funds could pit one country against another. Some analysts argue that the investments of sovereign wealth funds should be part of international trade negotiations. In other words, investments would be subject to the regular rounds of trade negotiations. Bureaucrats would sit in positions of control, deciding, after negotiating with their international counterparts, how much investment to let in, as well as the nature of and targets for that investment.

Badian and Harrington point out that such a bureaucratic approach could produce a new spate of protectionism. The barriers to foreign

investment, particularly in economic sectors deemed of strategic importance, are rising rapidly. Of course, defining the word *strategic* is ripe for
bureaucratic mischief. To a certain extent, most of a nation's economic
activities, if need be, could be defined as "strategically important."

Complicating matters is that the lines between restrictions on foreign private versus government ownership are murky. I recently spoke
with a senior decision-maker of a sovereign wealth fund and he was
indignant at the suggestion he was some political tool of his government. His main argument: As financial professionals, we succeed if the
sovereign wealth fund succeeds in achieving a predictable, attractive,
and safe return on investment. Complicating things further is that not
all sovereign wealth funds are created equal. Some indeed are the
appendages of governments, while others are truly independent entities interested only in attractive passive investments, which are the
kind that will stabilize and strengthen the world economy.

Many of these latter funds engage in buy-and-hold strategies. As
long-term investors, they are among the first to jump into the market
and buy when the price of an asset falls. Yet other sovereign wealth
funds clearly exist in part to gain strategic national advantage for the
country back home.

If all of this sounds ominous, it is important to remember how
enormously the United States has benefited from a global system of
free-flowing capital during an amazing quarter-century of unprecedented wealth creation and poverty reduction. Moreover, the McKinsey Global Institute estimates that the investments by the oil exporters
and Asian central banks alone (by purchasing U.S. Treasury securities)
have lowered U.S. long-term interest rates by as much as 75 basis
points. Those bond purchases and other investments are likely to
increase in the coming years. In addition, apart from the strategic
complications posed by sovereign wealth funds, millions of well-
meaning foreign investors from hundreds of national economies have
found the United States an extraordinarily safe and profitable target
for broader investment, and the results are undeniable. Moreover,

although the Chinese, Russian, and Indian sovereign wealth funds grab the attention, benevolent Singapore claims the majority of cross-border sovereign wealth fund investments, over 50 percent of the total since the beginning of 2007, according to the *Financial Times*.

During the past twenty-five years of financial globalization, America amazingly (until the current recession) was in recession only 5 percent of the time. In the previous quarter-century before globalized financial markets, the U.S. economy was in recession 22 percent of the time. Despite disappointments over the uneven nature of wealth distribution, Americans benefited from the robust equity markets and low interest rates brought about by this new financial system, a scenario, however, that is changing quietly as the economy weakens as a result of a decline in confidence and trust in the economic future. Moreover, Americans may soon learn that there is no certainty about the future, as other nations position themselves to reject the globalization model.

Note that as this global financial power shift has occurred, Washington's political leadership has played the role of the naive fool. Most of the time, the politicians operate as if the global financial system doesn't exist. But occasionally the politicians produce a round of demagoguery, arguing that many of these nondemocratic economies fail to play by the rules (some don't) and that somehow America retains the option of opting out of the system. It doesn't, without experiencing brutally negative consequences in the form of dramatically higher long-term interest rates and soaring joblessness, as U.S. companies retrench.

What American politicians fail to realize is that they have only one option in this strange new world with its new dangerous ocean of capital. It is, to repeat: to make the American economy on a long-term basis the most attractive destination for global investment. That means reforming the capitalist model of the past quarter-century, making the financial system more transparent and its distribution of wealth more even. This is something today's political candidates abhor as they increasingly worship at the populist political shrine of antientrepreneurial demagoguery. It also means establishing a new financial order to enhance more universal trust in the global financial system.

In December 2007, just before Christmas, I was having coffee at a Washington, D.C., Starbucks and ran into an old friend, David Lipton. A gentle, unflappable man, he was one of the bright lights in the Clinton administration's Treasury Department, where he served as the crisis manager during the late-1990s Russian default.

We began our chat by discussing the rising global power of the sovereign wealth funds. We both agreed that politicians in both Europe and America would soon try to mount a challenge to allowing China, Russia, Saudi Arabia, and other nondemocratic regimes access to meaningful ownership of European or American industrial and financial interests. We concurred that a broad, bipartisan consensus that these investments need to be heavily monitored if not stopped will likely quietly emerge. "That is why these are dangerously unpredictable times," I interjected.

"Yeah, because it's not as simple as they think," Lipton countered. "If U.S. and European officials woke up tomorrow to a full-fledged global financial crisis, the first five calls ironically would go to the sovereign wealth funds in an appeal for help in achieving stability." Concluded Lipton: "Nobody else holds that kind of capital. Certainly not the International Monetary Fund. They [the sovereign wealth funds] could be our only hope."

That, in the end, is why America needs to maintain policies that continue to make it an attractive destination for investment. America also needs to correct its fiscal imbalances. The challenge, however, is to devise policies that will correct imbalances without jeopardizing the wealth and jobs created by the entrepreneurial capitalist system. The key is to avoid killing the last several decades' spirit of entrepreneurship. At present, there is a real danger that the policy prescriptions offered by a political community now infatuated with class warfare and protectionist rhetoric will end up killing the patient. As I will demonstrate in the following chapter, it is essential to understand what makes an economy grow and prosper. That means appreciating the role of the champions of today's new economy—the entrepreneurs—and how they are financed. But as I will also later point out, policies to promote a climate of economic risk-taking creativity must be complemented by policies that promote the broad-based nurturing of human capital. Ultimately, in the twenty-first-century global economy, it is human capital that matters the most.

3

Entrepreneurs in a World of Private Equity and Hedge Fund Troublemakers

---

One day in the summer of 1988, Paul Tudor Jones, then a young hedge fund investor who today ranks among the *Forbes* 400 richest Americans, called me, asking that I stop by his office on my next trip to New York. I had never heard of him, but our subsequent meeting taught me a lot about the nature of those in an entrepreneurial economy who provide capital to society's risk-takers.

A week or so later on a sweaty afternoon, I found myself roaming the lower section of Wall Street in what seemed a hopeless search for his office. Finally, I followed an almost invisible, trash-strewn staircase (the elevator was broken) next to a fast-food restaurant up to a seedy second-floor office with no sign, no receptionist, no one in sight, and not much air-conditioning.

Ten, then twenty, minutes passed and no one arrived or even responded to my calls throughout the empty offices. As I stood in the entranceway getting ready to leave, suddenly, up the stairs and into the small disorganized quarters bounded Jones. A scrappy-looking man of medium height in his early thirties in a sweat suit and with what appeared to be a cowlick, he introduced himself and led me into his personal office just across from the front door. Friends had suggested that someone named Jones, a Tennessee-born former commodities trader, had the previous year earned a fortune by brilliantly predicting the U.S. stock market crash. But surely this couldn't be the same guy, could it, I wondered?

"What do you think of the dollar?" Jones immediately queried as we sat down, his southern drawl so thick and exaggerated I began wondering if this was all an elaborate act, some prank pulled by a mischievous college friend who had hired a bit actor to play Paul Jones. Jones appeared to be just off the farm. Before I could respond, my eye caught something strangely out of place, just to the right of him. It was a fully clothed, life-size department store mannequin sitting next to his desk and staring right at me.

I suddenly became self-conscious. It was like two interviewers in one. Quickly I glanced around and sensed something quite familiar: The entire room exhibited the feel of the frat house in the movie *Animal House*. This was college dorm central, complete with a foot-long, yellow No. 2 pencil. Perhaps most disconcerting: The mannequin wore sunglasses, so there was a sense of realism as the two pairs of eyes stared at me, the mannequin's and Paul's. Was the mannequin a market spy for some French bank? I laughed to myself.

I answered the dollar question, suggesting that the foreign exchange desk at the Japanese Ministry of Finance (MoF), more than the markets, held the cards in the short run on the yen-dollar rate, so it was important not to risk being blindsided by the MoF going into the upcoming G7 meeting of the industrialized world's central bankers and finance ministers. However, about forty-five seconds into my explanation, Jones broke in: "You're hired! Now how much do you charge?" Financial traders in the hedge fund world often make instantaneous judgments, relying on gut instinct.

On several occasions, Jones invited me to his four-thousand-acre preserve on the Eastern Shore of Maryland, a hunting paradise he referred to as the "Disney World of Hunting." Twenty-six employees catered to our every hunting need. One day, several years after we met, we found ourselves standing in a field waiting for the staff to force pheasants out of towers to be shot by the guests (Jones, looking a bit like Rambo, wore camouflage army fatigues; another guest and neighbor, former Treasury secretary Nick Brady, stood about twenty feet away). While waiting, Jones and I began talking about what life would have been like outside of the markets. "How would you define your dream job if not in the markets, Paul?" I asked. Jones, a billionaire and by then a born-again environmentalist (because of a wetlands mishap on his own property that led to the imprisonment of his construction foreman), offered an unexpected reply. "My dream is to be U.S. secretary of the interior," he said rather earnestly.

I was shocked. Here was a financial superstar whose dream was to head a cabinet agency generally derided as a backwater inside the Washington Beltway. It dawned on me how even the most sophisticated players in the markets understood little of how tough it is to change policy in Washington from the inside, particularly relative to the power they could wield as well-funded outside promoters of causes. Despite all our advances in communications, the gap of understanding between government and the financial markets remained dangerously wide. Here were two worlds passing in the night. As a metaphor, it explains a lot about why the world remains dangerously unstable. Government policymakers and financial markets enjoy little understanding of one another's worlds. Two of the new global economy's main providers of entrepreneurial capital—the hedge funds and the private equity firms—remain enigmas to the political class.

Incidentally, today the offices of Tudor Investments can compete in their taste and luxury with any in the financial world. Jones dresses like a fashion model (probably advised by his wife, who *is* a fashion model). He has used his trading and business skills to create an impressive non-profit operation, the Robin Hood Foundation, for the disadvantaged in and around New York City. But he has never traded quite as well as when that mannequin sat by his side in the sweltering office above a fast-food restaurant, which continually reminds me that the most successful risk-takers in society usually operate, at least in the beginning, outside of the mainstream. They are seldom members of the "club." They don't start out resembling anything close to a success story. That is one reason they and their risk-taking cousins, the entrepreneurs, remain so mysterious.

I ended up working closely with most of the major hedge fund players of that era, and I know a number of the key players in the private equity world. Hedge funds are highly agile, largely unregulated, usually global funds for high-net-worth investors who can handle risk—far more than regulated market funds like mutual funds would allow. Private equity investors deal with firms not publicly listed on a stock exchange and reshape them through mergers, restructuring, or recapitalization (sometimes taking them public) to produce better performance.

Today both hedge funds and private equity firms have become the international financial system's new bogeymen—the horrible, greedy monsters blamed by frustrated politicians for the loss of control and occasional chaos associated with today's highly unpredictable capital flows. Even if there is a small kernel of truth to the bogeyman charge, this negative bias poses a danger to the international system and risks leading to a period of financial market stagnation. Indeed, it is true that while some hedge fund operators, who earn enormous fees, demonstrate an extraordinary level of generosity to those around them, others exhibit a level of greed that is almost beyond comprehension. It is that degree of avarice, combined with a certain play-outside-the-box mentality, that contributes to today's cauldron of political resentment and potential financial risk.

For example, one Wall Street trader I know, whose funds usually produce huge amounts of volatility, regularly consults a professional astrologer on trading decisions. This fact somehow fails to appear in his firm's disclosure documents for investors. Another hedge fund operator, worth a fortune and based in the New York area, sent his chief lieutenant to my office after he had been a client for about a year. The purpose of the visit was to discuss renewing our consulting contract.

Imagine my shock when the lieutenant actually began by saying: "We can *steal* the written part of your consulting service. What we can't get is the analysis from your client telephone calls. We'll pay you half of your consulting fee to get those calls." Flabbergasted, I quickly thanked the lieutenant for his candor and ended our professional relationship with his firm. Several years later, the same hedge fund manager was spotted in front of Carnegie Hall just before a concert was about to begin. He had purchased one ticket too many and was trying to scalp the unused ticket for the best price to passing pedestrians before the concert began. The billionaire's friends watching were mortified.

The private equity world, where the big money guys throw themselves $6 million sixtieth birthday parties, is no different from the hedge funds. There is a considerable amount of hypocrisy, too. For years, some high-profile, self-appointed leaders of private equity partnerships have complained that the low tax rate on the top bracket for individual income in America rewards the rich too handsomely while contributing to budget deficits. Sounds public spirited? Well, the fact is, partners of private equity firms don't pay the going individual or corporate income tax rates on the bulk of their income, which is classified as something called "carried interest." Instead, they pay only a 15 percent tax rate, less than half that paid by other businesses.

This is the situation that needs to be phased out. Doing so, however, won't be easy because other countries would like nothing better than for American private equity funds to move offshore. For example, discussions are under way in Switzerland to introduce legislation to offer New York– and London-based private equity firms the same 15 percent tax rate as an incentive for them to move their headquarters to Switzerland. Given the mobility of capital, such a move would not be as far-fetched as it seems. Financial services remains one of the industries in which the United States globally is competitively superior. The rest of the world would enjoy seeing its demise, which appears already to be under way as a result of the subprime crisis.

But here's the point: The greed of some hedge fund operators and the effectiveness of private equity tax lobbyists do not negate the value of these organizations to the global financial system. Private equity firms don't create distortions in the markets; they simply reflect distortions. If credit is too cheap and too readily available, and if the regulatory climate causes corporations to lean toward mergers and acquisitions over investment in new enterprises, then private equity firms rise up out of the woodwork of the financial system to be of service. Despite their outlandish fees, they are the effect, not the cause, of the existing climate.

In today's new uncertain world, politicians would like to eliminate hedge funds, the perceived troublemakers of the world economy. Call me biased, but these troublemaking institutions are the international economy's truth serum. They constantly challenge governments' conventional policy views and often cast a skeptical eye on the bogus explanations offered by the corporate captains of industry about their firms. Several years ago some critics argue that hedge funds engaged in market collusion, particularly in the area of commodities, and thus, it is charged, were responsible for the then higher commodity prices. My sense, however, is that by and large the big hedge funds were predicting a global economic slowdown, led by the United States. An investor in this scenario would have bet on commodity prices' dropping. After all, never before in history have commodity prices risen during periods of worldwide economic decline. Complicating this situation is that if sovereign governments, led by China, were indeed hoarding commodities, such a development would not remain a secret for long. Knowing of this development, the hedge funds, as wise money managers, would liquidate their "short" positions in the commodities markets and bet on prices' rising despite global economic softening. In this scenario, the hedge funds are reacting to, not leading, events.

The hedge funds are historically significant as the first series of actors in the great globalization drama. They were the first to figure out how to use to best advantage or arbitrage the new global financial structure. They began putting together investment portfolios reflecting many different international markets with different investment instruments, based on a broad, macroeconomic assessment of the entire global economy. Former Federal Reserve chairman Alan Greenspan calls the hedge funds "the bees that spread the pollen." I am convinced that if hedge funds did not exist, financial markets would experience far more calamities than they do now.

Rather than serving as a source of destabilization, as some critics maintain, hedge funds during the last decade of globalization, despite bouts of irresponsibility, generally have helped the markets converge and become more efficient. Indeed, hedge funds are critical to long-term market stability. Without them, inefficiencies can exist for a long time in the marketplace, suddenly igniting a large, potential shock to the system.

For example, before the development of hedge funds, companies and/or governments that supported cartels and monopolies (an approach sometimes referred to as crony capitalism) could hide their activities for long periods of time. Insider connections, not the free hand of the market, guided decision-making. In the old days, the market failed to fully discipline such behavior. Today a whole class of hedge fund speculators turns over every rock looking for market inefficiencies to exploit. One such inefficiency is governments that announce major reforms with great fanfare, knowing that they lack the political courage and will to follow through with their promises. Today, European financial officials would place the hedge funds in a straitjacket. The reason: The hedge funds are questioning the European banks' massive exposure to shaky emerging market debt.

Another example: bloated companies with excessive overhead and inefficient operations. The leaders of these companies have little vision for the future, nor the courage needed to run their firms with greater efficiency or enhance their competitive position. These companies are the hedge fund manager's dream. Traders take "short" positions in the companies, anticipating that their value will fall so that the hedge fund can reap the windfalls. The threat of this process also forces management at all times to think about constructive change, allowing their companies to avoid becoming globally obsolete.

Spend some time with politicians in Germany and you'll discover that hedge fund operators, in their view, are nothing less than the devil incarnate—"locusts," as some critics call them. Yet ironically, in recent years hedge funds, private equity firms, and their cousins, the global investment banks, have been restructuring and modernizing Germany's corporate and financial sectors. This has largely occurred without the knowledge of the politically stymied coalition government. Like most European governments, Germany for decades has tolerated double-digit unemployment and subpar economic growth while lacking the political will to reform the economy. In Germany in recent years, the hedge funds and private equity firms have forced change, which is why, as I'll show in a later chapter, a more productive Germany became more globally competitive relative to the rest of Europe. By contrast, Italy, an economy more closed to outside financial interests, fell further behind.

Critics counter that many of the newer hedge funds take on reckless amounts of leverage and therefore increase the risk to the entire financial system. It is true that the number of new hedge funds has exploded. When I began my market advisory firm, there existed only a few hundred hedge funds, with a couple dozen representing the cream of the crop. Today nine thousand hedge funds take on risk within the system, the vast majority of which I wouldn't touch with an eleven-foot pole (which is what I use for some things I wouldn't touch with a ten-foot pole).

In a hedge fund, seniority counts for little. The only considerations of success are bottom-line trading results. In this system, therefore, brilliant young traders often rise quickly to powerful senior positions. The problem is that a lot of the young traders working at these funds have never experienced an extended down market. At an average age of twenty-six, they were in grade school during the time of the 1987 crash. What they lack are experience and judgment.

That's the bad news. The good news is that the financial markets are correcting this situation. Since the beginning of 2004, a lot of global capital has moved away from the young upstarts and back to the more established hedge funds with long, safe track records. Currently, the hundred largest hedge funds control 75 percent of the total funds invested in hedge funds—and the figure is rising. At the beginning of 2004, that percentage was 50 percent. As for the upstarts, the market has begun to sort out the true talent from the imitators in the placement of capital. In the wake of the subprime crisis, this sorting-out process has accelerated as a lot of hedge fund financing through the troubled U.S. banking sector has been withdrawn.

In 1998, the collapse of the hedge fund Long-Term Capital Management (LTCM) nearly tanked the world financial system. By comparison, in 2006 another Greenwich, Connecticut–based hedge fund, Amaranth, lost almost $9 billion (in dollar terms, larger than LTCM's losses). But today's deeper, more modernized global financial system absorbed this loss with barely a hiccup. The same thing happened during the subprime crisis of 2007–2009.

Some hedge funds suffered huge losses and quietly went out of business. But the big story initially was not the hedge funds. It was the major banks and other large financial institutions that failed to offer a transparent picture of the risk to the markets. Over the coming years, more hedge funds will fail, but less because of excessive risk and more as a direct by-product of the banks' difficulties and the resulting withdrawal of hedge fund capital.

Most European and some American policymakers would again like nothing better than to place the hedge fund world in a regulatory straitjacket. What they fail to realize is that the large established hedge funds for the most part would like nothing better. New governmental burdens would serve as an impediment to newcomers setting up competing hedge funds, what economists call "barriers to entry." If the entry fee is $3 million in legal and other regulatory-related costs, a lot of talented traders, who come out of some of the best trading firms, such as Goldman Sachs, would be unlikely to strike out on their own. Large established businesses have a track record of attempting to achieve a monopoly within their industry, and the people who run the big hedge funds are no different. Enhanced competition could also jeopardize their generous fee structure, if newly arrived, talented traders on the scene are willing to cut prices.

In December 2007, during the early stage of the subprime credit crisis, Federal Reserve chairman Ben Bernanke offered this observation to a small group of market analysts: "When the crisis is over, the banks ironically could become much more the center of financial intermediation than they have been in the past." On the surface, this sounds like a healthy development. During the beginning of the crisis, the Federal Reserve, in one of its first actions, expanded its safety net through a new auction system to enhance bank liquidity. The Fed essentially circled the wagons around the U.S. banking system—and for good reason. If the banks collapsed, so would the U.S. economy and probably the world economy as well.

However, making banks even more the center of credit allocation in America, particularly when the world is de-leveraging, sounds reassuring, but it's not. The reason is that banks have a relatively poor track record in financing entrepreneurship. Bankers in general lack the imagination and vision to take a chance. There are also lots of laws and regulations that prevent them from doing so. The high-risk-taking entrepreneurs are the magic ingredients that allow an economy to expand rapidly and create jobs. Yet as every small town knows, the local banker is always aggressively willing to lend to anyone wealthy enough *not* to need a loan. The unknown, unvetted start-up firm backed by a brilliant business idea but with insufficient capital is turned away time and again. Today the question is whether the current financial regulatory reforms will eventually slow overall lending to the entrepreneurial sector.

Historically, hedge funds, private equity firms, venture capitalists, and the other vehicles for capital allocation have brought to the table a special quality—a curiosity about entrepreneurial creativity and an imbued sense that economic expansion stems from a destruction of the status quo. Most large firms, including the large banks, fixate on preserving *what is*. The tiny hedge funds and other capital allocators concentrate on replacing *what is* with something better. That is why they are so detested by the establishment. They are the original promoters of the notion that economic success stems from continual reinvention. In their eyes, the entrepreneur is almost a mythic hero.

But the question is whether today's political culture, influenced by the new politics of envy, will continue to tolerate an entrepreneurial class set apart from the rest of society that continues to earn incredible sums of money. The early returns are not reassuring. The most common political mantra today is the populist call to "put an end to corporate and Wall Street greed." But how as a society do we deal with the crooks at Enron and foolish bankers in general, without throwing the proverbial entrepreneurial baby out with the bathwater? How, in reforming the system, does Washington avoid crippling the U.S. financial services sector, a development that would warm the hearts of financial competitors around the world? How do we avoid cutting off financing to society's risk-takers?

The discussion of entrepreneurs as a separate and distinct societal class reminds me of a conversation I had in early 1990 at the home of Bundesbank president Karl Otto Pöhl. The powerful head of the German central bank had participated in many of the international economic conferences I organized in the late 1980s and 1990s, and we had become friends. Pöhl, of medium height and always tanned from a regular golf and ski regimen, may be the most charming policy official I've ever met. When he spoke to someone, that person felt like the most important person in the room. I am convinced that had Pöhl not gone into central banking, he would have become chancellor of Germany.

That evening, Pöhl had just finished the most controversial period of his career. In November 1989, the Berlin Wall had fallen and he had just labeled Chancellor Helmut Kohl's plan to unify a divided Germany under a single currency "a fiasco." The East German currency was, of course, far weaker than the almighty West German deutsche mark (DM), yet Kohl insisted on a risky one-to-one conversion rate to create, overnight, a single German currency in an attempt to unite his nation. This was high drama. The Bundesbank president and the chancellor of Germany were at war.

The German central bank president's home, a striking contemporary design, sat heavily guarded and surrounded by dozens of two-hundred-year-old oak trees in the small, charming town of Kronberg, forty minutes outside of Frankfurt. Fortunately, unlike Frankfurt, Kronberg escaped the Allied bombing at the end of World War II.

Despite his ongoing battle with the chancellor, Pöhl was in good spirits when I arrived. After exchanging stories about the international community over a round of drinks, I decided to gently take issue with the Bundesbank president, who was, at the time, the most important policymaker in Europe. "Karl Otto," I began, "correct me if I'm wrong, but didn't Germany in 1946 come back economically almost overnight against all expectations, so why can't East Germany today? What about a second German economic miracle?"

Pöhl's response said a great deal about why societies need the special breed that are entrepreneurs. "In every society," he began, "there is the top 15 to 20 percent which includes the leaders, talented managers and, most importantly, the visionary risk-takers. You are right: In 1946, against British and American expectations, this talented group after the war brought about the first German economic miracle under Ludwig Erhard, minister of economy. The risk-takers had no other place to go, but today is different. The moment the Berlin Wall fell, that high-powered group in East German society immediately raced across the border, fully confident they could compete in the West and immediately earn ten to twenty times their current incomes. Left behind are the less talented, the more dependent, and the more fearful. These people lack the ability on their own to rebuild that economy. And by implementing a one-to-one currency conversion, Kohl will be crippling the entire German economy for a decade." Given the relatively weak performance of the German economy until recently, dragged down by the eastern sector, it turned out Pöhl was right (although some analysts argue that, in the end, the real problem was the pushing up of East German wages).

Pöhl's analysis—which states essentially that in any organization the cream rises to the top—is reminiscent of a question I once posed to a friend, a high-powered New York management consultant. "What's the secret to being a great manager?" I asked casually one day over lunch. His crude response: "Tolerating crap!" His explanation: The well-known understanding among managers is that "every organization is comprised of the 80 percent or so who produce anywhere from the average to the mediocre, while the talented 20 percent spread throughout the organization bring about creative change, productive advancement, and generally make the difference between success and failure." He concluded: "As a manager, if you can't tolerate crap, you'll create an internal war for yourself. So the key is to nurture that talented group, to allow them to be highly productive, without offending the others."

Former Goldman Sachs CEO Henry Paulson, who went on to become U.S. Treasury secretary, once made a very similar observation during his time as the head of that prestigious investment firm. During a question-and-answer session at a Salomon Smith Barney conference in January 2003, he said, "There are 15 to 20 percent of the people [at Goldman] who really add 80 percent of the value. I think we can cut a fair amount and not get into muscle and still be very well-positioned for the upturn." This set off a firestorm of controversy, which was picked up by the press, and Paulson apologized soon thereafter in a firmwide voice mail. One wag later observed that there was no need for Paulson to apologize, because at the hypercompetitive Goldman, "everyone thinks they're part of the 20 percent, so no one was really upset by what Hank said."

This emphasis on one, exclusive part of society at first glance seems both wrong and unfair, particularly in a country like the United States in which all are perceived as "created equal"—and particularly at a time of growing class warfare. Left to their own devices, moreover, it has been my gut feeling that society's elites usually screw things up, whether in Vietnam or Iraq. As conservative columnist William F. Buckley once quipped, "I'd rather be governed by the first two hundred people in the Boston phone book than by the members of the Harvard faculty."

On the other hand, the idea that the entrepreneurial leadership group of risk-takers changes continuously is more compelling. The far more intriguing picture is of a churning meritocracy of risk-takers, succeeding and failing as they collectively develop innovations that propel an economy forward, constantly reinventing it along the way. In this cauldron of economic activity, of success and failure, membership is open to any and all with courage and a new idea.

Robert Litan, of the Brookings Institution and the Kauffman Foundation, has tried to quantify the U.S. entrepreneurial situation. His findings: About a half-million Americans launch companies each year and between 10 and 15 percent of all working adults engage in some kind of entrepreneurial activity, with a portion of these folks being the innovators who matter the most. More recently, the Small Business Administration has said that 672,000 new companies were started in 2005, more than at any other time in U.S. history. Clearly, at some point in the early 1980s a paradigm shift occurred, unleashing this explosive dynamism. This white-hot entrepreneurial meritocracy rocketed the U.S. economy upward.

Indeed, until the last few decades, the label "entrepreneur" implied something sinister. Entrepreneurs were perceived as the winners in a zero-sum game, leaving the economic losers cut adrift. They were the brutes who, through the sheer force of audacity, unfairly skimmed the cream off the top of the free market capitalist system.

What the last quarter-century has demonstrated is just the opposite. Swedish writer and defender of globalization Johan Norberg argues that entrepreneurs have done nothing less than "filled our lives with everyday miracles." Norberg points out: "If you lived several hundred years ago, you would wake up each morning with no electric lights, running water, or even indoor sanitation. You would have no car, bus or train and no antibiotics. You would toil for decades doing what a computer can do in seconds. Plus, your life expectancy would be less than forty years."

That is why, given the choice between being King Louis XIV of France in the late seventeenth century and a middle-class person in America today, I'd take the latter. The availability of antibiotics, new communications technologies—not to mention the riches that our culture has to offer through electronic media—would settle the matter for me once and for all.

Given the way entrepreneurs have improved our lives, they should be praised, not pilloried. They are society's risk-taking problem solvers who seek new opportunities against all odds. They are, as Norberg puts it, our society's "explorers who venture into uncharted territory and open up the new routes along which we will all be traveling soon enough."

Entrepreneurs often traffic in revolutionary ideas that, to the rest of us at the time, seem foolhardy. I am reminded of Chester Carlson, who in the late 1930s found himself with what seemed to others a foolhardy idea—an electrostatic printing process—which he tried to sell to the top mimeograph companies in America. Turned away time and again, he finally converted his kitchen into a workshop and went into business for himself. He experienced risk and a shortage of capital, but the tiny enterprise survived and prospered.

Today, we know it as Xerox.

Were Carlson alive, he probably would ask, "Whatever became of those smug mimeograph companies?" The answer is that they fell victim to what Joseph Schumpeter, the economic theorist, called the "creative destruction" of capital—the process by which a new idea enters the marketplace, making existing capital worthless. What sounds like some arcane process is at the heart of today's new global economy. Five out of six fledgling enterprises will go out of business, the majority within the first year, with new ones springing up to take their places. In the United States, Frost Belt or Sunbelt, such businesses fail at roughly the same rate.

This cycle of success and failure provides a perfect object lesson. The secret to maintaining a robust economy centers on more than efforts to modernize existing plant and equipment. The secret is creativity, allowing new firms with new ideas to rise up, while existing firms work every day to reinvent themselves to compete on a global scale.

The secret lies in a buoyant, free market global system. It exists in the enterprises yet unborn, the energy sources yet untapped, and the inventions yet untried. Many of these fledgling entrepreneurs will fail, but others—like Chester Carlson, with his original entrepreneurial instinct—will replace today's capital and products with new and better ones, to the benefit of us all. And where is Xerox today? It appears to be nowhere, because ultimately it too failed to engage in the process of continuous reinvention while more competitive firms have appeared on the scene. Indeed, Xerox invented the so-called computer mouse, but failed to see its potential and therefore never benefited from its own invention.

Many U.S. policymakers, and even more so those in Europe and Japan, find entrepreneurial capitalism disconcerting. One reason may be that it is hard to represent politically the interests of an entity that does not yet exist, or a young, struggling enterprise virtually invisible on the economic landscape. But it also may result from the great frustration over the unpredictability, and lack of controllability, of the entrepreneurial process. It is difficult to provide a blanket of total economic security in an entrepreneurial society. Entrepreneurial capitalism involves the dynamic process of two competing forces—success and failure. And perhaps most frustrating, it continues to depend directly on the creative implementation of new ideas from individuals who, in the eyes of elite society, often appear unpolished and relatively inexperienced.

I remember watching Ted Turner in the early days of CNN arrive one morning in Washington to testify before Congress. With his thick southern drawl, Turner came off as a wild-eyed hayseed, not the cunning billionaire of his later reputation. A bunch of no-name Senate staffers, sitting behind their bosses at the hearing, snickered at Turner's less-than-polished demeanor and audacious start-up venture. Who are the fools today?

Entrepreneurs tend to appear to be a little bit crazy. They are the illogical dreamers, even though many enjoy an inner genius for success. They are nonetheless our society's main creators of jobs and wealth. While entrepreneurs may be crazy, they are crazy like a fox.

Most underestimate the risks. Some make reckless overestimations of their chance for success. They have to. Otherwise, they wouldn't try. Still, as society's daring playmakers, they will endure incredible risk—far more than the average business executive—for the possibility of great psychic and monetary returns. At the heart of today's globalized new economy rests the notion that every individual is a potential entrepreneur, in the sense that entrepreneurship is not limited by social status or wealth. Notice that this is not simply capital formation, but capital mobilization. Capital is more than money. Capital is productive ability and thus exists in the minds, hands, and hearts of people. The challenge for policymakers is how to encourage these potential wealth and job creators to undertake the risks in the first place.

In recent years, the role of the entrepreneur in the industrialized world has undergone a transition. Not long ago, Western businesses began relying on the computer for tasks once accomplished by humans, from the revolution of the supply chain for goods and services to management of inventories. But with the emergence of the low-cost Chinese and Indian markets, efficiency alone is not enough to assure success.

Instead, the essential ingredient for success has become a steady stream of innovation. Harold Evans, the author of *They Made America: From Steam Engine to the Search Engine: Two Centuries of Innovators*, notes that if you Google the entry for "CEO," there are today a startling twice as many entries for "CEO and innovation" as for "CEO and efficiency." Says Evans: "Our future depends on groundbreaking innovation. Yes, we must implement and develop the lead with efficiency, but in that management process never lose sight of the animating vision that created the innovation in the first place, or the lead will surely vanish."

It is difficult to say what prompts the entrepreneurial sector to take risks. It would be a mistake to suggest that tax policy or money alone led to the explosion in risk-taking the last quarter-century. Bill Gates, in nurturing the start-up firm Microsoft in the early 1980s, was propelled forward by a bold vision, not by tax advice from his accountant. Entrepreneurs initially don't take the risk largely for the money. They do it because it is to be done and has never been done before. Some do it for ego. Eventually, entrepreneurs realize the idea needs to be economic, which can eventually lead to great wealth.

In 2006, the World Bank issued an amazing study called "Where Is the Wealth of Nations?" which explored this question: Why do highly industrialized countries like the United States succeed economically while some less developed economies with ample natural resources do poorly? Put another way, why are developing-world immigrants in America four to five times more productive than they would be had they stayed at home? The study concludes that the difference is that the United States and other industrialized economies enjoy an enormous amount of "intangible wealth."

Total wealth in an economy involves more than compiling a list of a country's physical and financial assets. Wealth involves intangible assets such as property rights, an honest and efficient judicial system backed by the rule of law, a workable government, an appreciation for and nurturing of human capital, and, I would add, a tolerance of and even appreciation for entrepreneurial creativity and risk, combined with a rejection of class warfare. In other words, intangible assets include something as simple as a society's tolerance for successful risk-takers becoming rich. And achieving riches is what successful entrepreneurs do.

However, just as the theory of "economic man" responding only to his own, greedy desires is less than satisfactory in explaining what motivates the entrepreneur, so is the notion that money doesn't matter. Levels of taxation and the general political climate toward entrepreneurship and risk matter enormously. This is particularly true in the early stages of a new venture. The level of taxation can be a strong motivator. Entrepreneurs are counting on the fact that if they make a lot of money, it won't be largely taken away by the government. That is why tinkering with this new global system to make it seem fairer, or to use confiscatory taxation to try to create a feeling of a greater security for society in general, carries with it the potential to produce unintended consequences. For every policy action, there is the potential for a negative reaction. Why? Because when all is said and done, entrepreneurs enjoy the capacity to be mobile. Let me offer one striking example.

The rock star Bono, the lead singer for the rock band U2, is known for his philanthropic efforts. Experts in the field of poverty reduction tell me that Bono at his core is an individual with a heart of gold. Here is a man who has it all—wealth, rock star status, and more. Yet his heart bleeds for AIDS-choked Africa and for suffering among the poor around the world. A major star in an entertainment industry known for its hedonistic impulses has also retained his soul.

Yet his business manager, to the surprise of the world, announced that Bono was moving a significant part of his business operation from Ireland, where taxes on the entertainment business had been raised, to the Netherlands, where the tax on artistic royalties by comparison is low. Bono found himself attracted to a better risk-reward ratio. He suddenly came face-to-face with a more entrepreneurial Netherlands seeking to develop a base in the entertainment world. And this was a man who had become perhaps Ireland's greatest iconic figure to the world.

If Bono would do that to his beloved Ireland, how can Washington's class-warfare politicians be sure a hefty segment of the American entrepreneurial class won't move offshore seeking a better venue for risk-taking and wealth creation—or leisure—in the event of major, class warfare–inspired changes to the current U.S. environment? I suspect competing economic policymakers elsewhere in the world would hardly object. This is why U.S. policymakers should approach the fragile phenomenon of entrepreneurship gingerly and with extreme caution and sensitivity. Here's an even greater irony. In April 2008, the British Labour government announced a major review of the competitiveness of the United Kingdom's system of taxation. The reason: A number of large British firms announced that they were relocating their headquarters to Ireland, attracted by the lower Irish corporate tax rate.

The latest tax development in the United Kingdom is the effort to force non-British residents to pay taxes on all their overseas investments (or simply pay the government a $70,000 annual fee to avoid disclosure). While such a fee is an insignificant rounding error for, say, a Russian oil tycoon living in London, the fee represents an enormous disincentive to the senior and midlevel executives of foreign firms based in the United Kingdom. As a result, even more of these firms are planning to leave. Particularly in today's service-oriented industrialized economies, mobility is a fact of life. The British government's efforts to tinker with the tax code have already initiated a negative psychological effect in changing global attitudes toward Britain as an international financial center. And what are the alternative locations of the future? Many experts list the following, in order of likelihood: (1) Ireland, (2) Switzerland, (3) Singapore.

But don't get me wrong. Not all highly compensated executives are fairly paid. There is something troubling about failed senior executives such as Robert Nardelli, the former head of Home Depot, Inc., being fired from his job with a $210 million payoff. This demonstrates a complete and total breakdown of effective corporate board governance. Today's overly generous level of executive compensation in public companies is, almost across the board, a disgrace. This unrestrained greed at shareholder expense has seriously undermined political support for the market capitalist system. The attempt by Wall Street banks to use taxpayer money to provide large executive retention bonuses is both absurd and insulting.

And it does give one pause that a new enterprise, unproven but with potential, can go public during periods of excessive credit and bullish stock markets, reaping rewards in the hundreds of millions of dollars. This is particularly true when it is compared with, say, the senior management of a proven existing firm, making prudent decisions to maintain healthy levels of employment, guiding the firm forward for decades, which never sees any such financial windfall. With entrepreneurial capitalism, there are times when it seems the system is one big, unfair lottery.

The problem, however, is that in a highly entrepreneurial economy, it is difficult, if not impossible, to micromanage wealth distribution without negative countereffects. To some extent, the system must tolerate a certain amount of ugly distributional "unfairness" with the greater goal of producing an explosion in wealth creation, greater job creation, and broad-scale poverty reduction. In my view, the turbocharged entrepreneurial capitalist model is more than worth the trade-off because it offers the potential to create opportunity at all rungs of the income ladder.

How? The entrepreneurial economy of continuous innovation, the purest form of meritocracy, by definition moves risk-takers up and down the income ladder in a climate of ferociously chaotic dynamism where the people at the top are seldom there for long. Look at the *Forbes* 400 list of the richest Americans, and the major industries they represented, for the year 1980. A lot of those people and industries are missing on today's list.

There has been a similar phenomenon at work with the *Fortune* 500, the list of America's top companies. In the 1960s and 1970s, an average of just twenty companies per year fell from the ranks of the *Fortune* 500. By the 1980s, it was forty companies per year. Between 1990 and 1995, two hundred companies had been displaced. And of the top one hundred companies on the 2005 list, nearly three-quarters were not on the 1980 list (though a small percentage still exists through mergers under other corporate names).

The fact is, just as capital roams the world seeking the highest return relative to safety, so do global entrepreneurs enjoy the ability to choose their venue for operations based on regulatory and legal conditions, as well as the risk-reward relationship. Today's policymakers fail to realize that in the new global economy, where services make up the bulk of economic activity, people and institutions are highly mobile. Adam Smith two centuries ago may have been the first to notice this phenomenon:

> Land is a subject which cannot be removed; whereas stock easily may. The proprietor of land is necessarily a citizen of the particular country in which his estate lies. The proprietor of stock is properly a citizen of the world, and is not necessarily attached to any particular country. He would be apt to abandon the country in which he was exposed to a vexatious inquisition, in order to be assessed to a burdensome tax, and would remove his stock to some other country where he could either carry on his business, or enjoy his fortune more at his ease. By removing his stock he would put an end to all the industry which it had maintained in the country which he left. Stock cultivates land; stock employs labor. A tax which tended to drive away stock from any particular country would so far tend to dry up every source of revenue both to the sovereign and to the society. Not only profits of stock, but the rent of land and the wages of labor would necessarily be more or less diminished by its removal.

Consider the fallout from the Enron situation. In response to the Enron collapse and other scandals, the U.S. Congress in 2002 passed a corporate reform act, known as Sarbanes-Oxley. It was based on the belief that America's capital markets could only maintain their preeminent global position if major reforms were implemented. The effort backfired. While the concept of the reforms made sense, the implementation was heavy-handed, requiring new mountains of paperwork. The law required corporate CEOs to "certify" their books, meaning that if serious mistakes were found down in the accounting department, the CEO upstairs became criminally liable.

The precursor to Sarbanes-Oxley in the United Kingdom was the Cadbury Commission, which took a less draconian approach to corporate governance in its 1992 recommendations. The U.K. approach proved particularly successful at not throwing the baby out with the bathwater, by reaching a broad-based agreement for corporate structures that separated the offices of chairman and CEO.

Not surprisingly, with the advent of Sarbanes-Oxley in the United States, London became the world's preferred financial center, with New York being the loser. True, Sarbanes-Oxley defenders try to suggest that price competitiveness and robust growth in international markets caused the shift to London. That may be partly the case, but considering the curious timing and huge size of the shift out of New York, the argument that Sarbanes-Oxley bears no responsibility seems a huge stretch.

The bottom line is that a governmental response to the scandals of the Enron era, where thousands of pensioners lost their futures, was vital. The problem was that Sarbanes-Oxley, Washington's well-intentioned medical procedure, geared toward tinkering with a problem, produced the unintended consequence of killing the patient. London gained a leg up in the financial world, which has hardly helped a U.S. dollar already under downward pressure. The disastrous mark-to-market accounting rules that came out of this era, and helped sustain the banking crisis, are another case of unintended negative policy consequences.

Ultimately, the failure stemmed from an inability to realize that risk-takers are a mobile breed. In today's global system, they can take their fledgling company public on the London exchange just as easily as they can in New York. Or maybe even Hong Kong or Shanghai. That is why raising the regulatory barrier or otherwise tinkering with the risk-reward ratio, while it may offer a soothing sense of fairness and safety, can produce swift and ugly complications. That is why, in a curious sense, entrepreneurs are dangerous.

They're dangerous to the careers of the politicians who take the elusive nature of our entrepreneurial creativity sector for granted and fail to think carefully before making rash tax, regulatory, or legal changes. They are dangerous for industrialized world policymakers who fail to appreciate that their economies, when viewed from an entrepreneurial perspective, are competing in a global war of ideas and risk-taking in which there are no breaks for the weary, the restless, or even the big success stories of the past. At any time, entrepreneurs can pick up and take their creative initiative elsewhere, and they will be welcomed with open arms in most countries around the world.

In a more fundamental sense, the problem is that the political process responds only to entities that can expressly define themselves and their needs, entities with real lobbying power. In a sense, you can't blame the politicians because the birth or reinvention of an enterprise involves an elusive, almost metaphysical quality that is unpredictable, which makes targeting and planning difficult. Inventions pop up in unlikely places from unexpected sources. Something as common and essential as the ballpoint pen was conceived by an insurance executive on his summer vacation. The automatic transmission, invented by a struggling supplier, had little if anything to do with the fancy engineering departments of the Detroit auto industry.

All that policymakers can do to establish a climate of dynamic entrepreneurship (besides providing the best possible education and training for their citizens and fair access to credit) is to provide a climate of economic buoyancy—avoiding legal, tax, and regulatory impediments that might stifle an individual from following his or her dreams—while avoiding any hint of class warfare. That is why, before making changes in policy, policymakers should always take this one-question test: With my proposed action, am I harming the climate of entrepreneurial risk-taking so essential to staying on the cutting edge of the global economy?

Today the international race is on to develop new competitive ideas that allow existing companies to reinvent themselves and new start-ups to flourish amid sweeping global changes. In this environment, it would be absolute insanity for politicians to tinker with the entrepreneurial sector, but that is what they are inadvertently doing. America, where the political culture is increasingly driven by anxieties over financial panics and declining real wages, is pondering trying to legislate or regulate a new era of economic security. Judging from today's political rhetoric, many of our leaders appear to be taking the previous era of opportunity and prosperity for granted, as if entrepreneurial risk-taking is like a never-ending waterfall. That's an enormously risky assumption.

As someone who was once involved in the policy world, I have to constantly remind myself that the global economy and financial system cannot be easily controlled or managed, and that includes through Washington bailout attempts, and overly ambitious regulatory schemes, that provide an illusion of enhanced financial security but turn out to severely limit financial risk-taking. The American economy in particular is not an island. What happens elsewhere in the world doesn't stay elsewhere in the world. That includes unfolding economic and financial events in China, which sits at the center of the global storm. In the next chapter, I will demonstrate how absolutely nothing about the churning cauldron we call China can be taken for certain. Indeed, China, with its rising social, political, and financial instability, represents perhaps the strongest case for why the world is not flat. If transparency is a key to the long-term stability of global financial markets, what do any of us really know about the future of China?

4

Tony Soprano
Rides the Chinese Dragon

In the mid-1970s, when I first arrived in Washington, many policymakers talked in hushed tones about someone named Herman Kahn. He was usually referred to as "the super genius Herman Kahn."

Too curious to leave the matter alone, I tracked him down. Kahn had founded a think tank called the Hudson Institute, after having gained fame at the prestigious RAND Corporation. Friends told me that it was impossible not to admire the extraordinarily provocative mental gymnastics of the man, especially his forecasts about future geopolitical trends, so I attended my first Kahn lecture. A burly man with a beard, Kahn stood before a lectern and mesmerized the crowd with uncanny insights and predictions. Kahn was, at the time, perhaps the nation's top trend forecaster, and the crowd could not wait to hear his grand finale. By the beginning of the twenty-first century, he confidently predicted, one country will emerge as the dominant industrial power in the entire world. Which country would dominate? China? India? No, not even close. The country that would dominate the world stage would be . . . France.

Since that time, I have become intrigued with the process of extrapolation. That's because examining current conditions and projecting out several decades to arrive at a conclusion can be so dangerous. Something in the human psyche makes us hold tightly to "absolute certainties," which of course quickly turn into conventional wisdom. Even though conventional wisdom is almost always wrong, we seek comfort in it anyway.

Perhaps nineteenth-century German chancellor Otto von Bismarck, in describing the difficulty of predicting the historical flow of events, captured this frustration best when he noted that "political genius consists of hearing the distant hoof-beat of the horse of history and then leaping to catch the passing horseman by the coattails."

Consider the track record. In the late nineteenth century, Europe's most important geostrategists were debating which country would be the next great world power by 1920. In some circles the top choices, believe it or not, were the United States and Argentina, as both nations enjoyed abundant natural resources. (Argentina's were more balanced and more diverse. The U.S. population was much larger; its GDP higher.) Most British elites who engaged in this debate picked the United States, but a number of Continental experts opted for Argentina as the next great world power, emphasizing its strong tradition of European influence and lack of racial problems that existed in the United States.

Here are more predictions: Several years ago, a senior Japanese official dropped by my office in Washington, mostly to talk about China. He produced a copy of a *Foreign Affairs* article written in 1957, which argued that the Soviet economy, at the time growing officially three times faster than the U.S. economy, would become the dominant economic force by the mid-1970s (a conclusion reached by many other experts at the time). Later in the 1970s, the conventional view was that Germany would globally dominate; in the late 1980s, it was Japan that would run the world. So much for conventional wisdom.

Today's conventional wisdom is that China will dominate the twenty-first century. In this chapter, I will explore how China is a huge unpredictable force with the power to help or sink the world economy. I'll argue that U.S. policymakers have no choice but to try to make our cumbersome, often frustrating relationship with China work.

For the global economy, China represents an enormous paradox, which I will begin by describing in a nutshell. On the one hand, China has no choice but to try to expand at unheard-of rates of growth. Slower growth rates mean few jobs and thus the potential for greater— and potentially dangerous—political and social tensions. On the other hand, China as it expands rapidly also risks becoming a menacing economic and financial bubble to the world. Already in China, bureaucratic decision-makers continue to stockpile commodities with the goal of fueling an ever growing economic machine. Surging stock markets are beginning to show a dangerous instability.

But nothing here is simple. When the Chinese bubble bursts (and bubbles always do, in one fashion or another), China could instantly become a deflationary threat to the world. In the resulting slowdown scenario, China could have no choice but to dump those stockpiles of commodities and finished goods onto world markets. This would potentially cause global price levels to plummet, presenting huge complications for industrialized world policymakers. Under such a scenario, commodity prices upon hitting a tipping point would decline viciously, because some of the price increase pressure had been the result of speculators' betting on higher prices. Once the upward trend began to reverse, the speculators would quickly pull out and run for the hills, causing prices to plummet.

Another paradoxical element about China: the role of capital flows. On the one hand, China needs industrialized world technology in the form of a constant infusion of specialized direct capital investment from abroad. On the other hand, China is a major capital exporter. It uses its central bank reserves (which are huge today in part because Beijing keeps its currency deliberately undervalued) to make investments abroad for strategic advantage. The bottom line is that China represents a delicate balancing act for industrialized world policymakers, a scenario involving a kind of Rubik's Cube set of variables that make strategic planning for crisis management extraordinarily difficult.

While China's economic performance over the past decade has been more than impressive, with an annual growth rate north of 10 percent, the Communist Party leadership nevertheless faces an enormous challenge: integrating into its workforce people from inland provinces. Given the numbers, this is a huge undertaking. China has to integrate what amounts to more than two-thirds the population of Canada, each year, for the next twenty-five years, as the country phases out its corrupt and inefficient state-run enterprises. Such a goal requires annual economic growth rates to remain close to 10 percent. It requires unprecedented high rates of investment and increasing rates of consumption. Maintaining those rates while controlling inflation will be extraordinarily difficult, if not impossible. Because of China's daunting challenge, the world is a house of cards in a way no one in the world yet fully comprehends.

There is no doubt a successful China will bring enormous benefits to the world economy. A booming Asian economy that purchases greater amounts of American exports, moreover, is one of the most effective means, short of a global recession, of reducing the huge U.S. current account deficit. But it is simply not a slam dunk, to use Warren Buffett's favorite phrase, that China's growth will continue at the same torrid pace. While the West continues to seek new and better ways to invest in China, a growing number of Chinese elites are questioning the political foundations of their system. And, once again, politics is at the center of the uncertainty.

The greatest danger is that China is becoming the latest economic and financial bubble. A bubble is a period where economic decision-makers find themselves irrationally attracted to an investment in which expectations of ever higher price increases create a cycle of ever higher expectations. As all recent bubbles reveal—the 1980s Japanese real estate bubble, the 1990s U.S. dot-com bubble, and the great Western housing bubble at the beginning of the twenty-first century—nothing lasts forever. Occasionally a bubble slowly deflates, but most of the time bubbles burst, with devastating consequences.

When the Chinese bubble bursts—and it likely will burst, not slowly deflate—the consequences for the rest of the world could be catastrophic. Someone recently asked me to detail a likely scenario for when the Chinese bubble bursts. The fact is no one can be sure of the exact outcome. The first act of Chinese administrative authorities could be to quickly sell into world markets the vast amounts of commodities currently being stockpiled to fuel ever higher future expansion (stockpiled in part because of China's negative real interest rates, a recent development I will describe shortly). Next, the world would be flooded with massive amounts of Chinese goods at fire sale prices.

For the rest of the world, declining price levels would wreak havoc with the financial system. Suddenly central bankers worried about inflation would be forced to contend with declining price levels, or deflation. Business contracts based on expected future rates of return would become meaningless. A round of job layoffs would appear immediately. Global stock markets would collapse as investors, seeing the likely outbreak of a protectionist fight along with the sharp drop in price levels, panic and sell their stocks and mutual funds and instead purchase U.S. and European bonds. Fairly quickly, hordes of pension funds would announce their inability to meet future obligations because of the stock market's poor performance. The Big Four— sovereign wealth funds, oil producers, hedge funds, and private equity firms—would withdraw their global investment stakes as fast as possible, moving into cash. As with Japan in the 1990s and the entire world in the 1930s, price levels that decline too swiftly and by too great a magnitude represent the potential for long-term economic stagnation. Economic planning becomes impossible. A generous price that a company anticipates receiving for a product or service today may no longer remain so generous in the future.

But there is another possible scenario. China's leaders, fearing a social collapse, could panic and, in a move of irrationality, withdraw their massive reserves from the global system to use that money simply to buy off angry political constituencies back home. This scenario, dependent on a climate of irrationality, would sharply raise world interest rates and force foreign central banks to increase the money supply to buy up China's bond holdings. The result, theoretically, would be higher world inflation, not deflation.

Whatever the doom and gloom scenario, most of the world would likely retaliate against China by setting up protectionist barriers, which would produce immediate retaliation by the Chinese against foreign firms based in China. In the meantime, global central bankers would continue to flood the world with liquidity in an attempt to keep markets from collapsing. But as we saw with the Great Credit Crisis of 2007–2009, the recovery process could be slow and painful. That's because global investors in such a panic would quickly place their money in the industrialized world's safe short-term government debt markets, believing stocks and even highly graded corporate bonds are far too risky. Therefore, global credit markets would seize up. As during the subprime crisis, the panicked central bankers would be limited in their ability to exert much influence or control.

In the final analysis, we really don't know what is about to unfold in China, and a single jolt could be all that's needed to topple the whole structure. During China's three great social and political upheavals since World War II—the Great Leap Forward, the cultural Revolution, and Tiananmen Square—China's GNP growth plummeted from the 10–13 percent range to the 4–5 percent range. This is the situation China is experiencing with the current collapse in global trade and growth.

In the interest of full disclosure, I have to say that I am a bit negatively biased toward China's situation. That is because in the early 1990s, I joined a small group in an investment called China Cement. The group included some of the world's leading economists, a Nobel Prize winner, and the current head of a central bank. We purchased eight Chinese cement factories spread mostly throughout China's northern provinces, in areas where it was clear big-time infrastructure spending was coming soon. China had just emerged as the hot new economy. This was the new frontier, the late-twentieth-century gold rush. We saw an opportunity and hoped to take advantage of all of the excitement by developing the company and taking it public on the Hong Kong stock exchange.

Instead, the investment bombed. Like all new frontiers, including the beginning period of the American economy's industrialization, corruption was rampant. The company's accounting system, because of questionable input from the Chinese senior management, became a form of creative writing and metaphorical expression. We hired an ex–Goldman Sachs executive as CEO to try to make sense of things, but to no avail.

China Cement never went public. We sold the assets at a loss to the French cement company Lafarge. We were all sucked in by a good story. Simple mismanagement and a lack of understanding of the Chinese system contributed to our getting clipped. But in the process, I learned an important lesson about the Chinese market: Never, ever leave money on the table that is not tied to some relatively immediate exchange of a good or a service. Buying widgets for a fixed cost is one thing, but operating an ongoing company based on trust in accounting data, or virtually any other objective measurement, is hugely problematic. For foreign investors, this lack of trust will become particularly problematic during times of economic or financial panic in the wake of the bursting of the bubble.

Clearly, a number of Western companies manage to make money in China. The CEO of a major European auto parts company notes how he keeps successfully expanding his Chinese operation despite problems with intellectual property theft (which he described as "about as bad as Taiwan was thirty years ago"). In China he utilizes only early-generation technology. "I'd never expose them to our latest stuff or they'd steal it," he said.

In the end, my investment in China Cement proved to be a godsend. Why? In the coming years, I avoided losing money on other, potentially more expensive ventures. When approached by friends or acquaintances with a proposal, I would always respond: "I have a rule that I invest only in things I know something about." I then lay out the story of China Cement, concluding with the rhetorical question, "What did any of us know about cement, or China?"

So consider this a "glass is half empty" analysis, which is probably useful because all but the most sophisticated media paint a picture of China as the great Asian Promised Land. Perhaps it will be. But in my view, China is attempting to accomplish something never achieved in the history of mankind—to marry a market economy with a Marxist political regime. This means avoiding the ills of official corruption, massive resource waste, environmental degradation, and massive economic inequality, while expecting the global economy to expand unabated and the trading system to remain open. That's a tall order.

Deng Xiaoping stands out as a bold leader, but I suspect even he failed to grasp the extent of the power of this new economic engine. The Chinese have unleashed a dynamic that is beyond anyone's capacity to control. They wanted a prosperous market economy, but they got something that may not be sustainable. Now they are operating under the false assumption that this monstrously explosive economy can be controlled by official edicts. But that, of course, is not how the new global system works.

The country's economy, with a population of approximately 1.3 billion people, has long surpassed the point where it can be saddled and easily ridden or intimidated by Beijing, which has relied on policies such as the one that Chinese officials sometimes describe with the tag line "To scare the monkey, kill the chicken." An example of this was when a health official a few years back was caught taking bribes and given the death penalty.

Indeed, if the U.S. economy is the equivalent of a twenty-first-century state-of-the-art jet aircraft, the Chinese economy would be a 1990 jet, but with sixties-era controls in the cockpit. In other words, without adequate tools of monetary policy to stabilize the economy, the Chinese still rely heavily on crude government control techniques, which are sluggish and imprecise.

Despite these drawbacks, China has become a global economic power of great weight but little leadership. It benefits from an unheard-of trillion-plus dollars in central bank reserves (the most of any country in the world). China has more billionaires than any other country but the United States. Seven of the world's largest shopping malls are Chinese owned. Yet, strangely, China seems unable to step fully onto the global stage other than to engage in unrealistic posturing largely for domestic political purposes.

With the United States, China has established a new codependency that is historically unusual. The world's most advanced economy is connected at the hip with an economy far behind in sophistication, technology, and adherence to the rules of the international system. The consequences are serious, as evidenced by recent scares of dangerously tainted pet food and unsafe Chinese toys. Today most commentators fixate on China's dollar recycling, which helps support the U.S. debt market, yet the trade relationship may be even more important. With Hong Kong included, China now represents America's third-largest export market, behind Mexico and Canada. Yet Americans have started to become skeptical about Chinese goods. The growing concern is that Chinese manufacturing firms lack proper regulatory guidance. The unknown here is the Chinese response to purchasing U.S. and European products and services in the event of an American or European consumer pullback from Chinese products.

Because China's geographical size is about the same as that of the United States, but with a population four times as great, forecasters argue that China's economy will exceed the size of the U.S. economy within three or four decades. That is based on an assumption that growth will merely continue at its current pace. Maybe, yet nothing is as simple as it seems.

According to economist Angus Maddison, in 1820 China produced about a third of the world's GDP with roughly 36 percent of the world's population, with a per capita GDP about 90 percent of the world average. By 2005, despite nearly 10 percent economic growth annually for the last three decades, China produces only 5 percent of the world's GDP with 20 percent of the world's population. Over nearly two hundred years of intense social change, China's productivity dropped from 80 percent to less than 25 percent of the world average, and while it has been recovering, the country still has a long road to travel. The world fixates on what China could be. But as of now, the economy is only roughly three times the size of the Netherlands, as measured using World Bank dollar exchange rate figures (ten times if measured on a purchasing power parity basis).

China's fundamental problems, moreover, should not be underestimated. Several years ago, I asked a Beijing official why his government needed such a large standing army in today's era of high-tech warfare. After all, notwithstanding the U.S. Seventh Fleet's presence in the South China Sea, China appears to face no significant land threat. The official's answer (translated into my own idiom) put the finger on China's central problem: We need the army, he said, to keep them down on the farm. Without the army, the poor and rural population would rush into urban centers, causing China's largely coastal cities to triple in size overnight. This, in turn, would cause these cities to collapse. Moreover, China's decades of a one-child policy has created a surplus of males over females. The army helps absorb young Chinese men who will never find mates.

Since 1980, more than one hundred million rural Chinese have moved to the cities seeking the Chinese version of the American dream. In the next two decades, at least several hundred million more are expected to try to make the same move. Several decades from now, more than three-quarters of a billion eager and hopeful Chinese could be crammed into roughly 150 or so largely coastal cities, seeking the lifestyle of the middle class. Despite efforts to improve the safety net and to move jobs to the country, social unrest and violence in rural China are already rising rapidly—and these have been the good times. Western news reports rarely mention this growing problem, even though Chinese police statistics monitor its growth. That's because it's in the world's best interest for China to succeed, and harping on the country's internal strife won't accomplish anything.

Japanese strategists tell me that China's coastal cities still have plenty of investment liquidity in the pipeline, but move inland, and there is a surprisingly widespread shortage of capital. The provinces, which have their own paramilitary forces, operate in relative independence from Beijing. There is widespread sentiment in inland regions that in the 1990s the coastal cities have enjoyed a boom with the move to a market economy. Unfortunately, this "party" has provided very little benefit to the inland provinces. In addition, the rural Chinese migrants have not been very happy once they resettled in the cities. This could be due to a number of factors.

The World Bank observes that sixteen of the world's twenty most polluted cities are Chinese. Over 70 percent of the water in China's seven major rivers is already considered undrinkable. The Chinese today face by far the world's highest levels of airborne sulfur dioxide, mostly from the broad-based use of the crudest form of coal furnaces. According to the U.S. State Department, "respiratory and heart diseases related to air pollution are the leading causes of death in China." Unfortunately, the Chinese are unlikely to change their environmental policies. For instance, the main argument against the U.S. Senate legislation that would begin to control greenhouse gas emissions (the Lieberman-Warner bill) is the unlikelihood that developing economies such as China and India will cooperate. Indeed, these developing economies will be quick to claim that the legislation is inconsistent with the rules of the World Trade Organization. Yet China, with a far smaller economy, now surpasses the United States as the world's biggest source of greenhouse gases. Chinese emissions, according to the International Energy Agency, are increasing at a rate faster than the capacity of all developed nations to reduce emissions. China's environmental policies are on a collision course with its trade goals.

There is another basic problem plaguing China: the lack of reliable information about the country's economy. A number of years ago, a senior Chinese official having cocktails in Beijing with a group of international bankers was asked whether his country was getting serious about efforts to achieve "macro" transparency of the financial system. The official surprised the group with his forthright response: "Our model," he said, "is that the best fishing is done in murky waters." So far, he seems to be correct.

Despite murky waters (i.e., a lack of transparency), huge amounts of foreign capital have poured into China, first as direct foreign investment but more and more as portfolio and real estate investment. While betting on China may seem a great and sensible point of portfolio diversification, do global investors fully understand the assets they are acquiring? Do they really know the Chinese companies' ownership structures? Do they really appreciate the shortcomings of Chinese accounting and auditing practices? Will they have much to rely on when the bubble bursts?

For the past ten years, the Chinese have aggressively wooed foreign investment. Still, the government has consistently restricted foreign investment in strategic and other sectors, including insurance, banking, retailing, shipbuilding, media, telecommunications, and real estate. Several years ago, for instance, out of the blue, most cross-border mergers and acquisitions began to face a complete round of new obstacles. Nobody fully understands what's fueling this pullback, other than that some political shift had occurred, which has only added to the mystery and obfuscation.

Sometimes it seems the Chinese themselves are not sure what is going on. In April of 2005, a senior International Monetary Fund (IMF) delegation visited China, met with the highest levels of the official community, and was told a significant upward revaluation of the Chinese currency was "a 100 percent certainty" (one official's phrase) the following weekend. To the embarrassment of the IMF, the bold currency adjustment never occurred (which may have been fortunate because the IMF was thinking of a 20 percent revaluation, while the Chinese were thinking of far less than 5 percent). Also embarrassed, according to a senior IMF staffer, were officials at the Chinese finance ministry and central bank. These officials actually took the unorthodox step of formally but quietly notifying their G7 counterparts that they (members of the Chinese central bank and finance ministry) should no longer be seen as responsible for controlling key decisions such as currency reform. Instead, the State Council, a mysterious body of the most senior Communist Party elites, makes all the most pivotal decisions.

President Hu Jintao, for example, despite his best intentions, is said to approach any council meeting with no more than three votes in his pocket, not nearly enough to achieve a quick majority on the nine-member council, no matter what he has promised an American president or European prime minister. A member of the European Central Bank Council once said to me of the Chinese: "Their decision-making structure is a complex web. We asked them several years ago what the various European central banks can do to help them establish a more modernized central bank infrastructure. It took the Chinese nine months to figure out how to respond."

That is why, in my own thinking, I picture today's Chinese official power structure metaphorically as a large, fancy Beijing office building with a small, shabby lobby. Sitting in the lobby greeting the international guests from tiny, makeshift, cardboard receptionists' desks are the Chinese equivalent of Alan Greenspan and Ben Bernanke—highly intelligent, honest, forthright, and globally sophisticated Chinese officials. In my mind's metaphor, even President Hu sits in the same reception area. They earnestly greet the guests, identify with China's obvious problems, and yet wield little power.

By contrast, the rest of the building contains floors of plush oak paneled executive office suites occupied by the folks who wield the real power, the party hacks. They remind me of a kind of benign, usually nonviolent version of American television mobster Tony Soprano and the operators of the Bada Bing Club. A group estimated at anywhere from a dozen to several hundred, they control the Communist Party apparatus just as Tony Soprano controlled northern New Jersey. I have a vision of a bunch of feet-on-the-desk pols smoking Cuban cigars and chatting about what all political operators talk about: how to hold on to their power. In this case, it is how to keep power and stay atop this unpredictable, highly chaotic, bruising Chinese political and economic beast. Please note that I am not suggesting any malicious grand conspiracy here. This power crowd is simply trying to figure out how to survive in their own house of cards of domestic politics.

But make no mistake, China has achieved economic wonders in spite of, not because of, the penetration of the economic structure by this party elite. This situation reminds me of the private comment made recently by the chairman of a large European bank. This individual, on business in China, was asked by a competitor while standing in the lobby of a Shanghai hotel: "You're not doing much business here in China, are you? Don't you see the reforms in the banking system?" The European banker's response: "Oh, it's not the reform of the banks that's missing; it's the reform of the political system that affects the banks."

A few years ago, Chinese officials stunned many global market participants with the announcement that China's largest bank, the state-run Industrial and Commercial Bank of China (ICBC), is now the most highly valued bank in the world. Within several years, ICBC will be making global acquisitions. Indeed, the bank has already been informally sniffing out the possibility of purchasing one or both of two significantly sized European banks.

Yet individuals involved say Western investors, many of whom have done highly successful initial public offerings (IPOs) with ICBC and the four or five other state-owned banks, appear to have little idea that the octopus of the Communist Party is still deep into the structure of bank decision making. When the Communist Party goes on weekend retreat, one ICBC observer noted to me, virtually the entire senior bank management clears out. This is true in the Beijing branches, but particularly so in the regional offices. Party officials dominate not only credit risk assessment, but also human resource decisions. Therefore, efforts at structural reform made by serious government reformers at the top (yes, there are some) and the international investment bankers are being ignored, both at the headquarters and at the provincial and bank branch levels. This situation is similar to what happened in the early years of Japanese banking reforms. Meanwhile, the pile of nonperforming loans and even larger pile of underperforming loans keep being rolled over. And the way the Chinese banks have dealt with this situation has been to increase the issuing of *new* loans aggressively. As a result, the ratio of bad loans to all loans goes down, creating the appearance of normalcy. The obvious tipping point of this Ponzi scheme is when handing out new loans becomes more difficult, which often occurs in an inflationary environment.

If you are not convinced of the seriousness of the risk within the Chinese financial system, take a close look at the prospectus of any of the Chinese banks that have recently gone public. These are thick documents. Somewhere in the section marked "Risk" you will find page after page of descriptions such as: "Mr. Wang of our Hong Su branch was arrested for embezzling $2 million. Mr. Hu, the branch manager in our office in wherever, was arrested for stealing $10 million." The list goes on and on. The section marked "Risk" also acknowledges that the bank has no risk management system to monitor credit. In some cases, there will be the admission that the bank has in place no liquidity management system. Yet the bank, having gone public, enjoys $100 billion plus in market capitalization. That is what happens in an environment of massive, excess capital . . . that is, until the bubble bursts.

Does this sound like hyperbole? The latest story among Western investment bankers working in China relates to the IPO initiated a few years ago by one of China's largest state-run banks. Knowing of Western concerns with risk management, the Chinese hired as the bank's senior risk officer a Westerner who had worked before at a well-known American investment bank. That all sounds prudent except for one small detail: The new risk manager did not speak Chinese. Yet he was asked cynically by the bank's Chinese leadership to sign off on all the papers backing the IPO. He refused and eventually quit. Another

Western investment banker noted: "Didn't he know he was hired precisely because he doesn't speak the language?"

Let me reiterate: The Chinese banking structure, under the thumb of Tony Soprano, will be attempting to buy up major industrial and financial institutions worldwide. Talk about a coming world of discontinuities, with severe twists and turns. Picture European Central Bank president Jean-Claude Trichet, Federal Reserve chairman Ben Bernanke, and a Chinese Tony Soprano all at some international banking conference talking about financial transparency, with Tony telling Ben and Jean-Claude the line about fishing in murky waters and Ben and Jean-Claude having to remain mute because of their own banking problems. This is not a question of ideology; it is a question of whether a party-run state ownership system is compatible with economic decision making in today's highly sophisticated, globally competitive market where adequate financial transparency is the difference between a climate of healthy growth and outright panic and collapse. Compared to the Chinese banks, today's troubled, large American and European financial institutions look like paragons of financial purity.

The Chinese party-run banks simply do not understand credit risk management, not to mention even the rudimentary rules of financial transparency. Because banks are considered social and political instruments in China, the party chiefs have an overriding interest in maintaining the existing system. But there is also a sense of fairness here. The West, through individuals and firms, invests heavily in China, seeking majority control of its investments. Why shouldn't this arrangement work both ways? Why are we surprised that the Chinese government, which controls most investment going outside of China, wants to buy and control major companies in the West?

In early 2007, China's premier, Wen Jiabao, announced, using vague wording, that China was in the process of changing its management policies toward its trillion-dollar-plus pile of central bank reserves. Clearly, the Chinese are about to embark on a buying spree. No, they will not do anything intentionally to hurt the U.S. dollar, which would diminish the value of their reserves. Instead, they will follow the Singapore model, concentrating first on energy and commodity investments, where they have felt most vulnerable, but soon moving on to international financial institutions. In the process, Chinese officials may seek precisely the kind of majority ownership control that they do not let others acquire in China.

We see China as one nation, but it is really a collection of interdependent but different regions, with Beijing vying to act as command central. One reason operating a single broad macroeconomic strategy is so difficult is the great Chinese disparity: Shanghai's GDP is now higher than prosperous Malaysia's, while living standards in many other areas resemble those of impoverished Bangladesh.

I recall a decade ago when the mayor of Shanghai boasted to me that his government demanded more than a yuan equivalent in services for every yuan of tax revenue sent by Shanghai taxpayers to Beijing. It was as if Shanghai were allowing Beijing to save face. The tax transfer was covering up what was really going on in China: that the Chinese central government was losing influence over a highly decentralized economy.

True, the 2008 Beijing Olympics represented a point of national pride, unity, and stability. With internal unrest in villages and small cities growing exponentially, the government, in the buildup to the games, initiated an effective crackdown, using the argument that the Olympics should show China in the best light to the rest of the world. The fear, however, is that the Olympics became such a focal point for creating order that the post-Olympic years could eventually reverse the situation—worsened, of course, by the collapse of global trade and GDP. In the event the economy slows further, China could see an astounding increase in instability in a kind of reverse eruption of pent-up emotion in coming years.

Some worry that wealthy Chinese will become the new scapegoats for resentment of economic inequality. The cleavages are already significant. There is tension between Beijing and booming Shanghai, between the rich coastal provinces and the poor inland provinces, and between the crony capitalists and migrant laborers. All of this tension is exacerbated by a layer of Communist Party influence and representation. Five percent of China's 1.3 billion people, roughly sixty-five million, led by a special elite cadre of several hundred, enjoy the front row seats for no particular reason—other than that they are part of the party. Predicting the consequences of China's political transition will be tricky. Perhaps Martin Wolf of the *Financial Times* put it best when he suggested that "China has a tiger by the tail: that tiger, of course, is China itself."

China's economic situation is suspiciously reminiscent of the Japanese experience in the late 1980s and early 1990s. In Japan, there was first a large run-up in the stock market, followed by a real estate and stock market bubble, followed by a restrictive or tight policy that eventually led to a bursting of that bubble. In China, the tightening and the collapse haven't occurred fully yet, but the Shanghai Composite Index jumped 500 percent in the period 2006–2007 and in 2008 began to seriously correct, dropping in value by more than half between October 2007 and April 2008, only to rebound in 2009. For the first time, China's stock market capitalization exceeded its GDP. In certain sectors, real estate prices soared by similar magnitudes. Note that some analysts argue that China could also follow the path of Taiwan in the 1990s—a soaring stock market followed by years of collapse and economic underperformance. This would be a situation similar to Japan's but without Japan's large, globally competitive multinational corporations to serve as an economic shock absorber for the rest of the economy. Don't forget that despite a booming economy, Chinese consumer spending strangely has plummeted from nearly 50 percent of GDP in 1992 to 36 percent in 2006.

Want to know the ultimate reason the Chinese in recent years found themselves on a slippery slope with soaring real estate and stock market investment, and commodities stockpiling out of control? The concept is difficult to comprehend, but the reason is that real interest rates in China, the rate after subtracting for inflation, were negative, or at best zero percent (in other words, if the interest rate is 3 percent, but inflation is 6 percent, the real interest rate is negative 3 percent).

Inflation in China soared, but the administratively controlled interest rate, heavily influenced by political insiders, was not being raised fast enough. This is one downside of not allowing financial markets to function freely.

When an economy experiences negative real interest rates, investors borrow as much as possible and buy as much as possible. For a while, they buy stocks as well as physical assets such as commodities and real estate with reckless abandon. That is why the Chinese in recent years have roamed the developing world, including Africa, locking in long-term contracts for the purchase of commodities. Let me state again: Normally, an economy with rising inflation would also experience rising interest rates and a strengthening currency (eliminating a negative real interest rate scenario). But China's interest rate market and currency have been administratively controlled. Thus the climate of real negative interest rates has contributed to an expanding economic and financial bubble. That was the game in China—to borrow and buy as many assets as possible because nobody believed the bubble would burst or that global trade would plummet, causing Chinese exports to collapse. Of course, sooner or later, bubbles always burst. Just ask the Japanese about their experience in the 1990s, or U.S., U.K., and Spanish homeowners in more recent times whose home values have sunk, in some cases well below the level of their mortgages.

One of the themes of this book is that policy changes often have unintended consequences. When the Federal Reserve slashed short-term interest rates in the wake of the subprime crisis, the result was like dropping a financial atomic bomb on the Asian economies, particularly China. Even as the U.S. economy slowed and Asian exports therefore decelerated, the Asian economic climate of excess capacity (overproducing) continued. As a result, Chinese and Asian price inflation accelerated, a phenomenon that caused wages to increase. Although Chinese economic data are not always reliable, by mid-2008 wage inflation jumped to a rate of 20 percent a year. Yet real wages (after accounting for inflation) were at best flat. During the same period, the prices of food and energy jumped by more than 20 percent. Rice prices in a nine-month period between 2007 and 2008 jumped 300 percent, a phenomenon that caused riots in more than thirty countries throughout Asia and Africa, not only in China.

Let me state again that Chinese economic data can be unreliable, but the one area of some trust involves the measure of the money supply. Using money supply measurements to forecast inflationary trends is a tricky business, particularly in a financial system as sophisticated as that of the United States. Nonetheless, the Chinese situation is telling. From mid-2006 to mid-2008, the Chinese money supply grew at a 16 percent annual rate. Inflation during this period jumped from 2 percent to over 8 percent. Yet the *real* money supply (after adjusting for inflation) was rapidly decelerating.

Note too that as a result of globalization, international wage inflation for a while spread widely. In Vietnam, for example, wage inflation also soared above the 20 percent annual rate. Until recently, the Asian economies have been driven by a steady stream of capital expenditures. Several years ago with the rise in inflation, the rate of Asian capital expenditures started to dramatically decrease. This situation worsened with the slowdown in the U.S. economy, which shrank America's current account deficit but also global liquidity. That, of course, is not a positive situation for either the United States or the Asian economies. One of the bright spots in the initial aftermath of the subprime crisis was the emergence of American multinational corporations as a trade export machine, exporting mostly to Asia. In the first nine months after the crisis, the U.S. economy failed to deteriorate as thoroughly as many analysts had predicted, precisely because of a huge surge in American exports. Not anymore. The resulting shrinkage in capital expenditures, trade, and consumption caused the new U.S. export machine's pistons to seize up.

More than a decade ago, the Japanese were among the first to pour massive amounts of investment capital into China, with a number of Japan's elite opinion leaders believing this new relationship would partly offset Japan's increasingly tiresome economic relationship with the United States. Not anymore. The Japanese severely retrenched on

Chinese investments in 2005 and 2006, and for a while created mass confusion in Beijing.

In the Japanese view, there were a number of troubling developments, mostly tied to seemingly reckless Chinese decision-making. For example, China had tried to corner the world market in iron ore with little regard for world demand for steel or for the fact that the world already produces ample amounts of steel to meet global needs. China's planned steel-producing capacity at one point was large enough to meet not only its own needs, but also those of the world's two giant economies, Japan and the United States.

China currently produces 450 million tons of steel per year. By contrast, Japan produces 120 million tons; the United States, less than 100 million tons; and Europe, about 150 million tons. In China, about a third of steel production actually goes to building more steel-producing capacity, another third for the export of products made of steel, and the final third for domestic consumption. China's steel market, therefore, represents a huge danger for the world market as Chinese demand deteriorates and the global economy flattens.

The Chinese had embarked on this ambitious steel-producing venture despite having an economy still only three times the size of the economy of the Netherlands. The danger of such an approach is the creation of large stockpiles of commodities, which at first leads to artificial price rises, but at the risk of a swift and brutal price collapse once the global commodities market reaches a tipping point of uncertainty about sustaining the new price levels. The Chinese government has been massively stockpiling other commodities as well, all the while oblivious to concerns about global overcapacity and actual global demand.

In 2007, a baffled Japanese auto executive noted privately that the Chinese, already in the car production business, told him they are about to increase auto production dramatically. The numbers, if they can be believed, are astounding. In 2006, Chinese domestic car-producing capacity amounted to roughly six million units. The Beijing planners decreed that by as early as 2012, automobile production capacity should reach twenty million units, more than a 300 percent increase. This is similar to the scenario involving steel overproduction where there appears to have been a dangerous bureaucratic overestimation about the future levels of global demand for automobiles.

By 2012, for instance, Chinese *domestic* demand for automobiles is estimated to be, at best, only nine million units. So where will the remaining eleven million vehicles be sent? The Japanese believe China's economic administrators have been ordered to put in motion a plan to become the largest automobile exporter in the world, regardless of global auto capacity or demand. The goal: to fight competitively for and hold on to market share, ironically, a game the Japanese know very well. I was initially skeptical of the Chinese supremacy-in-auto-production story until hearing about the Chery Automobile Company, a Chinese state-owned independent automaker. Recently Yin Tongyao, Chery's chairman and general manager, announced to the *Wall Street Journal* that by 2010 his small company alone will be producing one million units annually for global and domestic sale, compared to fewer than one hundred thousand units at present.

Perhaps the main reason Japanese strategists are so skeptical toward Chinese overproduction is that China today is highly reminiscent of Japan in the 1960s. During that period, the Japanese economy grew at 10 percent annual rates, led by massive steel production. Once Japan reached a level of overcapacity such that the steel bubble began to deflate, Japanese annual growth rates dropped from 10 percent to the 4 percent range.

All of which is reminiscent of the Japanese Dark Theory about China. Several years ago, at a dinner in Tokyo with several Japanese government officials (non–Ministry of Finance), the discussion turned to China. After a never-ending flow of drinks, one of the officials bemoaned the fact that after all of Japan's U.S. investment failures in the late 1980s and early 1990s (led by the Rockefeller Center investment), Japanese firms appeared to be losing money in China as well. "Our companies have largely stopped any net new direct Chinese investment," the official said, adding, "It's too difficult to make a profit.

Vietnam is much more intriguing as a low-wage market." I immediately felt better about China Cement.

The conversation did not end there (nor did the drinks). The talk only grew more intense, which is when the official offered what I have come to call Japan's "Dark Theory" about China, the kind of talk one only hears in late-night sessions after tongues have been loosened, and lubricated, by a heavy dose of sake. What is the Dark Theory? It goes something like this: China's senior leadership—Tony Soprano and the gang—already know they can't meet their economic goals despite tremendous economic progress to date. Under even favorable conditions, achieving 10 percent growth and 40 percent investment rates for twenty-five straight years seems like a near-impossible goal, exacerbated by the hundreds of millions of new workers who need to be absorbed into the cities. But China's task is even more daunting for one additional reason—demographics.

While Europe, Japan, and, to a lesser extent, the United States face serious demographic pressures ahead, their task is a simple one compared to that of China, whose one-child policy of the 1970s and 1980s has created no less than a demographic monster (though some analysts argue Japan's demographic problem will be just as difficult).

By 2045, one of every three Chinese will be of retirement age. As analyst Chi Lo wrote in *The International Economy*, when the labor force is shrinking faster than the population, the standard of living inevitably falls, creating a vicious chain reaction. The chain starts with a lower return on capital, which lowers the capital stock, which lowers living standards. "We suspect the [Chinese] leadership's goal in this situation is to respond as most people in power respond—figure how to keep power," the same Japanese official said. "They have lots of liquidity for now and a window of about twenty years before the demographic problems set in. We suspect they'll use that liquidity to modernize and enhance the military, not solely or even primarily for external purposes, but like the Saudi military mostly to maintain domestic order." (In Saudi Arabia, the nation's large security force is geared toward controlling a 30 percent Shiite minority that happens to live near the most important Saudi oil fields.)

Note that this conversation in Tokyo occurred *before* March 2007. I know because I was, at first, quite skeptical of this Dark Theory on China. Then, on March 4, 2007, the Chinese government announced plans to boost military spending by a whopping 18 percent for the coming year, the largest announced military spending increase in a decade. Like most data in China, the true number is probably considerably higher. My immediate thought: They're preserving their power base. The Dark Theory may be correct.

At this point, you are probably asking yourself what in the world the Japanese are smoking. After all, China represents a world-class economic success story. By holding down the value of the yuan, exports have exploded upward at a 30 percent annual rate, while the growth of imports has been much slower. What's wrong with having official reserves—an official slush fund—of nearly two trillion dollars, 90 percent of which is held in relatively safe U.S. assets, while holding 15 percent of total U.S. debt? Having nearly two trillion dollars in reserve, while administratively controlling the exchange rate, represents a heck of an insurance policy in the event of a global financial meltdown. What's not to like?

The answer is that artificially undervalued currencies and the massive buildup of reserves represent a giant distortion to the global financial system. This distortion not only creates financial bubbles, but for Chinese officials themselves, it also makes the job of managing the economic system during the catastrophic bursting of those bubbles extraordinarily difficult. The normal healthy forces of market equilibrium necessary to achieve global financial stability remain offset by this governmental intervention aimed at currency manipulation.

None of this is to deny that China's economic performance has been impressive. China has been the final assembly point for a wildly successful low-cost Asian manufacturing behemoth that sends a big share of its final product to the United States. As a result, more than half of China's imports come from outside-funded companies, meaning that they are for reexport as finished products. More than half of China's product exports are made from components imported from elsewhere in Asia. This phenomenon has made the entire Asian region extraordinarily price-competitive worldwide as relatively low-wage Asian labor keeps downward pressure on prices.

In the process of spearheading this growing manufacturing giant, China consumes or stockpiles one-third of the world's annual supply of tin, coal, zinc, and iron ore. It has also, meanwhile, established troubling relationships with brutal oil-exporting regimes, including Sudan and Angola. These alliances have kept China somewhat apart from the global community. The U.S. government has openly criticized China for not doing enough to discourage inhumane practices, calling on the country to be a "responsible stakeholder" in the international community of nations.

Despite these criticisms, the Chinese juggernaut moves ahead. At least one hundred million Chinese workers today already earn more than $5,000 per year. That may not sound like much, but Reed Hundt in *America* magazine pointed out that the new Chinese middle class not only equals about two-thirds of the total American workforce, but their standard of living already resembles in many ways the average American's living standard because the Chinese equivalent of a dollar goes a long way in China. Shanghai apartment dwellers, for instance, pay a $5 monthly fee each for cable TV and telephone service. A personal computer costs $200. In Beijing this middle class can afford to hire domestic helpers to clean, cook, and do valet service. Compare that to the United States or Europe, where there are many dual-income, middle-class households and the majority of the middle class do their own cooking and cleaning.

In the next decade, economic strategists expect an additional two hundred million Chinese to also participate in this middle-class lifestyle. Today the Chinese consume about one-third as much as American consumers purchase (in physical terms). Within two decades, assuming political strife is contained, with several hundred million more joining the middle class, Chinese consumers are on course to influence global trends and technology as much as Americans do today.

What's more, there is no denying that China's economic impact on the rest of the world, to date at least, has been largely positive. China's ability to combine a nominal exchange rate pegged to the dollar with low domestic inflation and rapid productivity growth in the past decade has helped keep worldwide inflation and long-term interest rates low. Indeed, low-cost Chinese exports have helped to tamp down U.S. core inflation. In the absence of such exports, U.S. core inflation might be a lot higher. The problem, however, is that the imbalances of China and other developing nations have caused the world to seriously underprice financial risk.

On paper at least, China's future looks bright. China's surplus saving is continuing to swell. While China's personal saving has been falling, the savings bonanza is coming from corporations in the form of undistributed profits. In China, corporate savings are now higher than personal savings. Niall Ferguson, a professor at Harvard, and London economist Moritz Schularick argue that Chinese companies "have made enormous gains in market share, leading to record company earnings. . . . Chinese manufacturers have continued to make massive gains in price competitiveness [helped by the fact that] the renminbi [or yuan] is cheaper today than ever before."

Already, the professional extrapolators are suggesting the potential for China's global dominance. Hundt states that while no one yet knows the outcome, "if Asia falls like night on the West's long summer day, it will look like this: Chinese and other Eastern firms will make almost everything for nearly everybody in the world, and nobody else will be able to say or do much about it."

The implications of what happens in China are huge. But the issue is not whether China is growing; the issue is whether China has grown by an unsustainable rate. While Chinese data are not wholly reliable, it appears the Chinese, to contain political and social tensions, put the pedal to the metal a lot sooner than many Western analysts realized. China's levels of economic growth has probably been significantly higher than the official data suggest. Thus, the chances for the bursting of the bubble and resulting increased social unrest are more significant than we realize. The more recklessly things have soared on the upside, the more brutally they could plummet on the way down.

Here's the dilemma: Chinese officials stress that an 8 percent–plus growth level is the bare minimum needed to avoid serious political disruption. What would happen if, over the next decade, growth drops to, say, 7 percent? That's still a growth rate that represents extraordinary economic performance anywhere else in the world. Would China experience a political meltdown? Most Western experts suggest that if the Chinese growth rate drops to below 7.5 percent, serious unemployment would set in, furthering political unrest and threatening the stability of the entire economic system. During 2009, the economy officially grew between 6 and 7 percent.

Is a bursting of the financial bubble an unrealistic outcome? China today has 102.5 million trading accounts, with an incredible 300,000 new accounts opened each day. In 2006 alone, more than 24 million new Chinese investors began buying and selling stocks on the white-hot Shanghai exchange. The vast majority of these newcomers are novice investors. Equity or stock ownership, still limited to less than 10 percent of the population, is nonetheless expanding at an explosive rate.

Yet the system lacks the stabilizing effect of a financial futures market to reduce risk. That's because the government banned exchange-traded financial derivatives in 1995. In February 2007, for example, a seemingly modest market glitch caused the Shanghai Composite Index to drop by more than 9 percent in a single day (rumors had spread that the government, to deflate the wildly expanding equity bubble, was itself about to sell shares in some of China's largest companies). The Dow responded by plummeting by more than 400 points. And this is only the beginning of the phenomenon in which the murky Chinese financial system becomes entwined with the world financial system. Five years from now, in a crisis, financial developments in China could easily become the tail that wags the global financial dog. Even today, the Chinese stock market is still expensive by any measure. By early

2008, the Shanghai market's price-to-earnings ratio reached a point greater than Japan's stock market just before its market collapsed more than a decade ago. In the period thereafter, the Chinese market dropped dramatically from its highs.

As an object lesson, look at what happened during the worldwide Great Credit Crisis of 2007–2009. Initially, the Chinese financial system seemed strangely, if not bizarrely, unaffected. But the situation provided little comfort elsewhere. As the rest of the world struggled with credit problems relating to the subprime mortgage mess, Chinese A-shares (only domestically owned) during the first four weeks of the 2007 crisis actually jumped by more than 20 percent. Strangely, stocks soared even though one of China's largest lenders, the Bank of China, announced it had a $9.6 billion exposure to U.S. subprime mortgages, with other Chinese banks also announcing significant exposure.

The entire Chinese market should have reflected immediately the seriousness of the subprime situation. Why? China is still a heavily export-dependent economy. With the world economy collapsing as a result of the subprime fiasco, the Chinese exports to the world would have been the first to take a hit. The Chinese equity markets, in the wake of the outbreak of the crisis, only eventually reflected that obvious danger after a significant rally of bizarre robustness. By early 2009, with global stock markets collapsing, the Chinese stock markets achieved healthy growth. How? The state-run banks used the government's fiscal stimulus funds to buy the stocks of the state-run enterprises.

In 2007, I asked several senior strategists at the European Central Bank to lay out China's options for safely operating this economic behemoth. The goal of any economy is strong and steady growth, but growth restrained enough to avoid an overheating and bubble-bursting scenario. The Europeans believe the Chinese had four possible approaches: (1) quantitative intervention (administratively guiding the system such as by issuing government edicts calling for less or more consumption); (2) interest rate hikes; (3) allowing the currency to strengthen; and (4) administrative efforts to promote economic and financial outflows and to hinder inflows (deciding, for example, what global imports to purchase and how much).

In the European view, only one of these choices would be an effective option—allowing their currency to float and thus strengthen. They point to the 1970s when Germany, like China today, was experiencing strong growth and heavy capital inflows. The only measure that proved effective in safely slowing the economy was a stronger currency. For Germany, nothing else worked. And European officials have told that to the Chinese on a number of occasions.

But despite some strengthening of the currency to date, further dramatic Chinese currency appreciation is no simple affair. Indeed, the United States and China, now joined at the hip, face a currency situation where there is no easy way out. Clearly, the provincial governments prefer investment-led growth (as opposed to consumption), which is far more open to control and corruption. Obviously, if Beijing stopped the central bank's intervention in the market, the yuan would further strengthen significantly and foreign goods sold in China would likely be more competitively priced. But by allowing the yuan to further strengthen, China's inefficient, uncompetitive state-owned enterprises would risk collapse, creating mass unemployment (China's trade surplus represents a whopping one-seventh of GDP). Yet by keeping the currency artificially low, and with America's low rate of saving and its huge oil purchases, the U.S. current account deficit has risen to an extraordinarily high level of over 5 percent of GDP. This situation of imbalance is not beneficial to either China or the United States.

It is not that American officials have been complacent. Goldman Sachs CEO Hank Paulson, a true market heavyweight who is highly respected on Wall Street, was called to the rescue and took office as Treasury secretary in July 2006. Although Paulson knew financial markets, his selection stemmed from one other qualification—he was a China expert, having traveled there on business more than seventy times. Paulson's appointment represented a "two-for-one" for President Bush. Paulson could calm the financial markets in a crisis. Plus, he could peer into the inner sanctum of the Chinese and begin to address in earnest the range of bilateral disputes, including the yuan-dollar relationship.

By early December 2006, Paulson had decided on a course of action. By then more than thirty-five trade-action bills had been introduced on Capitol Hill, most charging the Chinese with currency manipulation. Paulson organized the highest-level U.S. delegation to visit China since Richard Nixon was in office. Most of the Bush cabinet and even a reluctant Federal Reserve chairman Ben Bernanke departed for Beijing. And how did the Chinese respond? Paulson returned home with nothing, and there was not much the Treasury secretary could do about it without the Chinese retaliating in two areas highly influential in Washington—financial services and agriculture. If the Chinese ended or curtailed their U.S. agricultural purchases and restricted American financial investment activities in China, the resulting situation would prove to be highly damaging to the U.S. economy.

During a meeting at the Bush White House in early December 2006, an official suddenly began talking about Paulson's trip. The official, clearly not a Paulson admirer, expressed surprise that the lineup of Chinese officials he met was, as he put it, "surprisingly no different than the people hapless [former Treasury secretary] John Snow would have seen were he still in office." The delegation met with China Central Bank governor Zhou Xiaochuan and Vice Premier Wu Yi, but the real power players stayed out of sight. No Tony Soprano, nor the others who pull the strings (though Zhou is occasionally listened to).

Officially, the U.S. Treasury excused China's poor response with the explanation that China is in political turmoil, a situation likely to remain unresolved for the next year or two. President Hu, with a minority of votes on the State Council, may be pushing for currency reform, but the remainder of the group is nervous about upsetting the inland provinces with the loss of markets and jobs in a whole set of marginal industries. "We'll wait for a reshuffling" was the common excuse for inaction when I queried various U.S. officials involved. The Chinese currency reform lip service is likely to go on a lot longer than we think. European officials appealing to China on the currency issue have faced the same Beijing brick wall.

There is a reason for this resistance: The politically powerful but highly inefficient domestic (often state-run) enterprises fear the negative effects of a dramatically stronger currency. Today, foreign-funded companies in China employ a mere 3 percent of the workforce (25 million workers) but are responsible for 55 percent of exports, 80 percent of export growth, 22 percent of GDP, and 41 percent of GDP growth. By contrast, domestically funded companies employ 97 percent of the workforce (775 million workers) and are responsible for 45 percent of exports and 78 percent of GDP. For the foreign-funded sector, labor productivity may be as much as nine times higher than it is in the domestically funded sector.

Therefore, the Chinese leadership resists further currency appreciation for precisely one reason—it believes that China's domestic (many of them state-run) companies operate with such low productivity that an abrupt strengthening of the yuan would destroy their export competitiveness. Moreover, increasing the productivity of this 97 percent of the economy (i.e., the domestically funded companies) would require something that is unlikely to take place anytime soon—an independent monetary policy requiring a complete modernization of the financial system. This would have to include an immediate dismantling of the corrupt state-run banks, which for political reasons is not about to happen.

A related question is whether further Chinese currency appreciation would significantly reduce America's huge trade imbalance much anyway. Morris Goldstein and Nicholas Lardy of the Peterson Institute for International Economics argue that Chinese exporters have not been that vulnerable to a change in exchange rates because in China there is seemingly no floor for wages. Forever lower wages can compensate for the effects of the strengthening currency—that is, unless rising social tensions and labor unrest significantly increase the restrictions on hiring and firing practices, thus providing a floor for wages. And as noted previously, those employment restrictions are just now appearing on the horizon. In the more advanced industries, however, where Chinese workers must have sophisticated technical skills, Chinese companies have actually experienced labor shortages, a development that has put a floor under wages.

The solution to the current account imbalance requires both the United States and China to address the imbalance issue together in a way that rebalances the savings-consumption relationship. The solution requires, but is not limited to, an upward adjustment of the Chinese exchange rate.

It is true, of course, that the Chinese currency has been allowed to appreciate since 2006, which on the surface has led to a significantly better U.S. position for net foreign exports. But the currency has not been allowed to appreciate far enough.

I suspect one issue, and one alone, will drive further decision-making on the currency. It is an issue that may even supersede the concern with the negative effect of a strengthening currency on large domestic Chinese firms. That issue is inflation. If once the global economy recovers and inflation creeps up in China, particularly affecting food and clothing, the outcome will produce even greater social tensions. In the end, the Chinese leadership could be forced to confront a nasty choice between protecting the domestic and state-run enterprises while accepting the politically and socially destabilizing effect of higher inflation, or accepting a stronger currency, which will throttle back the economy a bit and potentially control prices, but jeopardize, at least in the minds of officials, the survival of many state-run enterprises. This crucial choice, when made, could affect the entire global economy.

One of the broad themes of this book argues that economic success stems from the ongoing innovations by a risk-taking entrepreneurial class that allows an economy to continually reinvent itself. If that is the case, then China should have a strong entrepreneurial class and be riding high. On the surface, China, a place where market trading and business risk-taking seem to be in the national DNA, would appear to be a likely candidate as the world's haven for entrepreneurs. But like most things in China, the situation is far more complex. As Columbia University economist Jagdish Bhagwati put it, "Because China has an authoritarian regime, it cannot fully profit from the information revolution, thus inhibiting the technology that is at the heart of growth today. The PC (personal computer) is incompatible with the C.P. (Communist Party)." True, Chinese entrepreneurs have proven to be awesome capitalists throughout Asia, but in China itself, their prospects are limited.

One of the perks of owning a magazine is that publishers regularly send free copies of books for review. One bitter cold day in early 2007, I was sitting in my Washington office reading a new book called *Wiki-nomics: How Mass Collaboration Changes Everything* by Don Tapscott and Anthony D. Williams. The book's "bottom up" thesis, noted earlier, argues:

> The growing accessibility of information technologies puts the tools required to collaborate, create value, and compete at everybody's fingertips. This liberates people to participate in innovation and wealth creation within every sector of the economy. Millions of people already join forces in self-organized collaborations that produce dynamic new goods and services that rival those of the world's largest and best-financed enterprises. This new mode of innovation and value creation is called "peer production," or peering—which describes what happens when masses of people and firms collaborate openly to drive innovation and growth in their industries.

As I read these words, I thought that what the authors were really saying is that the Internet now represents the new tool for mass, collaborative, bottom-up entrepreneurial reinvention. It made sense. My twentysomething kids live their lives through the Internet. If, for example, I say I saw an interesting article in the *Washington Post*, with the newspaper sitting right next to them, they will by habit stand up and walk across the room to the computer to check it out. In the

coming decade, the already vibrant entrepreneurial culture will be turbocharged again, turning the economy upside down in a kind of
second-round "online" populist entrepreneurial revolution.

As I was ruminating on this interesting book, I suddenly noticed a
headline running across the Bloomberg screen on my desk. The headline seemed too bizarre to believe, too out of touch with today's globalized system, but read something like: "Chinese President Urges
Internet Censorship." The gist of President Hu Jintao's troubling
comment to the Political Bureau of the Central Committee of the
Communist Party was that the government was gearing up plans to try
to police the Internet. The government, he said, would implement
"new advanced technologies" to assure that Internet content promotes, among other things, "the development of a socialist culture . . .
and the security of the state."

President Hu's intention, of course, was not to stifle entrepreneurial initiative. On the contrary, the official community is in fact
attempting to do just the opposite, and recent efforts to establish private property rights and a more uniform tax system are cases in point.
It is simply that trying to police the Internet threatens the new culture
of bottom-up entrepreneurial initiative. Officials appear not to know
any better. Most troubling is that they fail to comprehend the essential
role of freedom in the entrepreneurial process.

In China, much of the original political energy of Tiananmen
Square was cleverly redirected into entrepreneurship and away from
political change. But it is a breed of entrepreneurship different from
what we know in the West. In America, as Reed Hundt astutely puts it,
entrepreneurs disrupt order; in China, they perpetuate it: "Entrepreneurship fills a vacuum once occupied by the Communist state's system of production."

It may be that Chinese entrepreneurs find Internet policing tolerable
because they often are already saddled with having to partner with government bureaucrats (who, for example, help them defy environmental
restrictions as the outpouring of pollution increases exponentially).
Some entrepreneurs are even members of the Communist Party. Wildly

disparate estimates range from a low of 17 percent to a high of 76 percent of the entrepreneurial class being official members of the party.

Some experts go as far as to suggest that China's level of entrepreneurship peaked in the late 1980s and early 1990s. Since then, particularly in cities, the tentacles of the bureaucracy have slowly grabbed on to the risk-taking system. In 1999, for instance, thirty-two million people were listed as "self-employed." By 2004, that number had dropped to twenty-four million, suggesting the possibility that the latest period of phenomenal economic growth stemmed a lot more from the benefits of a cheap currency and domestic cost-cutting than from a continuously reinventing entrepreneurial revolution. If that is the case, China is in more trouble than we realize.

But don't think the leadership has given up. Still heavily dependent on foreign technological know-how, the Chinese today outspend the world in trying to dominate pockets of entrepreneurial and technological leadership, buying overseas what cannot be accomplished at home. Some analysts call this an attempt to create a "host of champions," particularly in textiles, oil, chemicals, and information technology. It is the ultimate—and most likely futile—attempt to ride herd on and contain a dynamic process that is, and must by its very nature be, uncontainable. The major problem is that new technologies often become quickly obsolete. Just as the ink has dried on China's long-negotiated contract to purchase some cutting edge technology, a new break through somewhere in the world has abruptly made that technology obsolete.

Will the predictions that China will run the world someday have more accuracy than the earlier predictions about Japan, France, the Soviet Union, and Argentina coming out on top? Perhaps. But don't count out India, the dark horse candidate. I have avoided writing a separate chapter on India because its economy, compared to China's economy, poses a significantly lower threat to the global system. India is not a major capital exporter. Of its roughly one billion people, fewer than five million work in manufacturing. If anything, India represents not so much a threat to the world as a threat to China.

The fact that China has achieved 10 percent economic growth rates for more than a decade is without precedent anywhere in the world. Less well known is that India in recent years has achieved an impressive 8 percent or better average annual growth rate.

Clearly, the Indian economy, with its huge, well-educated, English-speaking middle class, is in a takeoff phase. If China is the world's factory, India is the world's back office. In general, the back office offers a lot more long-term stability than the factory. Whereas the China model depends on unpredictable and not completely controllable external variables—exports and the inflow of foreign technological direct investment—India enjoys an economy driven largely by domestic demand, albeit with more short-term capital inflows. India, moreover, operates under a relatively reliable, Anglo-Saxon-style rule of law that, while not perfect for outside investors, remains a stark contrast to the nebulous, even nonexistent, Chinese legal situation.

True, India's economy has historically been hindered by inflation, by relatively inconsistent political leadership, and, perhaps most of all, by poor infrastructure, which is why a huge, decade-long, unprecedented infrastructure spending process has finally begun. (Today India's manufacturers pay twice as much for power and three times as much for rail transport as Chinese manufacturers because of China's head start on infrastructure spending.) During the past fifteen years, inflation has been impressively reduced from 14 percent to 5.5 percent, but still needs to be reduced further. Moreover, India has become more vulnerable as a result of its growing current account deficit.

Nonetheless, the larger point is that China, which opened its economy in 1979, benefits from a twelve-year head start over India, which did so in 1991. Yet India may be in a better position than China was at this stage of development. India's direct foreign investment, today over $50 billion, is roughly the same as China's at the fifteen-year mark after reform. China's growth was higher, but India's more stable, with a financial sector potentially far less burdened with nonperforming loans.

India appears to be more technologically savvy. Will Hutton, in his book *The Writing on the Wall: Why We Must Embrace China as a Partner or Face It as an Enemy*, argues that India has moved far ahead of China in computer technology: "Despite massive investment . . . China trail[s] far behind." He agrees with me that Beijing's attempts to police the Internet have not helped. "Yahoo, Microsoft and Google are part of the cultural yeast of globalization, yet each has been at the receiving end of China's Internet firewall of censorship."

So the issue is not what India has done, but what it could do in the decades ahead if infrastructure needs, restrictive labor laws, and other impediments to growth are corrected quickly, as the government has promised. Note too that if manufacturing reaches a point of global saturation, and China attempts to compete globally in the services arena, India will be its greatest headache.

In the end, China is, above all, a momentum-driven economy. Its momentum stems from the need, as least for now, for a ferocious incoming stream of technical know-how and an aggressive outpouring of exports. Anything that trips up this momentum—be it a slowdown in investment, a drop in exports, a global-warming-induced trade war, or some technical blunder by the Chinese leadership—has the potential to create negative multiplier effects throughout the Chinese system, and no doubt the rest of the world. A further thing to watch: a European or American demand for investment reciprocity that the Chinese, for political reasons, can't or won't offer.

The global implications are serious. Together the new "G2," the United States and China, until the outbreak of the financial crisis was responsible for more than 60 percent of the cumulative growth in the world's total GDP. Face it: America has, when all is said and done, married itself off to the Tony Soprano family. And, to a large extent, so has the rest of the world. The entire global system is increasingly tied into a murky Chinese political, economic, and financial system of limited transparency. With China, we have little concept of what is around the bend, yet there is no turning back. Indeed, if we are to preserve today's new global economy, we need to help Chinese officials learn how to cope and work with the rest of the international system.

We desperately need a coordinated effort to try to guide this impressive yet dangerous beast that has the capacity to lift the world to a new era of prosperity—or drag us all down into chaos.

Back in the mid-1980s, when I began my market advisory business, Japan was in a strikingly similar situation to China's positioning in the global economy today. Japan, the largest source of global savings, with its impressive industrial might, was expected to dominate the world economically. Because of a series of policy blunders in managing interest rates and its currency and in conducting bank regulatory policy, things didn't quite turn out as planned. As I demonstrate in the next chapter, free financial markets may at times produce terrifying volatility and uncertainty. The only system worse, however, is a system where flawed human beings, through administrative control and government edict, attempt to manage the outcome of a sophisticated economic and financial system within a globalized economy.

5

Japanese Housewives
Take the Commanding Heights

In the mid-1980s, Japan was being talked about in awe. If Britain dominated the nineteenth century and America the twentieth century, Japan was fully expected to own the twenty-first century. This is similar to what the experts now predict about China and, to a lesser extent, India.

Indeed, if you were a Martian just landed on planet Earth, Japan economically the past decade might still look pretty good. Many Japanese multinational corporations dominated major world industrial sectors. Toyota, for example, eclipsed General Motors as the largest automobile manufacturer in the world. The Japanese stock market for a while successfully rebounded from its lows of the 1990s. Foreign ownership of Japanese equities increased every year for most of the last two decades until the crisis.

In addition, Japan has sat on the world's largest pool of private investable savings. It purchases the government debt of other countries, keeping global interest rates low. The so-called low-interest-rate "yen carry trade" has financed economic expansion worldwide (because Japanese interest rates for the past decade have been far lower than the rates throughout the rest of the industrialized world, global investors have borrowed huge amounts of capital from Japanese financial institutions to invest globally). Given all of these strengths, what is not to like about the Japanese economy?

The answer is that Japan is the perfect object lesson for how *not* to run things in the new global economy. No, Japan doesn't resemble the kind of threat China poses to the international system—some reckless, unpredictable, out-of-control force. Japan simply represents what happens when policymakers make serious policy blunders. The result has been a decade and a half of ugly underperformance and the end of Japan's economic leadership role in the world. For Americans in particular, the lessons of Japan are particularly timely and relevant. That's because Japan's recent past has the potential to become America's future.

In this chapter, I will show the pitfalls of an economy loaded with debt. I'll show what happens when a financial bubble bursts, when price levels actually drop too low, and when central bankers become powerless to come to the rescue. I'll explain how Japan went from a soaring, bubble economy in the late 1980s, with an extraordinarily strong currency, to a period of deflationary weakness in the 1990s described as nothing less than a "lost decade." And I'll point out the risk that America could stumble into its own lost decade.

Most important, I'll explain how Japan's big corporations almost alone have benefited big time from this deflationary, low-interest-rate period—and how Japanese housewives, stuck with the losing end of the deal, managed to fight back. A number of years ago, a friend of mine, Dan Yergin, coauthored the book *The Commanding Heights: The Battle for the World Economy*. "Commanding heights" is a reference to a speech by Vladimir Lenin describing the parts of an economy that effectively control and dominate the other parts. In the economy of the twenty-first century, Japanese housewives, as hard as it is to believe, find themselves perched atop the commanding heights. They unwittingly have become big players in the Japanese and world financial systems—a major financial force right under the noses of Japan's initially unaware economic establishment. Here's how it happened.

From a distance, Japan enjoys the image of great strength and maturity. Roughly thirty-five to forty world-class, well-funded multinational corporations—among them the Toyotas, Mitsubishis, and Canons—enjoy the ability to compete head-to-head with any equivalent company in the world. Using Japan's low interest rates and relatively weak currency, these companies continuously restructured their firms to become ever more efficient and competitive. Today they are still lean and growing, earning profits on the products they sell abroad despite the decline in global demand. Japan's megafirms represent roughly half of the companies listed on the Japanese stock market. On the surface, the picture still looks impressive.

Yet the picture is two parts illusion and one part reality. While the highly successful megafirms represent half of the stock market, and thus keep that market stable, the market itself reflects only 10 percent of the actual Japanese economy. The other 90 percent, the neglected part not reflected in stock market valuations, is going nowhere fast. Japan's economy has been below its nominal peak growth rate of 1997, according to Lehman Brothers and has now fallen into recession. Since that year until 2007, the euro area economies grew by more than 50 percent; the U.S. economy became 70 percent larger. Not surprisingly, class warfare and resentment over income distribution in Japan are beginning to grow.

To understand what has happened to Japan economically over the last several decades, begin with the yen. In Japan, the yen exchange rate is a driving force in everyday life. Americans and most people in other countries are generally unaware of their own currency's specific valuation against other countries' currencies. In Japan, the man on the street fixates on the Japanese currency. Currency exchange rates flash constantly from electronic signs on the sides of skyscrapers in downtown Tokyo and other major cities.

The story of Japan's currency is reasonably straightforward. This explanation may at first sound a bit tedious, but the yen is a useful lens through which to examine the Japanese economic system. Beginning in the mid-1980s, the yen soared in strength against the U.S. dollar (encouraged by an agreement among the industrialized nations called the Plaza Accord to allow the dollar to weaken to reduce global trade friction with the United States). The yen jumped from 254 yen to the U.S. dollar in January 1985 to 127 by late 1990 (the lower the number, the stronger the yen). By 1995, the yen had strengthened to 80 yen per U.S. dollar.

It was specifically during the yen-strengthening period from 1986 to 1989 that global commentators talked of a new, supercharged Japan as buying up the world, led by the Japanese purchase of an American icon, Rockefeller Center in New York. At one point during this golden period, it was said that the value of one square mile of real estate surrounding the Emperor's Palace was worth more than the real estate value of the entire state of California.

The famous "bubble economy" became a seminal event. Asset prices, including the price of stocks and real estate, soared. One reason for the real estate boom is that Japanese banks during this period recklessly financed commercial real estate and commercial land at unheard-of prices. This was not unlike the way American banks in recent years financed mountains of unqualified subprime mortgage borrowers. During bubble periods, everyone tells themselves, "It's not a bubble. This time, things are different." The price of virtually all Japanese real estate initially soared. I remember a friend, an independent Japanese financial strategist, who invited me to his condominium in a fashionable section of Tokyo. The apartment was an attractive, several-bedroom affair that would have cost perhaps $500,000 in Washington or perhaps $700,000 in New York. It was appraised for $10 million. By December 1989, the Nikkei stock index nearly hit the 39,000 yen high mark (by comparison, the market in 2004, a decade and a half later, was at the 7,500 level).

But the great Nippon bubble burst, as all bubbles do. Why did the bubble burst? Part of the reason was the nature of financial euphoria itself. Markets that irrationally get ahead of themselves generally abruptly reverse course once time passes and common sense throughout the market eclipses the euphoria. But the bubble burst also because of human error. Throughout this book, I have warned of the negative unintended consequences of well-intentioned policy actions. Japanese officials the last two decades are a prime case in point. When the yen began to strengthen after the Plaza Accord agreement, Bank of Japan officials, intending to cushion the effect of the stronger yen on the global competitiveness of domestic exporters, lowered short-term interest rates five times. They should instead have allowed the strengthening yen to force the economy to restructure so as to continue being able to compete globally. Nonetheless, by February 1987 the short-term interest rate (called the official discount rate) had been dropped to 2.5 percent. By late 1989, realizing their mistake as the bubble grew larger by the month, Bank of Japan officials reversed course and raised short-term interest rates in relatively quick steps to 6 percent. To control skyrocketing real estate prices, the government implemented a new land holding tax and placed restrictions on bank lending for real estate.

Not surprisingly, by January 1990 the stock market collapsed. Bill Emmott, the former editor of *The Economist* and a Japan expert, describes how the Japanese central bank, after the stock market collapsed, actually continued to raise interest rates (to crush the asset-price bubble) until September 1990. Then officials waited to ease until seventeen months after the crisis began, a policy failure of monumental proportions (and one thankfully not repeated by the Federal Reserve during the 2007–2009 credit crisis).

The Japanese economic and financial system in this yo-yo scenario took a nosedive. The yen eventually dropped like a stone. More important, job creation screeched to a halt, wages declined, and so did consumption. Corporate profits, which had been softening, went into a tailspin. Tokyo insiders thereafter called the period of the 1990s Japan's "lost decade." Many Japanese lost faith in their future.

Worst of all, the economy, rather than experiencing modest, gradual inflation, as most economies do, fell into a deflationary spiral.

Prices dropped dangerously through the floor. As a result, domestic demand throughout much of the economy collapsed. After all, why buy a house or a major appliance under those conditions if you expect the value to drop precipitously? Hold off and wait for the lower price.

Chapter 7 is titled, "The Incredible Shrinking Central Banks." Perhaps the strongest evidence in support of that title is the Bank of Japan. During this crisis period, the "shrinking" Japanese central bank officials blundered further as they tried to respond to declining prices. They cut short-term interest rates, but by too little, too late. This placed the central bank far behind the curve. Chasing the deflationary spiral downward, but always one step behind, was a policy failure of spectacular proportions.

During this "lost decade," government policymakers blundered in one other way. The economic nosedive caused a lot of borrowers to fall behind on their loans, and the regulators did not move aggressively enough to force the banks to address their nonperforming loan problem (a euphemism for loans where the borrower is actually bankrupt or soon to go bankrupt). A paralyzed banking community, loaded with nonperforming loans on its balance sheets, all but stopped new lending.

But here's the point that is key to today's policymakers in the United States and worldwide. From that point on, monetary stimulus became virtually powerless to affect the level of prices. Economists call this situation a "liquidity trap." Interest rates are so low that bonds and cash are virtually interchangeable. Thus the central bank is unable to expand liquidity by buying bonds; it simply exchanges one asset for another that is virtually the same. During Japan's "lost decade," relative prices dropped by 25 percent compared to the United States. This is what happens in a deflationary spiral. The actual decline in the yen's value was almost 50 percent against the U.S. dollar. Even worse, the central bank lost its ability to affect long-term interest rates (central banks control short-term interest rates but the financial markets control other rates, including the long-term rate). Long-term interest rates had been 7.5 percent in 1990 at the peak of the bubble period.

Bond investors in Japan earned healthy returns on their bond purchases. By 1999, the markets dropped long-term interest rates to below 1 percent. The central bank had no choice but to cut its overnight interest rate to zero percent. But it was too late; monetary stimulus had become ineffective. This raises the question: Could a similar scenario, brought on by a series of foolish policy blunders, unfold in America or Europe?

During this period of a weak yen and rock-bottom interest rates—what some have dubbed an era of cheap money—there were winners and losers. The economic mix proved to be beneficial to Japan's leading corporations. These firms, because of the weak currency, were able to compete aggressively in the export markets (in other countries, many Japanese imports became cheaper relative to the price of the same or similar domestic products). Borrowing at absurdly low interest rates, the big corporations could buy new, more efficient machinery and equipment to restructure for future global competition. Today they are positioned to earn ever higher profits from their activities abroad as a result of globalization.

The bad news is that Japan's medium and small enterprises, by contrast, are underfunded and in poor shape. More labor-intensive, they suffered big time during the low-interest-rate, weak-yen period. One reason is that the weak yen made the price of imported energy supplies hugely expensive. This is key because Japan imports all its energy. These smaller firms, the big losers, represent 75 percent of Japan's employment and are largely domestic demand oriented. Therefore, they need a *strong* yen to reduce the cost of imports, including oil and other commodities.

By the late 1990s, Japan's zero-interest-rate policy also allowed the large banks to start to clean up their disastrous balance sheets, shedding the glut of bad real estate loans from the previous decade. Like the giant multinational corporations, they too were big winners. During this period of cheap money, the banks took in deposits and could pay savers next to nothing because interest rates across the board were so low. Then the banks took those deposits and bought risk-free

Japanese government debt, which paid 1.5 to 2 percent higher than the interest paid to savers (this profit is called the spread). With the steady income from the spread, the banks were able to gradually write off their nonperforming loans. At long last they cleaned up their balance sheets. But this process of the banks loading up on government debt has placed Japanese monetary policy in a dangerous straitjacket that still exists today.

During this period, one other entity—one other loser—fell victim to this cheap money policy mix: Japan's household sector. Japanese households financially suffocated because their savings accounts, which once yielded reasonably healthy returns, again were achieving tiny returns. And in Japan, an aging, high-saving country, a lot of people traditionally have depended on savings account returns to supplement their income. Household interest income from savings accounts, thirty-nine trillion yen in 1991 (from six hundred trillion yen held largely in bank deposits), plummeted to a mere three trillion yen (from over seven hundred trillion yen in savings account assets) by 2005.

It is hard to overestimate how Japan's policy blunders even today frustrate the lives of average citizens. As recently as the period 2005–2006, for example, the bottom 50 percent of Japanese citizens actually saw their incomes drop. The middle 40 percent experienced flat annual income, even with company bonuses figured in. Given these realities, it is little wonder that the long-ruling Japanese Liberal Democratic Party in recent years has fallen on political hard times. That will happen to American and other industrialized world politicians if the so-called Japan disease of declining prices and neutered monetary policy proves to be a global event in coming years.

Here's where the housewives come into play. By the beginning of the twenty-first century, the frustrated housewives (and/or heads of households) had had enough of the economy's poor performance, particularly its poor returns on savings account investments. Using the words *housewives* and *capital flows* in the same sentence may seem bizarre, but it's not. Going back to the 1950s, the housewife in a typical

Japanese family controlled the finances. This is certainly ironic given the fact that Japanese financial institutions continue to be male-dominated. This financial role for the housewife reflects the lifestyle of a typical family. The husband, the salaryman, often works ten-hour days, suffers through two- to three-hour commutes, and is regularly forced to partake in drinks and dinner with the boss until late at night. The salaryman is seldom home, or at least not during waking hours. As a result, the housewife has naturally assumed the role of financial matriarch.

Starting in the early 2000s, the housewives, taking financial matters into their own hands, began to hunt for a greater return on their savings. They found these more robust returns in *foreign* bonds and other overseas investments. In the process, as incredible as it sounds, the housewives overnight have become one of the largest behind-the-scenes forces in the global foreign exchange market. They collectively control major amounts of Japan's household savings and have become extraordinarily savvy at shopping for and buying far higher-yielding foreign bonds.

Today, roughly one-fifth of all currency trading worldwide during trading hours in Tokyo involves Japanese private individuals, many of them women. In the world of currency trading, a common question lately has become: "What are the [Japanese] housewives investing in these days?"

Perhaps most interesting, the housewives often bypass the large Japanese financial intermediary institutions when making their investments. Instead, they increasingly invest directly through the Internet.

The numbers involved are astounding. Three-quarters of Japan's financial assets are held by an aging population dependent on the financial return on their savings. Overall liquid financial assets of Japanese households amount to roughly twelve hundred trillion yen, or over $11 trillion, with significantly more than half of that amount in savings accounts and other instruments. This is big money. A mere 1 percent of this household liquidity would make the housewives the largest player in the global foreign exchange market. Two percent potentially would be enough to overwhelm the global currency market in one fell swoop if the housewives moved collectively. To be sure, the housewives educated themselves and developed an extraordinary level of computer savvy almost overnight.

For the rest of the world, here's why the Japanese housewives are so significant. In one sense, the housewives' investments might be thought of as a stabilizing influence in the world financial system. With their computers, the housewives have access to a wide array of global financial investment opportunities, so they can seek out the best rewards. But, here they are, millions of individual decision-makers directing the largest pool of money in the world, and they are beyond the immediate reach of the people whose job is to maintain the stability of the financial system. As a force, therefore, the housewives are a powerful and unpredictable entity. In 2008, for example, the housewives abruptly changed their approach. They curtailed their foreign purchases and began buying domestic financial assets as the rest of the world in response to weakness lowered short-term interest rates. As a result, Japanese net capital outflows rapidly began to shrink. Indeed, by mid-2008 the largest source of capital outflows stemmed from U.S. and European bank borrowing from Japanese banks. As the credit crisis continued to grind on, Tokyo became the last resort for a Western financial system desperate for liquidity. The yen soared in strength.

This newfound housewife flexibility in making investments is not reassuring for global crisis managers. Not that long ago, in the event of a full-scale global financial panic, U.S. Treasury officials could pick up the phone and call Japan's Ministry of Finance (MoF) officials who, if they saw fit, would then order the insurance companies and other large financial firms with excess savings into coordinated action. That is what happened during the 1987 stock market crash. Back then, the government bureaucrats could influence capital flows because the Ministry of Finance exerted regulatory control over the large financial institutions. Things have changed. Today in a global crisis, who knows how housewives would react? In the event of a global financial meltdown, which housewife leader would, or could, take the telephone call

for coordinated help from Washington? We face the frightening reality that one of the tried-and-true members of the global crisis management team—Japan's Ministry of Finance—no longer has control over a
large bulk of Japanese savings flows.

None of this is meant to denigrate the historic importance of
Japan's governmental leadership. In over twenty years of traveling to
Japan, I have been fortunate to know many of the great bureaucratic
operators at the Ministry of Finance. Japan is a place where the best
minds go to the University of Tokyo and then University of Tokyo
Law. Afterward, they begin work not in the private sector but at one of
the government bureaucracies.

The smartest and most talented go to the Ministry of Finance
where, in recent years, they are expected to manage a financial system
that is increasingly unmanageable. Names come to mind such as
Toyoo Gyohten, Tomomitsu Oba, Eisuke Sakakibara ("Mr. Yen,"
because of his clever backstage efforts to influence markets), Makoto
Utsumi, and Hiroshi Watanabe. All were internationally oriented vice
ministers who, when they spoke, rattled global markets.

Ironically, one of Japan's broader problems today is its superb history of bureaucratic control. It is not easy in today's volatile global
financial system for bureaucrats to feel comfortable with a chaotic
form of entrepreneurial capitalism involving risk and, more important,
continual failure. In Japan, there is something unnatural about the
market volatility of a liberalized financial system. Bureaucrats are bred
to prohibit failure. But that is precisely why Japan's economy keeps
tripping up; its bureaucrats don't know how to deal with the entrepreneurial uncertainty and failure that are essential to economic success.

Perhaps the most forceful bureaucratic strategist I have known was
Makoto Utsumi, who was vice minister for international finance from
1989 to 1991. I first met the dapperly dressed Utsumi, then the Japanese embassy's economics minister, in 1985 for breakfast at the Four
Seasons Hotel in Washington. I was trying to persuade him of the
merits of my first conference, the U.S. Congressional Summit on the
Dollar and Trade. Raised a Methodist in postwar Japan and now a Zen

Buddhist, he sat during the initial stages of the breakfast with his arms folded across his chest and a scowl on his face. I could read his mind: "You, in your early thirties, want me to risk my entire career by sending word back to Tokyo that our most senior financial officials should fly to Washington for a silly conference?" Utsumi then started to study his watch.

I could sense things were going nowhere fast, so I came to the point: "The existing pure floating exchange rate regime, Mr. Utsumi, is unsustainable because the rising dollar threatens to heighten trade restrictions on Capitol Hill. The current yen-dollar rate of 260 is a recipe for a coming trade war. Global currency and trade relationships have become inseparable. What does the Ministry of Finance have to lose in participating, given the private nature of this gathering? Moreover, if your people don't participate, Japan could be the point of attack in the trade and currency discussion. Japan's absence will potentially build resentment on Capitol Hill."

Utsumi's face brightened, then brightened some more. A mental switch appeared to flip. "There are no promises," he said, "but we may be able to help out." Makoto Utsumi helped out, and then some. By the time of the conference, the powerful elite of Japanese financial officials, who until then had resisted such public exposure, were flying to Washington in force to talk about currencies. And at a private conference, to boot. Tokyo had decided it was best to place itself in the middle of the debate. Incidentally, in planning that first conference, I included the world's major central bankers in the discussions. Up until that time, the independent central bank community avoided any formal participation in official international meetings involving finance ministry or treasury officials. Jean-Claude Trichet, today the president of the European Central Bank, who attended our conference as a French treasury official, argues that our including the central bankers in this event made history. "You all but forced the official meetings of the industrialized world finance ministers from that point on to include the central bankers," he said in a speech in Washington in late October 2007.

As the U.S. economy picked up in the years after the 1981–1982 recession, the dollar had soared. Soon after our conference, officials from the industrialized nations (including the central bankers) met in New York and agreed on the aforementioned Plaza Accord, which addressed the themes brought up by our conference involving the currency-trade relationship.

Utsumi, by the way, was a master at the use of bureaucratic power. These were the glory days of the Ministry of Finance. In 1991, for instance, India faced a liquidity crisis. Back then, because of its ties to the Soviet Union and with the cold war still raging, India lacked the financial relationships with the industrialized world it enjoys today. Yet the heavily invested Japanese banking system could hardly afford an Indian financial crisis.

Utsumi flew to New York and quietly met with former J. P. Morgan chairman Lewis Preston, who was about to take over as World Bank president. Utsumi's offer: If the World Bank would give "the public green light," the Bank of Japan would secretly make liquidity available to avert an Indian financial collapse. The shuttle diplomacy—financial style—worked; the liquidity crisis faded.

Utsumi was also a master at projecting the *image* of power. I can attest to that fact based on a strange incident that involved me. Here is how the bizarre events unfolded. The incident demonstrates the extraordinary lengths to which the Japanese bureaucracy would go to project a sense of power and influence.

When a man named Ryutaro Hashimoto became finance minister in 1990, I visited him at the Ministry of Finance quite often. Our mutual friend, Utsumi, usually sat in on these discussions. In Japan, people thought Hashimoto a dead ringer for Elvis Presley, but I never saw the resemblance.

Making small talk at the beginning of one meeting, I suggested to Hashimoto that he come sailing with me on the Chesapeake Bay near Washington, at a time of his convenience. This was intended to be what is called a "Protestant" or "WASP" invitation where, in social circles, a person says, "We must have you over some time." In reality, they are thinking, That's not gonna happen. In this case, it happened. Utsumi had heard my invitation and, unbeknownst to me, began to mobilize, I believe both as a friendly gesture and also to offer a demonstration of the ultimate exercise of bureaucratic power.

Months later, about two weeks before an important G7 meeting of finance officials in Washington, someone from the Japanese embassy called: "Finance Minister Hashimoto and his wife would love to take you up on your kind offer of a day sailing on the Chesapeake Bay. It's their wedding anniversary. They will arrive on a Saturday morning and leave in the late afternoon, in time to return to Washington for the official G7 dinner [of the world's central bankers and finance ministers]." It all sounded simple, but it wasn't. Upon hearing of the visit I instinctively became a bit nervous.

The entourage was so large, eighteen people including bodyguards, I was forced to charter a large yacht, my own boat being far too small. As the day of the Hashimoto (a.k.a. Elvis) visit approached, I established my plan. We would leave from the Annapolis, Maryland, harbor, several blocks from the entrance to the United States Naval Academy, and sail for several hours on the Chesapeake Bay. Around midday, we would wind our way down nearby Mill Creek for lunch at a famous Chesapeake crab shack called Jimmy Cantler's Riverside Inn.

I had previously taken many Japanese friends there because of the famed steamed Maryland blue crab, the best example, many said, of a Western version of Japanese cuisine. Crabs were always an instant favorite. Our chartered vessel pulled up to the restaurant's dock and the restaurant staff was waiting to help grab the lines to tie up the boat.

Inside the restaurant sat pitchers of cold beer and mounds of hot, steaming eight-inch-wide blue crab "Jimmies" seasoned in a hot, slightly peppery spice, ready to be cracked open by hand with wooden mallets on tables covered with brown, disposable paper. Finance Minister Hashimoto, after several hours of meticulously dissecting the crabs in this seafood feast, proclaimed this the most enjoyable meal he had experienced outside Japan in thirty years of international travel. I thought to myself, the crab shack, by international standards, was a risky but worthwhile choice.

As lunch ended, the entourage slowly made its way back to the yacht. An avid photographer, Hashimoto stopped and took hundreds of photographs of the restaurant's waterman's surroundings. He seemed fascinated that something so delicate in flavor could derive from surroundings that, I'm sure to him, were the stereotype of Red Neck, U.S.A. As the vessel pulled away from the dock, we proceeded down Mill Creek out into the bay and back toward Annapolis. "It is getting late," Hashimoto's chief aide informed me. "We stayed too long taking photographs and must return to Washington for the G7 dinner. The minister plays a major role tonight."

Suddenly, a slight pang of worry hit me. Better tell the captain to motor back at full steam because time is of the essence, I thought. Right at that moment, the captain, as if he had read my mind, asked to speak with me in private. We went below deck, but the conversation was not what I expected. "We have a problem with the boat," he began. The slight pang of worry intensified. "The engine works fine, but the transmission gearshift has stripped," he explained. "The boat won't go into reverse, and there is no way I can dock this boat in the harbor's narrow channel without going into reverse. I don't know what to do."

At this point, I pictured in my mind the *Washington Post* headline: "Japanese Finance Minister Stranded on Chesapeake," with the sub-head, "Reckless Consultant Ruins Anniversary Celebration, Disrupts G7 Proceedings." Instantly I experienced a momentary numbness, followed by an overwhelming sense of anxiety. What have I gotten myself into? I thought. If I had only kept my mouth shut, I wouldn't be in this fix. Now what to do? In Japan, form and appearances are as important as substance. This kind of fiasco could destroy my reputation, and probably Utsumi's as well.

After several deep breaths, I began to concentrate. My only hope was the captain, but that required a bluff. The captain and I went below deck again for a serious discussion. "This trip was to be a test," I began, my mind racing for what I would say next. "If everything went well," I told the captain, "perhaps the entire world finance ministry and central bank community could regularly use your services when they visit Washington. You could be their hired yacht captain, maybe someday even for prime ministers, even royalty, but not if this test proves to be a failure."

At the mere mention of the thought of additional business, the captain's interest intensified. He began: "What if we drop everyone off outside the town by the nearby Naval Academy bulkhead? I can make it there without going into reverse. We can call over to redirect their limousines to pick them up at this new location." I immediately responded: "That won't work. Their limo drivers won't know where to go. Plus, for the sake of the Japanese, it is probably best they don't know we're all in trouble. That would probably create enough anxiety to ruin the spirit of the day. You figure something out. This could be big business, but I need to know this is a professionally run operation." I crossed my fingers.

By that point, my guests began wondering about my absence, so I came back on deck. Forty minutes later, we found ourselves approaching the Naval Academy bulkhead wall. I had no idea what to expect. Suddenly, the captain, with surprising confidence, addressed our entire group. "Mr. Minister," he began, "we have enjoyed serving you today. We are honored by your presence. And because your time is so precious, we have decided as an extra service to drop you off at the U.S. Naval Academy. We'll have limos there to take you back to your limos in town."

When we arrived at the bulkhead, I looked out and was stunned. How he did so in such a short period of time, I will never know, but against the backdrop of the United States Naval Academy barracks stood four local stretch limousines waiting for the Japanese. True, two were white and one a powder blue. All no doubt had mirrored ceilings, and were probably to be used that night at the Annapolis High School senior prom. It didn't matter. The Japanese entourage jumped into the limos and raced back to their own transportation minutes away in the small town for the trip back to Washington. Hashimoto's assistant thanked me for being so sensitive with the finance minister's time by arranging this quicker means of a return trip.

As the limos sped away, I collapsed on the nearby academy lawn. I wrote the captain a check with an enormous tip and later sent his advertising flyer to both the Japanese embassy and the State Department. But my plan frankly was to never, ever open my mouth again about the joys of the Chesapeake Bay. No more Protestant invitations for me.

Despite all this drama, Utsumi, ever mindful of the perception of bureaucratic power, had made his point: His friends in Washington enjoyed real clout. He could arrange for them to go sailing with a man who at the time was perhaps the most powerful financial figure in the world—and in the middle of an important weekend G7 meeting. This was also a message to markets of how powerful a global bureaucrat could be. Utsumi was no doubt counting on the fact that the Hashimoto visit would make the rounds on Wall Street; it did.

But the point is that the Japanese system, once brilliant at controlling bureaucratic image and substance, is today facing its own fragile world that is curved. Now millions of housewives and other market decision-makers care little about bureaucratic image and power. They care about information—facts and insights that reflect future rates of return and risk. They care little about bureaucratic power because, in today's brave new world, they collectively now *are* the power.

To be fair, the current Japanese leadership is hardly oblivious to this populist uprising. A consensus exists in the policy community that today's low-interest-rate scenario needs to return to one of equilibrium, though there are huge fights about the timing of raising interest rates.

Nor are Japan's leaders oblivious to the benefits of more liberalized financial markets and entrepreneurial capitalism, as exists in the United States and elsewhere. Tokyo officials have initiated some serious banking and small business bankruptcy law reforms to encourage investment in entrepreneurial initiatives. The Japanese policy leadership understands too that the economy needs more than higher-yielding savings accounts for housewives. The economy needs an entrepreneurial revolution.

Still, there is always this lingering feeling among many Japanese leaders that the "Japanese-style" market economy culturally has no choice but to be a bit less open, less transparent, and more regulated. High-profile individual risk-taking within an Anglo-Saxon-style open market is somehow inconsistent with the Japanese psyche. In the policy community, a new, more sophisticated, multileveled financial system for assessing risk and distributing wealth is still in the planning stages. After the anguish created by the Great Credit Crisis of 2007–2009, the plan is likely to stay in the planning stages and not become a reality for years to come. The subprime crisis has produced some ugly aftereffects, including, in many parts of the world, a cooling in enthusiasm for the Western-style entrepreneurial risk-taking model. (Policies earlier in this decade allowing foreign direct investment in Japanese firms—a key component of the globalization process—are also being reversed.)

That is not good news for the global economy, where strong Japanese entrepreneurial activity, both separate from and within large corporations, could raise the level of economic growth and cause an increase in consumption. Increased Japanese consumption of imports would help to dramatically reduce global imbalances.

Unfortunately, in terms of providing liquidity to its small- and medium-sized companies, as well as to start-ups, Japan is where the United States was in the early 1980s—in desperate need of a better means of assessing risk and distributing capital. The tiny number of large Japanese banks today, having merged and merged again, are hardly interested in investing in unknowns. This is particularly the case after the bank balance sheet debacle of the "lost decade."

Neither do fledgling enterprises wish to face the heavy interest payments of bank loans in the early stages of building strength. So it is very important that new ways be found to encourage capital investment in new ventures. Equity investment through sales of stock is particularly important in the early stages of a struggling but promising firm. Former Federal Reserve chairman Alan Greenspan has pointed out that "businesses must have equity capital before they are considered viable candidates for debt financing. Equity acts as a buffer against the vagaries of the marketplace and is a sign of the creditworthiness of a business enterprise. The more opaque the business operations, or the newer the firm, the greater the importance of the equity base."

In Japan, reforms that would make equity investment more achievable are slowly emerging. The question, however, is whether a sophisticated, multilayered, highly innovative system for alternative stock ownership capital investments—the kind initiated in the United States in the late 1970s and 1980s—can come soon enough. The question is also whether tightly controlled Japan can experience a cultural change that tolerates the independence, unpredictability, and outright "craziness" of the entrepreneurial sector.

Japan, Inc.'s general awkwardness and sometimes discomfort with the entrepreneurial process reminds me of one of my many trips to Tokyo, this one in early 1990. The following anecdote offers a stark reminder of why Japan, a closed, tight-knit system, finds entrepreneurial risk-taking so challenging. It explains why Japan can't be counted on to become a major locomotive for the global system anytime soon. And make no mistake, with the strength of the U.S. economy slipping and Europe accepting a long-term policy of slow growth, the industrialized world desperately needs a reliable, additional economic locomotive.

The day before the trip, I met in Washington with former Senate Republican leader and White House chief of staff Howard Baker. He had just returned from Moscow and had agreed to co-chair my next conference. This was a time of great turmoil in Russia—the new Wild West—with the social order breaking down. Baker casually commented that Moscow was so chaotic and crime-ridden, with no domestic security, that "the price of guard dogs had jumped 400 percent."

Several days later, I found myself in a Tokyo meeting with various bankers and traders. "What about the chaos in Russia?" someone quickly asked, referring to the headlines about Russian chaos on the front page of virtually every newspaper in the world. I thought for a moment and began with the line: "Howard Baker just returned from Moscow. Things are so bad, the price of guard dogs has jumped 400 percent." The line worked, as it captured what was happening in Russia. I repeated it throughout the week as the lead-in to my more serious analysis of the Russian economy, political risk, and the potential for debt default.

By the end of the week, I had lunch scheduled with former prime minister Noboru Takeshita, then age sixty-eight, who had also agreed to be co-chair of my next conference. Even after leaving the prime ministry, Takeshita dominated the Japanese official policy world. He was head of the original Tanaka faction, the Diet's most sophisticated operators in the widespread politics of government largesse. He was also the linchpin holding together the entire structure of the ruling Liberal Democratic Party. Friends of mine at the U.S. embassy expressed surprise at my closeness to Takeshita—"a rare development," they said. Therefore, I was honored to have the former prime minister host the small luncheon gathering.

After years of scratching and clawing his way to the top, the diminutive Takeshita was a bit strange in that, to outsiders in a public arena, he never showed any facial expression—no anger, joy, sorrow—nothing. It was as if, to stymie political opponents, he had taught himself over the years not to allow the display of emotion to betray his intentions as he maneuvered through political minefields. All anyone saw was a subtle, benign one-quarter smile. His face gave away nothing, but his piercing eyes were always at work. Every time I was in his presence in a crowd, his eyes continually darted skeptically back and forth across the room in rapid-fire succession, gauging the human landscape for political danger.

At the lunch, Takeshita brought along Finance Minister Hashimoto, the man who looked like Elvis whom I had earlier taken on the near disastrous sailing trip on the Chesapeake Bay. My friend

Utsumi, the master bureaucrat, was also present. Takeshita and Hashimoto in front of me both constantly teased the junior Utsumi, suggesting he was the grand "puppeteer" of the Japanese government, pulling all the strings of power. Utsumi's face turned beet red in friendly embarrassment. Why? Because at that point he *was* in many ways the grand puppeteer.

What was fun that day in the private room of a Tokyo restaurant was that Takeshita and company let their hair down. Normally using a translator, the former prime minister instead spoke slowly in English. Strangely, the mood was like that of a high school locker room with a lot of verbal towel snapping and a continual series of lighthearted gibes. This was totally atypical of most meetings between foreigners and Japanese. Normally, an invisible wall of subtle awkwardness, based on the vast cultural distinctions, keeps the visitors at bay.

After about twenty minutes, a crazy-looking member of the Diet named Morihiro Hosokawa arrived. He apologized profusely to Takeshita for his tardiness, bowing so many times and so aggressively—and artlessly—I wondered if he would lose his balance. Hosokawa was a bit strange. His cheaply tailored brown suit and his tie and shirt combination lacked the normal crisp blue tie, white shirt, blue suit uniformity of the typical LDP politician. What's more, Hosokawa bounded into the room like a young Jerry Lewis, immediately becoming the humorous fall guy for the others, the butt of jokes from his colleagues.

Former prime minister Takeshita, presumably in an effort to continue the levity, said Mr. Hosokawa—Mr. Jerry Lewis, that is—would soon become prime minister. That seemed preposterous. I'd be prime minister of Japan before this goofy guy, I thought to myself. At that point, Finance Minister Hashimoto (a.k.a. Elvis), in Japanese, imparted a joke at Hosokawa's expense that, when translated, sounded a bit confusing but ended with the words "errand boy." Everybody laughed, led by the goofy guy with a series of loud guffaws.

To my surprise, it turned out Takeshita had been right. The "errand boy" became prime minister several years later. He served in 1993 and

1994 as a kind of weak concession figure squeezed between two war-ring political factions within the Japanese parliament. I remember my total disbelief as I watched the announcement on television back in Washington. I later learned that Hosokawa's grandfather, Prime Min-ister Fumimaro Konoe, a member of the second most prestigious fam-ily in Japan next to the imperial family, played an important role in history. He was the prime minister who helped initiate World War II. His grandson played the comedian. But the entire episode taught me that power in Japan is seldom where you think it is.

Eventually, the luncheon discussion turned serious. We exchanged views on the world political and economic landscape. Then Hashimoto, my Chesapeake sailing mate, asked if I had any thoughts about the chaotic Russian situation. I prepared myself to respond, loading the good lead in my cannon—the Howard Baker guard dog story. But before I could begin, Takeshita, the most powerful politician at the time in Japan, intervened. "Excuse me, but before you begin," he said, "let me say that I'm told that Howard Baker just returned from Moscow. Criminals run the city. He says that the price of guard dogs has increased by 400 percent." I sat surprised, my mouth wide open.

Let me put this all in perspective: In less than five days, my quick introductory Baker story had traveled from the trading floor and offices of various financial institutions to the highest levels of the Japa-nese government. I suddenly learned Rule Number One in Japan: Sooner or later (and probably sooner) everybody within the elite power structure knows everything. And because everybody knows everything, individual entrepreneurial risk-taking can be significantly more difficult in Japan than elsewhere in the world. Japan is a system where consensus drives decision-making within a culture that slams down on the proverbial nail that raises its head above the surface of the floor. While the outside world often perceives a lack of transparency within the Japanese economic and financial system, the Japanese elite ironically seem to know everything about each other.

Yet to a large extent, entrepreneurial innovation entails a degree of secrecy—plowing ahead with a new idea that, if prematurely exposed to the rest of society, would be lambasted as foolhardy. Innovation also entails risk and potential failure, which are not easily accepted in Japan's tightly controlled system. It is a system that abhors chaos, prizes inventive organizational prowess, but historically has considered failure a sign of cultural and character inferiority.

True, policymakers are hardly complacent. Several years ago, signs of Japanese structural reform excited the world financial community. Experts on Japan from think tanks and other institutions raised the prospect that this could be the beginning of a productivity revolution— fueled in part by a breakout of entrepreneurial growth, a lot of it within large company subsidiaries. But as analyst Richard Katz described the outcome, "The reform lacked critical mass and soon 'reform fatigue' set in."

And that, in the long run, is bad news for the process of globalization. Without greater entrepreneurship and deeper economic reform, it is unlikely the Japanese economy can fully recover. Without a full Japanese recovery, the global financial system will continue to have access to Japanese capital, but at the cost of ever-continuing global imbalances. These imbalances will keep the entire global system a house of cards. After all, how can industrialized world policymakers heavily pressure China to stoke up its domestic consumption and stop relying so much on exports when Japan, a longtime member of the G7 policy community, is largely deploying the same policy mix?

Lest this all sound too negative, let me make clear that unlike the stillborn recoveries of 1995–1996 and 1999–2000, the latest Japanese recovery for a while achieved some modest success. But that was largely because the rest of the world was booming. Large Japanese firms made a killing in their overseas investment activities and exports, a situation that has changed as the global economy crumbles and the yen strengthens as capital is being repatriated back to Japan in the wake of the global credit crisis.

For the broader economy, things softened rapidly. The underconsuming economic system, heavily export-dependent, became highly vulnerable to the bursting of the Asian bubble. Recent data suggest that the Japanese economy is in freefall as even the healthy export sector is being seriously squeezed by the strengthening yen.

To be sure, Japan's Ministry of Finance and central bank authorities are quite aware that their economic policies are out of balance. Monetary policy desperately needs to be adjusted, with interest rates raised. But for several reasons, turning the ship in a new direction has proved next to impossible. Moreover, international trade has been growing at double the pace of global GDP. Therefore, policymakers need to find a way to boost domestic consumption without doing anything that would damage the export sector of large brand-name corporations that have been performing brilliantly.

Many Tokyo strategists, moreover, in the back of their minds also wonder whether the reason the rest of the economy has consistently underperformed relates less to the need for policy changes than to entrenched structural and psychological factors stemming from the rapid aging of Japanese society and a growing sense of risk aversion. Sadly a similar risk aversion has developed in the United States and Europe.

When all is said and done, Japan represents a crucial object lesson for America for another, far more important reason. The Japanese experience of recent decades demonstrates in stark terms the pitfalls of an economy burdened with excessive debt. Japan's national public and private debt load, as noted earlier, resulted from the mountain of Japanese government debt purchased during the 1990s era of cheap money, when interest rates were kept at levels too low in order to compensate for the yen strengthening of the late 1980s. By the 1990s Japan also went into a kind of defensive policy action. Policymakers enacted huge pork barrel spending budgets, with massive public spending for roads and bridges in the largely rural provinces of the Liberal Democratic Party leadership. This spending, however, just barely kept the economy afloat. Meanwhile, it seemed as if every institution loaded up with government debt.

In an earlier chapter, I noted how scaremongers, including investor

Warren Buffett, for years grossly oversold their disaster scenarios regarding the debt-ridden U.S. economy and the dollar. They underestimated the ability of the American system to import capital. Japan is the flip side of that argument. Japan is proof that there are limits to the amount of debt an economy can successfully carry. And American politicians should take heed as the U.S. economy over the next several decades faces an entitlement debt nightmare with the baby boomers piling into retirement and overloading the Social Security and Medicare systems (the latter being the real wild card for policymakers—a debt drain that could break the bank). The current level of spending itself is unsustainable.

Japan's mountains of debt have become the real obstacle to its achieving a rebalanced, healthier, strongly performing economic system. Monetary authorities know that today's absurdly low-interest-rate climate represents a dangerous distortion for the Japanese system. Yet once the global economy recovers, raising rates to reflect the nominal rates of the rest of the industrialized world will be difficult.

The reason, of course, is Japan's dirty little secret—its mountains of hidden debt have placed the economy in a policy straitjacket. Take a close look at virtually every institution in Japan, public or private. They are all chock-full of long-term government debt (called JGBs, the equivalent of the U.S. Treasury's ten-year bond). That's Japan's dilemma. Once recovery begins, if officials raise interest rates too quickly and by too much in order to improve the return to the average saver, Japan would suddenly have on its hands a national bond market crisis (because raising interest rates hurts bond prices).

That's the Japanese predicament. A bond crisis would strip the gears of the entire Japanese economy, forcing every institution to dramatically mark down the value of bond holdings held as collateral on the books as a result of the era of cheap money. The value of Japan, Inc., would plummet like a reverse tidal surge. This would present serious financial problems not only for Japan but also for the world. Interest rates around the world would soar, as would the loss of jobs.

Because Japan has become one of the world's greatest sources of financing, the entire global bond market—and the world economy—would suffer.

If this sounds like an exaggeration, it is not. As incredible as it sounds, the level of Japan's JGB bond holdings today as a percentage of GDP actually exceeds the level of long-term government debt held in 1944. During that year, World War II was still raging and a desperate Japanese government raised military spending to an all-time high. Today, the debt is piled everywhere in virtually every institution.

As odd as it sounds, however, some Tokyo analysts believe that Japan desperately needs to allow its long-term interest rates to rise regardless of the risk to the financial system. Currently, long-term interest rates are held down because the Bank of Japan continually intervenes in the financial market by purchasing long-term government bonds, to keep the yield or interest rate on those bonds low. This practice of supporting the JGB bond market also keeps the yen artificially weak. If the central bank simply curtails these purchases, the theory maintains, two outcomes are possible: (1) Bond yields (long-term interest rates) would go up (producing what economists call a steepening of the yield curve, meaning that long-term rates become much higher than short-term rates). This is a condition that tends historically to produce a dramatic increase in business lending. (2) The increase in bond yields could encourage Japanese savers to buy long-term bonds (moving out of short-term bond investments currently paying next to nothing). The upshot, many experts suggest, would be dramatically increased consumption. The issue, therefore, is not simply whether the Bank of Japan raises interest rates; the issue is whether the central bank is allowed to stop artificially suppressing interest rates. This, then, is Japan's central policy dilemma. It is a debate that is likely to dominate the 2009 general elections. Change is risky, but so is adherence to status quo policies.

The implications of Japan's larger debt problem are significant for the United States. Until now, the American economy has successfully carried its debt because of its ability to attract global capital, because its safe, modernized financial system has largely remained untouched by Capitol Hill tinkerers, and because the big debt torpedoes stemming from the great baby boomer entitlement squeeze have yet to hit. But the torpedoes are coming, swiftly and relentlessly making their way toward America and the other industrialized economies.

Somewhere, at some point, probably sooner than we expect, there will be limits to the level of debt an economy can carry. The debt creates distortions. It limits the effectiveness of central bankers to come to the rescue and can render central banks impotent. And when politicians, with the best of intentions, foolishly gum up the workings of the financial system, the debt can become even more deadly.

For those skeptics who doubt that excessive debt can paralyze an economy's policymaking structure, severely limiting its ability to cope and to adjust, look at what happened to the Japanese. For Americans, Japan is what the United States could easily become if U.S. policymakers are not careful. For Japan, this decade of disappointment didn't just occur in a vacuum; it resulted from serious, now historic blunders in which policymakers greatly overestimated their ability to both understand and influence financial markets. My concern is that policymakers elsewhere in the world today seem to be exhibiting the same lack of understanding and foresight about the current dangers of a global financial system far larger and more complex than it was in the 1990s when Tokyo policymakers made all their mistakes.

6

Nothing Stays the Same:
The 1992 Sterling Crisis

Google the word *change* and the list of quotations throughout history is impressive. Benjamin Disraeli stated: "Change is inevitable. Change is constant." Heraclitus pronounced: "There is nothing permanent except change." Winston Churchill suggested: "To improve is to change; to be perfect is to change often." And Alvin Toffler, the pop culture writer, added: "Change is not merely necessary to life—it is life."

This universal obsession with change raises the question—if change is so essential to the human experience, how come we as a society never see it coming?

If, for example, in early 2007 someone had written a book suggesting that American banks had hidden mortgage risk in a set of dubious, off-balance-sheet vehicles, reviewers would in unison have suggested that a series of typos had occurred. The author obviously meant the *Japanese* banking sector was hiding risk.

If the same book suggested that only an initial $200 billion of subprime mortgages in a world economy of hundreds of *trillions* of dollars would nearly topple global financial markets, the assumption would have been that this book belongs in the fiction department.

Had the book presented the image of Citigroup executives, as a result of this financial turmoil, being forced, tin cup in hand, to roam the world begging for sovereign wealth fund assistance, the manuscript would have been labeled as too derivative of a Tom Clancy novel.

For most of us, the status quo, not change, dominates our thinking. The status quo, we think, is not part of life; it is life. We assume what is will always be.

In the thinking of most people, for instance, the global trading system for goods and services, while perennially in trouble, will always survive. America will forever continue as the dominant economic power in the world. China will serve only as a positive influence for global economic prosperity. Central banks, in this new era of improved global productivity, will forever tame inflation and deflation. Global investors and traders will forever remain optimistic. Our institutions and freedoms will last forever, our financial assets forever secure. We will always remain prosperous mostly because the economic institutions and institutional arrangements in which we have placed our trust will, we believe, never change. The purring sound of the global wealth machine will forever remain a constant.

In this chapter, I'll demonstrate what can happen when policymakers and politicians make that erroneous assumption. As Isaac Asimov (again back to Google) put it, "It is change, continuing change, inevitable change, that is the dominant factor in society." I actually prefer an unknown named John A. Simone's offering in the context of today's economic environment. Simone said: "If you're in a good situation, don't worry, it'll change."

The story I will tell you in this chapter is about a European monetary crisis that occurred in 1992. It is a tale of ego, intransigence, and blindness. The story serves as a reminder that as much as we grab on firmly to the certainty of the status quo, change—often nasty change—is inevitable. This is particularly the case in economic policy when human judgment comes into play and the power of financial markets is grossly underestimated. Policymakers in particular never see the flaws in their actions, or periods of inaction, until the brutal forces of change come charging over the hill right down upon them.

Every serious player active in the financial world knows on an intellectual level that the global economy is an unstable and constantly morphing structure. But in their minds, the system is vulnerable largely in an abstract sense. They see change in the status quo as a distant threat, but not an immediate one. So they act as if the economy and its current institutional arrangements will remain intact for the time being.

As this story shows, such blindness to the realities of a changing world can be very dangerous. In this case, the result was the brutal collapse of the British pound, which explains why the British people still use their own currency, the pound or sterling, and not the euro. The events that unfolded in the autumn of 1992 were totally unforeseen, yet they reshaped the European monetary world and represent a phenomenon that continues to impact global economies.

This seemingly limited episode actually redefined the relationship between the policy world and global financial markets. The incident, in which I found myself in a unique position as a close observer, marked the beginning of the rise in power of the leveraged global financial risk-taker. And, like the situation with our liberalized financial and trading system today, very few thought an abrupt change of such magnitude was even possible. In 1992, few could have imagined that the financial markets, back then much smaller and more under the influence of policymakers, would be able to grab the entire European currency system, turn it inside out, and shake it violently to force unexpected change. But that is precisely what happened. Could a similarly destructive upheaval, or one of even greater magnitude, occur with today's global financial system? I'm not predicting when or where, but you can be sure that a scenario of abrupt change is a real possibility.

To fully understand the story I'm about to tell about the U.K. currency's blowup, let me first say something about the makeup of the broader European economy.

To understand the economics of Europe, past, present, and future, look to Germany. It makes up one-third of the eurozone economy. For a decade after West Germany's October 1990 unification with East Germany, the new, unified economy performed miserably. Once Europe's most powerful economy, Germany became the sick man of Europe as it struggled with the huge costs and other problems associated with unification. Yet in recent years, until the financial crisis, the German economy had achieved an impressive turnaround. A lot of the success stemmed from the economy's ability to export. In fact, the export "engine" became Germany's one reliable economic performer.

This economic recovery could have been far more robust save for the fact that Germany is not a great place to start or rejuvenate a business. For instance, if an employer is modernizing and restructuring a globally *noncompetitive* German company, and finds that two employees have the same job, it will take that employer five years of paid wages to remove the redundant worker.

That's why in Germany the unemployment rate is nearly twice as high as in the United States. In other parts of Western Europe, the jobless situation is worse. Most new jobs come from small business start-ups, which are not popping up fast enough in the large, established European economies. This is largely because of their highly counter-productive labor laws and overregulated economies. Why would anyone want to start a new company in this environment when other venues, even right next door in Eastern Europe, offer far more flexibility?

It is not that German political leaders are unaware of the situation. They understand that Europe stands to benefit enormously by competing in the new world economy. They understand the importance of a flexible, more efficient, entrepreneurial economy with more flexible labor laws. They simply cannot muster enough of a political consensus to change the system. The best they can come up with is modest tinkering involving, in some cases, temporary suspension of some of the more restrictive labor laws. Coming into office, German chancellor Angela Merkel suggested in her speeches some impressive economic reforms, but almost all have fallen by the wayside.

Europe's uninviting labor climate was vividly illustrated for me on a business trip that I took to Rome in early 1990. I was staying at the Hotel Hassler near the famous Spanish Steps. The Hassler is popular among Westerners because its rooftop restaurant offers a spectacular view of the city. Suffering from a bit of fatigue, all I wanted on that first morning was coffee and a hot breakfast. After three days of continental breakfasts consisting of small rolls and pastries in Frankfurt, I was ready for a real American breakfast of bacon and eggs. I headed for the Hassler's rooftop café.

When I arrived, the restaurant host escorted me to a table inside, away from the view. I politely objected and suggested a table outside, as the weather that day was perfect. "Not possible!" the host said rather sternly.

As I sat down and looked over the menu, I quickly spotted what I came for. Coffee came immediately—thick, dark, and powerful. I waved over the waiter, but noticed his uniform only half-buttoned, as if he had rushed in late for work. "I'll have the bacon and eggs," I said, adding, "and by the way, would you mind if I moved outside for the view? Most of the tables out there are empty."

The waiter stiffened and then stood erect like the comical Italian general in the movie *Casablanca*, chest out as if he were about to salute. "Sir," he began, "you may *not* sit outside and you may certainly not order fried eggs and bacon. A hard-boiled egg and maybe some sliced breakfast meats are possible, but bacon and eggs are out of the question."

I could feel a sense of annoyance building. Then I saw something more than troubling. Less than twenty feet away sat a couple sipping coffee with clear evidence that they had just had what I had ordered. Annoyed even more, I called over both the waiter and the host. "What gives?" I protested, trying not to be too much the ugly American. "No eggs, no bacon, no outside views? And that couple over there . . . "

The host abruptly intervened in a way that told me, in a humorous way, a lot about the eccentric nature at the time of the traditional European labor scene and labor laws. He began: "Oh, yes, we served *them* eggs and bacon. But that was forty minutes ago. Since then we are on strike. That means no fried eggs, only hard-boiled ones. No outside views, only inside." I responded, "Well, what about some hot oatmeal?" The host, looking puzzled, shot back: "Ummm. I don't know. I will have to make a call." I never saw him again.

Certainly Europe's labor markets today have become somewhat more flexible, and Europeans during most of the 2000s began to experience slightly higher levels of growth. But the story illustrates the power that European labor has historically enjoyed and its ability to disrupt business operations at any moment. Although this story represents an exaggerated situation, inflexible labor laws and other constraints on business have been a serious drag on economic expansion.

In recent years, however, Germany until the financial crisis has, by far, been the biggest surprise in economic growth. Despite the political stalemate of the Merkel government's economic reform plans, the German economy started to race ahead of the European pack. And how did this relative turnaround come about? As hard as it is for the official community to admit, the global hedge funds, private equity firms, and global investment banks discussed in chapter 3 quietly nudged the private-sector restructuring process forward.

Axel Weber, the distinguished German academic and now president of the Bundesbank, has described with blunt honesty how in the past few years before the global financial crisis the German economy began to be restructured. He admits that initially neither the government nor the central bank was fully aware of what was happening.

What happened is that the mergers and acquisitions of large and medium-sized German firms exploded in number. Today more than 50 percent of the shares of German stocks are owned by foreigners. Global investment banks and other outside financial institutions, unbeknownst to the government, then began demanding restructuring and reform of German companies. As a result, internal corporate restructuring of many bloated German firms developed far more quickly than anticipated. International shareholders demanded higher productivity, and the German export engine became even more of a global powerhouse. In the process, even the German financial system began to be transformed from a largely bank-based system to more of a capital market system. This produced an improved rate of return and an abrupt rise in investment spending.

Germany, the sick man of Europe in the 1990s, rebounded. German companies were allowed to hire from a second tier of available "rental" (nonunionized) workers not covered by the onerous labor regulations. Real unit labor costs decreased while productivity modestly increased. In the process, Germany strengthened its position of international competitiveness. The economy was helped by the fact that two important German export sectors were in white-hot global demand, particularly in Asia—luxury automobiles and precision instruments and machines. Of course, the global slowdown has seriously affected German exports since then.

Germany's recent success has put the rest of Europe in a disadvantageous position. As Germany continued to become more globally competitive, the rest of Europe risked falling behind. Germany, for example, is Italy's largest trading partner. Yet year after year Italy dangerously falls behind the competitive curve. Such competitive differences are the crux of the story I am about to tell about the fall of the British currency and brutal shake-up of the European exchange rate system.

The continued strengthening of the euro has added to the problem that, in essence, can be summarized as follows—not all European economies are created equal. The situation has also spawned a debate within the economics community over whether Germany's wage restraint and other productivity-enhancing measures are killing the European economy or saving it from being cast aside as globally irrelevant.

Over the last decade, the Europeans have done a masterful job of building the credibility of the new European Central Bank. Monetary union and the integration of the new currency, the euro, have been impressive. Some, but hardly all, foreign exchange experts argue that the euro within a decade could challenge the dollar as the world's lead, or reserve, currency. But European officials will continue to face one undeniable headache: Because of the differences in competitiveness among various economies, serious economic tensions will remain. For example, some European economies (such as Germany's) can tolerate a strong euro; others (Italy's, for example) are finding the strong currency a huge impediment, equivalent to an almost global economic death sentence. Because the German economy continues to improve competitively relative to Italy's, global financial market investment continues to fixate more on enhancing Germany's economic future than the future of the Italian economy.

After all, Germany successfully competes globally head-to-head with Japan in luxury automobiles, precision equipment, and other highly sophisticated industrial products. Throughout Asia, Mercedes and BMW luxury automobiles are ubiquitous. The same holds true for German precision machine tools and equipment. By contrast, many other European countries such as Italy export relatively simple, easy-to-duplicate consumer items. These items are forced to compete in the global market with exports from the rest of Asia. The big-name brand luxury European consumer goods such as Gucci and Ferragamo are of course in high global demand, but competing against the Asian countries in nonexclusive consumer goods markets is extraordinarily difficult, particularly with the ever-increasing strength of the European currency.

The notion of Germany, this powerful entity, dominating the European economic and financial landscape is hardly new. For decades going back to the 1970s, the Germans, backed by the enormous credibility of their central bank, the Bundesbank, have held sway over European interest rates, often to the dismay of the rest of Europe. In fact, some analysts argue that the rise of monetary union and the euro in the late 1990s was a direct attempt by non-German Europe to try to strip Germany of some of its policy influence.

This powerful role of Germany was on the minds of British policymakers back in 1992, just prior to the great currency turmoil of that period. What transpired in the fall of that year was a remarkable incident that shocked the world. Germany was at the center of the drama. A decade after the beginning of liberalized financial markets, the episode marked the beginning of the decline in power of the world's central banks. Government's ability to manage the global financial markets would soon come into question. The dangerous ocean of capital—including the leveraged hedge funds and other risk-takers I discussed earlier in this book—was about to confront face-to-face the tiny, largely unaware European central banking community.

The actors in this 1992 drama included a stubborn German central banker, a collection of hapless Italian finance officials, and a group of British officials who failed to accurately read a situation crucial to their currency's survival. The story line is complex, but it is important to understand because it illuminates the fact that abrupt change brought about by mighty financial forces often comes when we least expect it. The world isn't nearly as certain as we think it is.

But first, let me offer some background about how the currency market functions in general. By the mid-1980s, the world's currency system was called a floating system. An ocean of market traders, betting on each currency, made the world's currencies fluctuate in wide swings. The U.S. dollar was by far the most influential currency. To counter that influence, the Europeans, believing there is strength in numbers, linked their smaller individual currencies in an agreement called the Exchange Rate Mechanism, or ERM. The European thinking made sense on several fronts. Integrating the European currencies (and eventually the economies) would both enhance monetary stability and reduce the likelihood of the kind of economic tensions that contributed to two major European wars in the twentieth century.

For newcomers to the subject, the idea of a global currency system is difficult to comprehend. Here's a useful metaphor. Think of the world financial system as a giant swimming pool. In the pool, under water, are the global currencies in the form of expandable or retractable porous rubber balls. By far the largest ball in the pool is the U.S. dollar. The dollar ball expands and contracts based on the perception within the global capital markets swimming pool of the effectiveness of American economic policies, the level of U.S. interest rates, and overall economic efficiency. In most cases, but not all, if a country's interest rates are lowered, the rubber ball contracts; if interest rates are raised, the ball expands. If the currency rises after an interest rate hike (the ball expands), that is generally because the market believes there is less of a threat of inflation. When the currency falls after an interest rate cut (the ball contracts), that is usually because the markets believe inflation has become a greater risk.

In the 1970s, the European currencies were relatively small balls in the pool, particularly compared to the large dollar ball. Having by far the largest ball gave U.S. policy a subtle but important influence within the international economic system. The Europeans found that influence annoying. To gain advantage, the Europeans connected their various smaller currency balls together—again, calling the system the ERM. It was understood that each individual European ball would continue to expand and contract, but only by certain agreed-to amounts (called currency bands).

If the capital markets expanded a ball by too much or too little (relative to the agreed-upon valuation limits of the currency bands), policymakers had several options to keep the entire European currency arrangement from breaking up. They could "intervene" in the markets by buying or selling the currency, which had the effect of injecting or retracting water to affect the ball's size. They could also raise or lower the interest rate of the country with the currency in question, thereby affecting the size of the currency ball by increasing or reducing demand for it. Or, as a final measure if all else failed, policymakers could call for a "realignment" of the currency bands. In most cases, this would mean that the country realigning would accept that its ball, relative to the other European currency balls, would be permanently reduced in size. That country's goods and services might then become more competitive in trade with those of other European countries, but at the risk of higher inflation because the weaker currency raises the price of imports.

The European currency system, or ERM, was set up to allow for flexibility. These government-initiated realignments were intended as a relief valve from market pressure. They would allow an economy a bit of a breather in the face of stiff international competition. Today's new, completely unified European system lacks such a relief valve.

In theory, after a realignment, the now weaker currency again would allow the traded goods and services of the devaluing economy to compete more effectively with those of the other members of the European system. That's where the Italians come into play. Because of their relatively inefficient economy, the Italian policy community regularly attempted to boost its trade competitiveness by negotiating realignments with its trading partners. Italian realignments were commonplace and were seen as a bit of a joke in the international system. They were a regular sign of economic failure.

By contrast, the German currency, the deutsche mark, or DM, traditionally sat at the top (strong) end of the ERM band. The DM was the largest European ball in the swimming pool in part because of Germany's strong economy but mostly because Germany's central bank, the Bundesbank, was the most trusted by the markets as a credible, independent, anti-inflationary force. By contrast, the lowly Italian lira, backed by a government and central bank short on credibility, always rested at or near the bottom. Its currency ball was tiny by comparison.

By 1992, the fact that Germany's currency ball dominated the collection of currencies tied together under the ERM had created considerable envy across Europe. Non-German European politicians resented in particular the power and influence of Germany's central bank. Many Europeans believed the Bundesbank had placed a de facto stranglehold over European interest rate policy (keeping rates too high to fight inflation). The other Europeans couldn't cut their interest rates without risking that their currency ball would shrink even further relative to the German currency. Such a development would risk the financial markets, forcing the country cutting interest rates (unless Germany also cut rates) into a humiliating realignment. These tensions, lurking under the surface, remained unresolved.

I was keenly aware of this situation as I prepared for a business trip back in 1992 to discuss the macroeconomic situation with officials and economists throughout the various European capitals. When my business partner, Manley Johnson, and I walked into the Bundesbank in Frankfurt on September 11, my wife was less than a month from delivering our third child. I was nervous being so far from Washington. I discovered the Germans were nervous too, though for vastly different reasons.

The United Kingdom, Italy, Spain, and Portugal were all facing huge competitive pressures within the European currency system, leaving the potential for realignment. The Italian lira, however, was in trouble the most. Complicating this situation was that the so-called Maastricht Treaty to unify Europe under a single currency was to be voted on in France on September 20, less than two weeks later. Support for the Maastricht unification plan was completely uncertain; Denmark had already voted against it. It was thought that if France also voted it down, the already fragile ERM currency arrangement could unravel as well. That unraveling could kill any chance for a broader European monetary union under a single currency and, in the short run, create considerable financial uncertainty. I had come to Europe expecting a series of polite chats about the macroeconomic outlook. Instead, I found myself in the midst of an economic and financial tornado of historic proportions.

The Germans had raised interest rates only two months before as an insurance policy against future inflation. Now because of this financial market pressure against the lira, sterling, and other currencies, they were suddenly being urged, particularly by the British, to reverse course and cut rates. The British wanted Germany to cut its short-term interest rate to help relieve currency pressures within the ERM. If the rate was cut, the deutsche mark would be expected to weaken—its ball contracting—against the other European currencies, and the ERM currency relationships might return to normal.

It turned out that a number of big players in the financial market had already turned a skeptical eye toward the British currency. Investor George Soros, following the strategic advice of his chief trader, Stan

Druckenmiller, had quietly taken a market position a month earlier (by selling short 1.5 billion pounds' worth of the British currency). In essence, they were betting that the London officials were in over their heads. British monetary policy could not match the credibility of German monetary policy. Plus, the British pound within the ERM was priced at too high a level relative to the German currency. Soros and Druckenmiller were betting that the British would eventually be forced by skeptical financial markets to realign—that is, reduce the size of their currency ball. But it was only a relatively isolated bet.

Still, even at that early point there was broader talk in international circles that aggressive traders were watching European policymakers closely, poised to seize on the smallest of missteps and to take positions in the market to capitalize on those missteps. Moreover, these traders could use vast amounts of market leverage (borrowing for investment) to magnify the potency of their actions.

The Bundesbank was led by President Helmut Schlesinger, a humorless monetary policy technician who had worked in the trenches for years as the central bank's deputy. Schlesinger was straightforward, almost without personality, and religiously devoted to the Bundesbank's long-standing conservative principles in an environment in which many others acted politically. He also saw things mostly in black or white.

Schlesinger particularly detested the British for using their ERM membership tactically to try to wield control over European monetary and exchange rate developments. He thought the British were simply trying to manipulate the currency system against Germany with little commitment to broader European monetary integration. Several years earlier, without negotiating with the rest of Europe over the entry price level, the United Kingdom simply announced that it would join the ERM. After originally opting to stay out, the British decided to join at a self-chosen exchange rate of 2.95 deutsche marks to the pound sterling. The Germans in particular had always questioned the terms of British entry, believing the entry point unrealistically high for the

British currency. In other words, they perceived the British ball at the entry point as too large. This judgment was based on the fact that the U.K.'s economic fundamentals were weak. U.K. inflation was three times higher than Germany's at the time, with interest rates at an astounding 15 percent. That meant, in the German view, that the British currency would forever remain suspect in the eyes of financial market traders.

By joining the new ERM currency club, Britain's exchange rate would be forced to fluctuate (the ball would expand or contract) within a narrow range of only 6 percent. If the currency fluctuated by more than this amount, the U.K. central bank, the Bank of England, would be forced either to realign or to use its pile of reserves to intervene in the market. That would mean buying the British currency or selling the deutsche mark as a means of stabilizing the size of the British currency's ball in relation to the deutsche mark. Most policymakers at the time thought it unlikely Britain would ever call for a realignment, much less be forced out of the entire system. One final weapon would have the British raise short-term interest rates to try to impress the financial markets that it too, like the Bundesbank, could exhibit inflation-fighting credibility. The hope was that by raising rates, the sinking British currency would stabilize.

The Germans thought the British had picked the wrong entry rate and resented not being consulted on the matter. Now the U.K. was desperate for help. The British conservative government, particularly skeptical of the European Union, had thought the 2.95 deutsche mark entry point would lessen the German currency's influence within the ERM. This proved to be a significant miscalculation, again leaving the British currency dangerously overvalued in the view of many global currency market traders.

By the second week of September, the British situation had left President Schlesinger in a perpetually foul mood. The bitterness toward the British was palpable. Our Frankfurt meeting in the midst of this drama, though, was not with Schlesinger but with Otmar Issing, the Bundesbank's enormously influential board member, chief econo-mist, head of research, and Schlesinger's closest confidant.

You may wonder why senior officials met with outside market ana-lysts and journalists. The answer is that the central bankers found it dangerous to limit their discussions to in-house staff and found it use-ful to gauge international market and political sentiment. In the case of the Germans, they also felt a particular need to present their case to the markets and the American press, often correcting the negatively slanted perception of German policy offered by what they referred to constantly as "the London crowd"—a euphemism for the British financial press.

As we entered Issing's office, the normally vibrant, athletic policy-maker looked ashen, his hair rumpled, his back stooped as if he had been up all night. The meeting, originally scheduled for an hour, had at the last minute been reduced to twenty minutes. As we were about to sit down, Issing nervously asked to rearrange seats so that he could sit next to the telephone. "I'm waiting for an urgent call and I may have to leave at a moment's notice," he said.

For weeks, I had been predicting that the Italians would realign their currency, repricing it at a weaker level than the other European currencies. I was also fairly convinced that a Schlesinger-led Bundesbank was not about to comply with British demands to reduce interest rates absent an Italian realignment. Reducing rates without such a realignment would be tantamount to rewarding the Italians for bad economic policy behavior. It seemed possible, but not probable, that the British would join the so-called weak sister of Europe—Italy—in a realignment to devalue the British currency. The British could also opt out of the system altogether, but that at the time seemed absurd.

Most market players believed the United Kingdom had one defen-sive interest rate hike bullet left in its gun. As a weapon to scare off the traders betting against sterling, interest rate hikes theoretically, if timed properly, have the potential to increase the strength of a coun-try's currency. Further interest rate hikes, however, would risk pushing the British economy into a recession. If the financial market perception developed that the economy was about to weaken, the traders across the board would dump sterling, sending it into a free fall.

Several weeks before the beginning of this drama, Britain's chancellor of the exchequer, Norman Lamont, and French finance minister Michel Sapin had issued strange statements. Both implied that the European Community had decided no European realignments were necessary. This was a ridiculous smoke screen that made me all the more suspicious. Something was happening, I thought.

The head of one of the Benelux central banks had been in Washington around that time, telling everyone who would listen that "Italy realigning is almost a foregone conclusion." Italian prime minister Giuliano Amato, for years a major figure in Washington at the Brookings Institution, offered a group of economists visiting Rome his personal scenario: If the Maastricht Treaty is accepted by the French on September 20, Italy will realign or devalue by "5 to 7 percent." If Maastricht fails, the market traders will take control and a 10 percent or greater realignment would be inevitable. My question was whether Italy would make it until the French vote and what effect an Italian realignment would have as a tipping point of instability for the larger European currency system.

As I sat in Issing's office, his acute nervousness, however, was more than I expected. Why should there be such angst over an Italian devaluation? Such devaluations were routine. Plus the Italians, somewhat of a sideshow economically, were never part of the core membership of the European currency club. Something bigger was at stake, but it was not yet clear the British would become the central story.

That morning, September 11, Frankfurt was full of stories in the press about how British prime minister John Major and Chancellor Lamont had been ham-handed in making their case for a German rate reduction at the previous weekend's meeting of European finance ministers and central bankers in Bath. Non-German officials present noted that the unbridled, anti-Bundesbank onslaught at the meeting was so severe that Germany's Schlesinger almost walked out of the meeting. Lamont had demanded an on-the-spot 25-basis-point German interest rate cut, which is highly uncharacteristic of the protocol in the central banking world. The demand was repeated three more times. German finance minister Theo Waigel encouraged Schlesinger to stay, but it wasn't long before Schlesinger got an earful from, of all people, the Italians. They demanded that the Germans promise to endorse and defend the current ERM alignments, including the lira. This was an impossibly expensive proposition that would have required the Germans to buy billions of dollars in lira.

Not surprisingly, the meeting caused the German central bank, which enjoyed a long and deep history of resisting outside influence, to dig in its heels against an interest rate cut. And German resentment toward Britain thickened; the effort to manipulate the Bundesbank policy environment had backfired.

Complicating the situation further was the fact that the Bundesbank president made what he thought was a rather nonprovocative statement several days later at the monthly meeting of industrialized world central bankers in Basel, Switzerland. However, Schlesinger's words were distorted in a series of British press leaks to imply that a Bundesbank ease was "soon to arrive."

By the time I arrived in Frankfurt, the U.K.-German relationship had collapsed. Recognizing this turmoil, or what some have called a comedy of egos, the global market traders quickly began to focus collectively on the vulnerable British situation, preparing to sell short the U.K. currency.

To add fuel to the fire, an unnamed British official, speaking to the *Financial Times*, suggested that U.K. officials, should they choose, could expand Germany's money supply on their own by unilaterally encouraging massive European-wide intervention. This seemingly benign technical point was really a threat. Bundesbank official Gerd Häusler responded with the monetary policy equivalent of declaring nuclear war: "This is not a time for a declaration of war," he said, "but certainly the Bundesbank will sterilize [make largely ineffective] it all. If the United Kingdom wants to play the intervention game, we can cut the number of repos [daily injections of liquidity] down to zero. If that doesn't work, the Bundesbank could even cut discount quotas [limits on how much central banks can lend banks through the discount window] if it has to!"This verbal exchange was considered highly unusual in the world of central banking.

Suddenly, every market trader in the world took notice. After hearing of the *Financial Times* inquiry and the German response, hedge fund trader Druckenmiller walked into his boss George Soros's office and declared: "Those guys [the British and Germans] are at war. I just took an additional five billion dollar position shorting sterling." Responded Soros, "That's ridiculous! If you really believe that exchange took place, up that to ten billion."

The German view of these matters rested largely on economics, not personalities. If you bind currencies together via an exchange rate mechanism like the ERM, eventually economic policy convergence by the member economics is essential. The big question in European circles was convergence toward what? For the Germans, there was no question that convergence had to target the best economic performer, Germany. Yet Italy, France, and Britain wanted to target the *average* performance of the countries participating in the ERM. Beneath the surface, the rest of Europe dreaded being tied permanently to the tough-minded policies of the Bundesbank.

As I sat there chatting with the Bundesbank's Issing, I suddenly heard the loud but muffled noise of a helicopter. Suddenly, the sound of the blades grew louder. Then louder still. I was talking about the Italians, asking whether they, in their recent intervention, were throwing good money after bad to support the lira. Had the Italians made the budgetary adjustments and realigned earlier, Issing noted, the lira would likely be appreciating instead of plummeting. I countered that the Italian intervention (using deutsche marks to buy lira to support the Italian currency) seemed to be getting awfully expensive and that the markets assumed the Italians would soon run out of money. Italy's central bank reserves, which had been more than $75 billion not that long before, were about $20 billion according to my estimates—and dropping fast. In my view, the Italians would not make it to September 20, which could potentially throw into disarray the European unification efforts and place enormous strains on the broader European currency system.

It was at that point that the chopper's noise completely drowned out our conversation. Almost immediately, Issing took a quick phone call. Twitching nervously, he stood up and politely apologized but stressed that the meeting had to end. As we stood and gazed out the window, we saw what appeared to be the tall, bulky frame of none other than the German chancellor himself, Helmut Kohl, leaving the helicopter and entering the Bundesbank building in a rare appearance.

While the Italians and British may not have fully appreciated the dangers ahead, the Germans were well aware this was serious business. Potentially, both the ERM arrangement and the future unification of Europe itself were at stake if the currency system were to blow up. With surprising perception, the Kohl government knew that in this new age of globalization, the global markets were to be treated with a decided wariness. The new dangerous ocean of capital would move quickly and with brutal force in the event of a policy blunder.

The irony of this European squabble and anguish is that it arrived precisely at the time that the Bundesbank itself was subtly being urged by domestic political and economic forces to shift away from a tightening mode. Every professional Bundesbank watcher could see this subtle pressure emerging. This raised the question: If others saw this subtle shift at work in Frankfurt, why didn't the British government? Why, moreover, were the British so emotionally fixated on the Prussian personality of Helmut Schlesinger? Why did Chancellor of the Exchequer Norman Lamont allow the dangerous perception to develop that Britain was somehow manipulating the policy of another country's central bank? Clearly, long-standing resentment toward Germany was embedded in the British mind-set. My sense was that the Germans were aware of this resentment and were not comfortable with the discord as Europe was contemplating broader unification.

At one point later in this drama, a beleaguered President Schlesinger all but promised an ease in the event of an Italian devaluation. Yet the leader of Germany's Free Democratic Party, Count Otto Lambsdorff, himself a financially sophisticated leader in German economic policy-making, privately chided the Bundesbank for appearing to kowtow to the demands of a foreign ministry of finance. Lambsdorff labeled such behavior a "dangerous precedent." So little about the German-U.K. relationship remained neat and tidy.

After this remarkable visit in Frankfurt, we traveled to Paris for a day or so of meetings with various French market traders and with Jean-Claude Trichet, then head of the French Treasury. Trichet would later become president of the European Central Bank. We hoped that he could sort out for us this German-British mess.

Like the Germans, Trichet often met with private analysts and journalists to make a case for the special merits of the current policy and the economy. During the later run-up to European unification and the single currency, for example, Trichet, through his behind-the-scenes briefings with analysts, managed to convince a skeptical global market that unification would become a credible reality.

Incidentally, I met Trichet for the first time in Washington, D.C., during my first international economics conference. He arrived literally holding the bags of France's G7 deputy and Mitterrand's chief of staff, Jacques Attali. Watching Trichet stand alone, as the powerful Attali worked the room, I asked him if he'd like to join a small group I was forming for dinner that evening. He accepted. All of which proves the old adage that it is important to always be nice to the guy carrying the bags. He may someday be Master of the Universe. Just as we were about to leave Frankfurt, however, our meeting with Trichet the next day in Paris was canceled.

By the time we arrived in Paris that Saturday morning, the Bank of Italy, by my calculation, had all but run out of deutsche mark reserves. The Italian monetary army was weaponless. As a result, the Italians would be forced to open swap lines with the Bundesbank to borrow deutsche marks, which they would sell into the market to defend the lira. This would be an increasingly expensive proposition that later would require paying back those borrowed amounts from an Italian treasury already in deficit.

Manley Johnson and I had decided to meet for a drink at the bar at the Ritz, a small, velvet-encased chamber set to one side of the lobby with small tables and even smaller chairs, to wait for a meeting with the head of a large French bank. As we sat down, I immediately noticed the German tennis star Boris Becker sitting just two tables away, engaged in a ferocious argument with his agent. We moved across the bar to another table, but Becker's loud German yelling at his business companion intensified. At this point, apart from whether we should confront the boorish athlete ("You go first," I said to Johnson, pointing to the scrappy but muscular Becker), I struggled with two questions.

First, if an Italian realignment devaluing the lira occurred this weekend (such events often occurred over weekends), would it be so small that the markets would expect some follow-up move after September 20? I knew the Italians would be tempted to do a mini-realignment, believing the French in the end would vote in favor of the Maastricht Treaty. But if they were wrong, the markets would likely force a second realignment, devaluing the lira by a significant magnitude. This would add to the pressure on the broader European currency system.

Second, I wondered if the market was at a turning point. Would the Germans, despite the perceived British attempts at manipulation, trim rates enough to stabilize things, pulling the weakening lira and sterling back from the edge? Don't underestimate ego and national prestige, I kept reminding myself, but I was also aware that significant domestic pressure was building for the German central bank to reduce short-term interest rates. I suspect this was because, with inflationary expectations under firm control, the central bank was being told by German exporters that the DM, or deutsche mark, was itself strengthening unnecessarily from its already strong position.

By the same token, Frankfurt officials were well aware that if they mishandled the easing, particularly if they appeared to be surrendering to outside foreign pressure, the same "London crowd" lambasting Germany's tight policy would turn on a dime. They would argue that the almighty Bundesbank had compromised its independence—its so-called policy manhood. The central bank could lose a chunk of its hard-fought credibility.

The French banker arrived and immediately made clear that Paris was abuzz about the likelihood of an Italian currency realignment that weekend. Later, it turned out Trichet, Bundesbank vice president Hans Tietmeyer, and German G7 deputy Horst Köhler (now president of the German Republic) were secretly in Rome that very moment working out the details with the Italians. Upon hearing of the realignment talk, I knew immediately that the eyes of the world would quickly turn toward Frankfurt. And indeed, that Monday morning, September 14, at 9:00 A.M., the Bundesbank held an extraordinary emergency meeting to cut short-term interest rates in response to the Italian realignment. The thinking was that the German rate cut would stabilize the entire European currency system.

But the question remained: Would this emergency German policy change be enough to appease the markets to save the pound sterling? It suddenly seemed doubtful. By creating all this drama with leaks to the press, the British economic high command had exposed itself to a momentum-driven, highly leveraged, globalized ocean of skeptical currency traders, all of whom wondered what the British were working so feverishly to hide. All of the drama had placed a giant global spotlight on the British currency. Now a universal chorus of financial market skepticism asked whether the pound was seriously overvalued within the ERM. Even traders not normally involved with the currency markets joined in. The specific danger was that an army of traders would borrow lira and pounds and sell them for deutsche marks. Traders knew that if those first two currencies weakened dramatically, particularly after a realignment, the traders could repay the loans in devalued currency, taking the difference as huge profits. There was potentially big money involved, but also big risk. The trick for the central banks was to convince the markets of the risks of such an approach.

In the midst of this flurry of activity, we traveled to London on the evening of Tuesday, September 15. We were fortunate to have had a meeting scheduled with Terence Burns (who later became Lord Burns), an important G7 adviser to Prime Minister Major. We had made a request a month earlier to see him. The meeting was changed to dinner at the Inn on the Park (now the Four Seasons) in Hyde Park, a quick taxi ride from Buckingham Palace. Over a plate of lamb chops, the amiable Burns made clear his government was convinced the crisis was over. The German rate cut, they thought, had calmed the European currency markets. The consensus was that the remaining mess with sterling was nothing the Bank of England could not easily "mop up" over the next several days. In the great monetary stare-down, the Germans had blinked, he suggested.

Interestingly, Burns said that Prime Minister Major was now actually planning to use his "superb" handling of this crisis, and no doubt the taming of the Bundesbank beast, as a central focus in his reelection effort. He said that Major believed his successful crisis management style would quickly set him up as the major power of Europe, particularly with the British soon taking over the European Union presidency (which rotates every six months).

After Burns left, we sat at the table in stunned disbelief at his lack of awareness of the growing financial tidal wave surging in his direction. That same morning, September 15, the Bundesbank's Schlesinger had given an interview to the German newspaper *Handelsblatt* that was immediately translated into its sister paper, the European *Wall Street Journal*. The interview, which we read that same evening in London moments before our dinner, caused an uproar because the German central bank head, in somewhat ambiguous language, appeared to offer support for sterling. Immediately, however, the governor of the Bank of England called Frankfurt for a clarification. Schlesinger refused to come to the phone on the grounds that the interview had "not yet been authorized." Schlesinger's sudden unwillingness to speak out became public, and the situation ignited a speculative onslaught against sterling the following morning. Suddenly, armies of global financial traders joined in the hunt.

For that morning, we had a previously scheduled meeting with Eddie George, the deputy governor of the Bank of England. To our pleasant surprise, the meeting was not canceled, despite the emergency situation. We assumed the Bank of England would be a little more grounded in reality about the market dangers facing British policymakers than Burns had been the night before.

The Bank of England, located on Threadneedle Street in London's financial district, has the feel of some exquisite nineteenth-century exclusive club. Entering the impressive building, one gets the feeling of drifting back through history into a world of elite privilege. As we entered the deputy's office, I noticed that he too was in remarkably good cheer. George was dressed like a London investment banker, with a stylish checkered shirt and striped tie combination. I had just been on the phone with our office in Washington. One of our people who watched the market screens closely noted that a huge global army of traders had amassed on the U.K. currency border. The Italian devaluation and German interest rate cuts had not worked, I immediately thought. The *Handelsblatt* interview, and retraction, had ignited a raging brush fire the British couldn't control.

Like Burns the evening before, the British central banker George spoke confidently about the government's ability to avert a further currency crisis situation. It was not that he smugly suggested the Germans had blinked by cutting rates, as some financial columnists were already writing; it was just his air of striking confidence when he said, "We have it all under control."

Then he offered the following (which I'll paraphrase): If need be, and we have just made this clear this morning to the financial press, we are prepared (he paused and took a breath) to raise short-term interest rates by up to 100 basis points. But we frankly don't think that will be necessary (the expectation being that even threatening to do so by such a huge magnitude would help strengthen sterling and fend off the traders).

At this point, it was tough to know how to react. Could the British official community be so out of touch, so oblivious to the rapid globalization of financial markets and the unique, power-enhancing changes within the markets themselves not to be deeply concerned about losing control of the situation? Then again, maybe Eddie George was right. Traders in massively large positions who have borrowed a lot of money and who find themselves on the wrong side of a central bank policy move can see their entire careers snuffed out. To a certain extent, the power of a central bank rests in its occasional ability to "burn" an overly ambitious trader. It does not need to happen often because the message throughout the trading community is so powerfully clear.

I decided nevertheless to go for broke and asked: "Aren't you worried that you may have slipped too far behind the curve on this thing? That you may have waited too long to raise interest rates and now the move will be counterproductive?" George shot back a look of mild annoyance and was about to respond when the telephone rang. He answered it and stared down at his desk as he listened intently for about a minute. When the call finished, he slowly raised his head. His skin began to match the gray hues of his suit. "I'm going to have to end this meeting," he politely said in a soft tone. "I've learned we've just raised interest rates by two hundred basis points"—an abrupt, unheard-of policy move—at which point he stood up, politely shook my hand, and literally ran out of the room. Britain's own house of cards had come tumbling down.

In the world of trading, there is always the danger that a policy action will be interpreted not as a sign of powerful intent, but as a desperate sign of weakness and futility. The policy action then becomes a magnet, drawing in the entire global trading community like bees to honey, to mix metaphors. This is similar to what happened during the 1997–1998 Asian financial crisis. Asian central bankers, with the help of the IMF, attempted to support the Asian currencies and found their efforts completely counterproductive. The pound sterling was experiencing exactly that phenomenon in September 1992. British policymakers were attempting to prove their foreign exchange manhood with extraordinarily aggressive interest rate hikes. The market was not buying any of it.

Later that afternoon, the British tried again, threatening to raise interest rates by another 300 basis points the next day, to no avail. Later, a German official mentioned that the amount of money used by the central bankers to support sterling and the lira during this drama exceeded the amounts used to intervene during the last stages of the Bretton Woods system before it collapsed in 1971. Yet none of these exercises worked. By that evening, Norman Lamont had no choice, the market reaction being so brutal, but to humbly announce that Britain was actually leaving the ERM.

The Bank of England found itself overrun by the markets. According to press reports, George Soros alone took profits of over $1 billion. Other traders won big as well. Early in the crisis, Lamont had announced that Britain would borrow $15 billion to defend sterling, not realizing that two traders, Soros and Druckenmiller, had placed a trade approaching that amount, betting that the currency would collapse. Many other traders had also jumped into the fray. Here was an information mismatch in which policymakers appeared to have no clue of the immense size and speed of the ocean of capital moving throughout the world.

After the fact, the U.K. Treasury attempted to lowball the loss to the markets for political reasons, setting the cost of Black Wednesday at $5.8 billion. Officials conveniently left out the huge loss to taxpayers had the government, instead of using its $24 billion in reserves to intervene, invested those funds to earn a profit from the devaluing currency. But these efforts to obfuscate are understandable because the entire episode was unfair, and economically hurtful, to the British people. Market forces that would later restructure the German economy brought devastation to the lives of a great number of people in the United Kingdom.

By ignoring these powerful new financial forces, British policymakers created the conditions for a huge transfer of wealth from British taxpayers to the independent traders and money managers at the major financial institutions—and that did not need to happen. Within days, London political pundits began poking fun at conservative Prime Minister Major, asking aloud what the billions of pounds could have purchased for the British people had the government not frittered the funding away with the recent intervention exercises. The government responded with a twofold scapegoating campaign—blaming both the markets and "the Huns." There should instead have been a national discussion about Britain's future role in the European economy and currency system, including how to come to terms successfully with this raging ocean of liquidity. Are today's global policymakers taking note of the need for a similar discussion?

Ironically, for Britain itself, opting out of the ERM, though humbling, may have been the best thing ever to happen. The economy was restructured and, having escaped the ERM foreign exchange straitjacket, within several years began to prosper. Between 1996 and 2005, for example, the German economy grew by a mere 1.3 percent annually, while the U.K. economy expanded at an annual rate twice as high, by 2.7 percent. For their bumbling, however, John Major and the Conservative Party never recovered and took a drubbing in the 1997 elections.

The international enterprise of Trichet, Tietmeyer, Mitterrand, and Kohl, Ltd., of course went on to achieve their dream of a unified Europe, bonded together with a single currency, the euro. The Germans had set the Maastricht bar for adopting the euro—the budgetary requirements in particular—so high that the exclusion of Italy seemed a certainty. Yet the Italians, through a mysterious last-minute juggling of fiscal and financial data, managed miraculously to slip through the closing door. Since that time, international use of the euro has exploded.

I've presented this backroom account of the great 1992 sterling crisis not to dredge up ancient history but rather to show the perils of not recognizing and dealing with changes in the global financial environment. That's what British officials did back in 1992 before their currency world was turned inside out. They remained nonchalant that their chosen ERM entry point for sterling left the currency in a perennially unstable condition. It is a similar remarkably nonchalant attitude our leaders today display in the face of the current financial imbalances, growing protectionism and class warfare, dubious financial architecture, and reckless economic policies in general. The only difference is that the financial markets of the twenty-first century are twenty times more powerful, and more capable of economic destruction, than they were in the early 1990s.

Today's policy officials and politicians remind me of the Bank of England's Eddie George, who declared back then as we sat sipping coffee in his office the morning his world came to an end, "We have it all under control." I predict a similar outcome unless today's leaders open their eyes to the financial threats looming over the horizon. We have convinced ourselves that today's financial and trade systems will muddle through. But as the British discovered in 1992, in today's world of highly mobilized capital, nothing can be taken for granted. In life, nothing stays the same.

7

The Incredible
Shrinking Central Banks

P eople picture central banks as having magical powers. When a
financial market crisis develops, institutions such as the Federal Reserve simply wave their magic wands, lower interest
rates, and the financial landscape is once again restored to normalcy.
Dream on.

During my career, I have known most of the world's major central
bankers. In the United States this includes Federal Reserve chairmen
Paul Volcker, Alan Greenspan, and Ben Bernanke. All would be the
first to admit that the image of the powerful central bank is way
overblown. And the declining power of central banks may be the most
convincing argument for why the world is curved.

In this chapter, I will show how, when financial panics arrive on
their doorstep, central banks today lack the same effective options to
respond that they enjoyed even a few years ago. I'll show that there are
new limits to how aggressively central banks can reply with monetary
stimulus. This is troubling because at the same time, the raging ocean
of capital, through the use of leverage, appears to know no limits. And
I'll explain how the central banks have lost some of their important

statistical "radar." Indeed, in some sense, the central bank pilots these days have been "flying blind."

The latest case study of central bank limitations is the period in the United States in early 2008, after the initial unfolding of the subprime mortgage crisis. The policy dilemmas during this period explain why the job of central banker has become so difficult. The Federal Reserve at that time faced a nasty combination of rising inflation, a housing collapse, a bank lending crisis, and a weakening dollar, all of which threatened a complete meltdown of the American economy.

U.S. policymakers, to their dismay, discovered that there were no obvious solutions to their dilemma—or at least none that could be set in motion without potential negative consequences. *New York Times* writer Roger Lowenstein suggested that the Fed faced "a devil's choice." Officials would lose if they moved strongly in one direction and they would lose if they held back and did nothing.

Here were their options. Because of the weakening economy and unstable financial market conditions, Fed policymakers could resort to what I'll call Option 1. They could slash short-term interest rates dramatically, perhaps by as much as another full percentage point, in one fell swoop, with more cuts thereafter. Short-term rates had already been cut several times in late 2007, amounting to a full percentage point reduction. The goal of Option 1: to reposition monetary policy further ahead of the curve. This is what the Japanese central bank should have done in the early 1990s, but didn't.

However, such bold interest rate cutting, some experts at the time maintained, could raise the market's fear that even more inflation was on the way. It could, more important, also risk a collapse of the dollar. Under such a scenario, potential foreign and domestic purchasers of U.S. Treasury bonds, fearing a huge decline in the yields on their bond investments as a result of the Fed's rate cuts, might look overseas for higher-yielding alternatives. Even worse, foreign investors with excess savings—most notably the sovereign wealth funds—remained the best private sector bet for bailing out the U.S. banks plagued by mountains of subprime mortgages. A dollar collapse might scare away that investment.

The bottom line on Option I: Bold Fed rate cuts could successfully boost the economy. Or they could be interpreted as a sign of panic, prolonging the credit crisis while igniting a further rise in inflationary expectations.

Option II would involve more restrained interest rate cutting. This is the approach, in the minds of some of the more hawkish policymakers at the Fed, that would be most likely to avoid a return to a 1970s economic scenario. The seventies began with soaring oil prices followed by rising inflation and economic weakness. The goal of Option II would be the hat trick of containing inflation, limiting dollar weakness, and stimulating the economy. The risk, however, could be further economic collapse as a result of the Fed's moving too slowly and too timidly. The danger was in falling behind the financial curve. And once global financial market traders sensed that happening, they would sink the dollar in any event, taking it down to unprecedented lows.

I've outlined these two options as an important case study of the central bank's awkward and at times subservient relationship to financial markets in the twenty-first century. So which option did Federal Reserve officials choose in their internal discussions? Neither. The reason is that those discussions never occurred because the global financial market quickly took matters into its own hands. On January 21, 2008, a week before the Federal Reserve was to meet formally in Washington for their debate, Asian stock markets, fearing U.S. economic weakness, crashed. The next day, European stock markets plummeted. Germany's declined by a full 7 percent. The same day, the sudden discovery that a rogue trader at the French bank Société Générale had suffered a $7.1 billion loss tied to phony transactions sent global stock markets into a further tailspin. In the process, global financial markets made the decision for the Federal Reserve. End of discussion. The markets picked Option I. The morning of January 22, Fed officials were forced by the markets to announce an emergency 75-basis-point interest rate cut with another 50-basis-point rate cut at the upcoming official meeting a week later.

Perhaps Paul Volcker, who was the Fed chairman from 1979 to

1987, summed up the central bank's predicament best when he told the *New York Times* he thought Federal Reserve officials were "in a very difficult situation." Volcker concluded that "too many bubbles have been going on for too long. The Fed is not really in control of the situation." That's my central point as well. Today's raging ocean of capital has become so huge, complex, and fast-moving that central bankers today are at an enormous disadvantage.

Volcker's successor, Alan Greenspan, who served from 1987 to 2006, describes the central bank's current predicament. In Greenspan's view, the dividends emanating from the fall of the Berlin Wall and rise of globalization—declining global wages—gave the Fed for a while enormous flexibility in the conduct of monetary policy. That was during Greenspan's time in office. But globalization, in bringing about greater world prosperity, also for a while caused the price of commodities, including oil, to soar. Concluded Greenspan: Because of these price rises, the problems facing central bankers are, by a huge magnitude, far more complex and difficult than they were during his tenure. Not convinced? In mid-2007, U.S. long-term bond yields were about 5.3 percent, and the price of oil was about $65 a barrel. A year later, the price of oil had nearly doubled to over $125, yet long-term bond yields for some strange reason had *dropped* below 4 percent. Historically, bond yields don't drop in an environment of dramatically rising oil prices. In mid-2007, U.S. inflationary expectations (that is, surveys showing what people expect future inflation to be) were in the range of 3.2 percent. A year later, the inflationary expectations figure had jumped to 5.2 percent, the highest in twenty-five years. Yet during this period, long-term bond yields again *dropped* by more than 150 basis points. In the traditional rule book of central banking, as Fed watcher Ed Hyman has pointed out, the bond market is not supposed to behave that way. Rising inflationary expectations historically have a devastating effect on bond prices; they don't increase bond prices (and thereby lower bond yields). Yet in today's confusing era of globalized markets, that was precisely what occurred.

The life and times of former chairman Greenspan offer a perfect window through which to view the workings of a central bank. His tenure saw the shrinking of the central bank's influence as a policy-making institution. During his nineteen years in office, Greenspan himself was a talented policymaker, bobbing and weaving and often living by his wits. But he was playing what he knew was ultimately a losing hand. Slowly but surely, the global ocean of capital was winning all the cards. Put another way, the world's financial markets held not only the aces but all the picture cards as well. In this chapter, I'll demonstrate Greenspan's extraordinary skill at communicating monetary policy decisions to financial markets. Yet he himself admits to presiding over, and contributing to, the worst credit crisis since the 1930s.

Greenspan and I first met in 1985 at the offices of his consulting firm in midtown Manhattan. A private economic consultant before his rise to the Fed chairmanship, he had accepted my offer to serve as moderator of my first international monetary conference. Greenspan was extremely interested in the conference. Extraordinarily quick on his feet, he knew this was a venue in which he would shine. He would be a natural at exchanging ideas and banter with the world's finance ministers, central bankers, and leading economists.

Greenspan performed well, as I had expected. The two-day conference in 1986 was described by the late Hobart Rowen of the *Washington Post*, then dean of international economics reporters, as "the final nail in the coffin of the pure floating exchange rate system." The *New York Times* wrote about or mentioned the conference in six separate stories, and *Newsweek* wrote two stories in as many weeks. In addition, the conference received wide coverage in a host of other print media.

A WEEK AFTER the first successful conference in Washington, Greenspan and I met to discuss a second event. This one was to take place at the elegant Dolder Grand Hotel in the hills above Zurich, Switzerland. The location was perfect, secluded yet important because of the unique role of the Swiss banks transcending the U.S. and European financial systems in the emerging process of financial globalization. "Let me give you a bit of advice," Greenspan warned in a kind of Dutch uncle style as we sipped coffee in his nondescript office: "You hit it big with that first conference. You affected policy and that doesn't come around very often. Better declare victory and quit while you're ahead."

I went on with the second conference in Switzerland anyway. Greenspan moderated, and it too became an enormous hit. Senator Bill Bradley, a lead sponsor, proposed a new program of emerging market debt forgiveness. The U.S. Treasury officials attending failed to completely kill the idea. So the developing world bond markets rallied significantly.

These discussions led to wide-open talk of Third World debt forgiveness. The consensus eventually led to the issuance of so-called Brady bonds. These were dollar-denominated bonds to consolidate debt issued by emerging market economies in the 1980s and 1990s. The result was a significant boost to the emerging markets and thus the world economy.

When Greenspan took command of the U.S. central bank in 1987, most traditional economists still considered the United States a relatively closed economic system. The forces of financial globalization were on the move. Still, the perception existed that the all-powerful Federal Reserve controlled a contained U.S. financial system.

Even then, that was increasingly not the case. Global financial markets, with the emergence of the developing economies (which would eventually include China) were mobilizing. A broad-based rise in cheap, competitive developing country exports would eventually tamp down wage gains in the industrialized world. This would produce a decline in inflationary expectations in the United States and other industrialized nations, followed by lower long-term interest rates. The result was a near-perfect set of macroeconomic conditions. Central banks in everyone's thinking could do no wrong. This was especially true of the Federal Reserve, which enjoyed an image as an all-controlling force of wisdom and stability.

Part of this perception stems from what I call the "Cult of the Chairmanship." Since the consolidation of the U.S. central bank under the Banking Act of 1935, the system itself has promoted the "Office of the Chairman" as an omniscient, omnipotent force. It almost doesn't matter who assumes the role as chairman of the Fed; that person becomes the central focus of the cult. All seeing and all knowing, he can do no wrong. It is questionable, however, whether this cult status is good for today's turbulent financial markets where it is increasingly impossible to see all and know all.

Greenspan's predecessor, Paul Volcker, deserves enormous credit for breaking the back of the 1970s inflation. He also enjoyed cultlike status. However, Volcker and Greenspan employed dramatically contrasting operating styles. Both enjoyed exceptional instincts, but differed in how they arrived at a particular decision. Volcker assumed the style of almost a nineteenth-century patrician. Greenspan's style was more modern, attuned to the latest advancement in technology. Yet they both achieved relatively high levels of effectiveness. This proves there isn't one personality or set of skills that leads to success on the job. Those who criticize Greenspan's successor, Ben Bernanke, for his more restrained and collegial style should look back and examine his predecessors' differences.

On Monday mornings, for example, the tall, Germanic Volcker would sit in a Fed boardroom meeting, reading the *Wall Street Journal* while holding the paper in front of his face. He would smoke a cigar while a staff member offered the week's forgettable economic briefing. Volcker expressed no interest in arcane economic data and said once to a colleague: "I have one goal. I want to leave office never having looked at a computer screen."

His successor, Greenspan, took just the opposite approach. He loved data, the more arcane the better (usually consumed during off-hours in a legendary soaking tub where the chairman spun out verbal gems to be used in congressional testimony to encapsulate and sometimes obfuscate the near-term policy outlook). True, Greenspan benefited from good instincts. He had the ability to feel something in his bones, but this instinct came from meticulous study of, and fascination with, data.

Let me offer some examples. At one Fed meeting, the discussion droned on about the latest macroeconomic developments. Suddenly Chairman Greenspan broke in: "This is all very interesting, but does anyone know the latest price of tomatoes?" (There had been a freeze in California and some other parts of the country.) The staff went crazy, as did several board members. "What do tomatoes have to do with monetary policy?" one board member asked incredulously. Watching it all in frustration was the head of research. First, Volcker ignored his department. Now, Greenspan was running the staff ragged in search of seemingly arcane data.

Despite the differences in the operating styles of the individuals, the Cult of the Chairmanship endured. To a certain extent, the power of the institution itself rested on the perception that the Fed knew something the financial markets didn't. The Fed "knew" inflation was in check, so the financial markets remained calm. The market's data-driven inflationary expectations remained subdued. The Fed "knew" output remained strong, so bond markets remained stable and equity markets robust.

Volcker, Greenspan, and Bernanke would all admit that the Cult of the Chairmanship is overdone in a way that is perilous to the financial markets. Why? Because market participants develop false expectations that, however brutal the crisis, the central bank can always step in to save the day (under Greenspan's tenure, this expectation of Fed intervention became known as the "Greenspan put," an insurance policy or guaranteed floor in the minds of stock investors). Yet the rise of globalization has robbed central banks everywhere of a considerable amount of their ability to come riding to the rescue. This is a scary thought given the major uncertainties emerging throughout today's global financial system. Globalization has reduced central bankers' capability as lender of last resort (stepping in to stabilize things when markets take on too much risk). After all, today the value of all global long-term securities exceeds an amazing $100 trillion. With significant amounts of this ocean of liquidity traded each day, all at the push of a button, the actual reserves held by the Federal Reserve appear tiny by comparison. The obvious question: To what extent can the central bank still influence such a highly complex, volatile economy?

The answer to that question is more complicated than it seems. Since the early 1990s, the forces of financial globalization have led to lower long-term interest rates worldwide. As a result, stock market and real estate prices have soared. The problem is that risk in the market, particularly in the past dozen years, has been severely *underpriced* as global growth at one point reached levels not seen since the 1960s. Underpriced risk eventually leads to periods of stiff and bitter market corrections. A prime example of underpriced risk, of course, were the stock prices of U.S. companies engaged in the mortgage and housing industries in the years before the subprime crisis. Those stock prices failed to reflect the growing risk that the housing bubble would eventually burst. Indeed, the rising price levels of the U.S. housing sector itself in the years before the bubble burst represented underpriced risk given the fairly predictable history of market bubbles. Because average homeowners thought their homes had risen in value, they felt more comfortable increasing their levels of household consumption. Economists call this phenomenon the increase in the "wealth effect." But the risk that this consumption would not forever briskly expand was underappreciated by both policymakers and the markets.

The Fed does still have one powerful tool to stimulate economic activity or throttle back the economy to reduce risk. That tool is the Fed funds, or short-term, interest rate. In times of panic, the Fed traditionally has been quickly able to "liquefy" the markets (through the banking system) by slashing the Fed funds rates. In times of excessive growth and risk, the Fed traditionally has been able to moderate economic expansion and stem the risk of inflation by raising short-term rates. Changing the level of the Fed funds rate would directly influence long-term interest rates, the rates the market controls. And long-term interest rates in the United States and in most parts of Europe are the rates used to finance a great deal of economic expansion, including, in most cases, housing (one exception is Great Britain, where housing loans for the most part are tied to short-term rates).

Here's why the Federal Reserve faces a potentially dangerous situation. Beginning in 2004, the central bank's influence over long-term rates mysteriously began to wane. How do we know that? During that year the Federal Reserve began a lengthy series of short-term interest rate hikes. To the surprise of everyone, long-term rates, the rates that affect most of the economy, barely budged. In the past, long-term interest rates would have also gone up in parallel with short-term rates. In a sense, U.S. long-term interest rates may have to an extent become a captive of global financial forces. At times, long-term rates appear to be reacting more to global financial developments than to decisions by American policymakers. For Fed officials, that represented a sobering development. To a certain extent, Americans at times no longer fully controlled their own interest rate policy.

This change has transformed central banks from a storehouse of the most up-to-date data on the economy into more of a grand global theater. The central bankers—whether they like it or not—have become the lead actors. They tease and bluff markets about coming trends in the economy, but mostly about near-term decisions on short-term interest rate policy. Their readily available resources or tools are less than potent. Thus, the central bank actors have had no choice but to use their dramatic skills to try to persuade, cajole, charm, and intimidate. The reason is that global market traders make up the audience and, until recently, they have controlled long-term interest rates.

The situation was not quite like that in *The Wizard of Oz* with a little man behind a curtain pulling all the levers, but the analogy is not completely off the mark. At the end of the day, the question remained: Is the central bank credible? In particular, has the theatrical play's lead, the chairman, performed well onstage? This may all sound a bit silly, but with today's raging ocean of capital the central bankers have no choice but to play their parts as skillfully as possible.

Ben Bernanke acknowledged after his first six months on the job that he was initially, of course, aware that managing "the theater" (his words) was an essential component of his job. What has surprised him is how *overwhelmingly* important successful theater management has become.

Bernanke and his colleagues would prefer to move away from a system based on the cultlike wisdom of the chairman to a more objective approach in the form of setting and achieving certain target rates of inflation. This would gear all of the central bank's inner workings toward a transparent goal well known to the financial markets. This makes some sense, although during financial crises when the Fed and the markets are unclear about the appropriate policy option, it might be more reassuring to the panicked markets if the Fed remained a bit of a mystery so as not to hurt investor confidence in times of Fed uncertainty.

The Fed itself is still trying to figure out its role in crisis management. During periods of financial crisis, it is important that central banks remain pragmatic and avoid rigid rules. Clearly the markets look for credible and inventive leadership from the policy world, not adherence to fixed policy formulas. That is why Bernanke quickly acknowledges that, notwithstanding the goal of inflation targeting, role-playing is still the dominant part of the Fed's job and will likely remain so for the rest of his tenure and beyond.

The reason is that the world's major central banks have been operating in a world of huge excess savings far greater than actual safe, credible investment opportunities. During the past decade, a lot of the excess savings have piled into government debt investments, particularly the U.S. Treasury market. As a result of this massive investment in Treasuries, long-term interest rates plummeted, which caused asset prices, including stock markets and real estate, to soar. That is why financial bubbles continued to rise to the surface, to the central bankers' dismay.

In this new world, central bankers have had no choice but to sharpen their theatrical skills. As *the* lead of all lead actors and the man who controlled monetary policy in the United States for most of two decades, however, Alan Greenspan would be the first to say that playing the role perfectly is next to impossible.

Because Greenspan despite some serious regulatory blunders was a compelling figure on the world stage for so long, I think it would be useful to lift the curtain and provide a glimpse of his backroom maneuverings. The former chairman's operating style provides a unique vantage point to understanding how the central banking world's conduct of policy has changed so dramatically in recent years.

An economist with a dull, monotone voice, Greenspan appeared to outsiders as if he were oblivious to politics. Actually, just the opposite was the case. What surprised me was that Greenspan's political antennae were the most sensitive in Washington (his wife is senior NBC correspondent Andrea Mitchell, a major force in the Washington political establishment). This is probably because, unlike other figures of power, the position of Federal Reserve chairman lacks a broad-based political constituency. Americans never voted him into office. He had no choice but to bring an incredible amount of political sensitivity to his office. Over the years, Greenspan and I have had many conversations about politics. I always came away surprised by his shrewd ability to strategically assess the political landscape.

On the everyday working level, Greenspan's operating style was quite basic: To one-up competitors, he always arrived overly prepared. Even as chairman of the White House Council of Economic Advisers in the Ford administration in the mid-1970s, he never came to a White House meeting with President Ford without some useful surprise. For example, Greenspan at one point concluded that a company called Stone Container, a maker of cardboard boxes, was a good barometer for the economy. Why? Companies need cardboard boxes for shipping products but usually have no place to store them. Stone Container provided boxes on two or three days' notice. A typical Greenspan statement: "I just got off the phone, Mr. President, with the COO of Stone Container. He tells me the box orders lately have taken a nosedive. Clearly something negative is happening out there with the economy." The rest of the team, including the president, suddenly sat there feeling inadequate.

At another White House meeting, a different official was spouting off the top of his head a view of the current trend in consumer credit. Greenspan politely followed these comments with the suggestion: "It might also be helpful to know what the industry is saying. GE Capital

is the largest industrial bank in the United States, Mr. President. Yes-
terday, I asked the chairman of GE if he'd have his boys prepare a little
memo about how they see the capital markets. I read the memo last
night. Let me tell you what's going on."

Alan Greenspan's mantra as a central banker was that there is *always*
something out there we don't know, some useful piece of the puzzle
that could make the picture clearer. That is why he became almost
addicted to the search for seemingly arcane data.

While Greenspan was fascinated by electoral politics, he became an
intense student of the Fed's internal politics. He knew that both his
reputation and his survival were at stake. In the early 1990s, for
example, the *Wall Street Journal* ran an article claiming that Fed vice
chairman David Mullins, not Greenspan, was in control of the Federal
Reserve. Most Fed watchers knew what the article was all about:
Greenspan was not playing nice with the press. The innocent Mullins
was being used journalistically as a club to beat up on the chairman.
That's often the way the media's relationship with the official world
works. In journalistic jargon, you've got to pay to play.

The article came up in one of my own discussions with Greenspan.
A week after the Mullins *Wall Street Journal* article ran, Greenspan, my
business partner Manley Johnson (a former Fed vice chairman), and I
met for breakfast. As we were leaving, the chairman pulled me aside
and said with a certain determination in his voice: "Call me, Dave, if
anybody tries to convince you I'm not in control of what's happening
here." From then on Johnson and I referred to this tendency as the
"Greenspan manhood issue." Criticizing Greenspan's policy views was
fair game. Greenspan loved the intellectual give-and-take. However,
to Greenspan, any suggestion that he was not running the show
amounted to a declaration of war. Greenspan instinctively knew that
managing the theatrical part of the job meant making it absolutely
clear that he was the star of the show.

Ironically, Greenspan's colleagues, even after leaving so they could
talk with great candor, made clear the chairman never faced any significant internal policy opposition (except for a slight disagreement over a

technical detail involving the chairman's flexibility in an emergency situation to change monetary policy between FOMC [Federal Open Market Committee] meetings). William McDonough, as president of the New York Federal Reserve for a decade, was the Fed's premier expert on financial markets and deserves some credit for Greenspan's success in monetary policy. He summed up the former Fed chairman's tenure best when he said: "There was never anyone even close to being in his class." Yet that *Wall Street Journal* article had seeped into the chairman's consciousness.

It shouldn't have. A typical Greenspan-led FOMC meeting went like this: All the voting members, many of them gifted and a few woefully out of touch, would first present their views. Then the president of the New York Federal Reserve would give his assessment on how the *financial markets* would likely react to various proposed actions. There was no mystery here because the New York Fed president (who, for more than half of Greenspan's tenure, was McDonough) and the Fed chairman, by the definition of their positions, always made sure their policy positions were largely in synch. Once the two reached a consensus, Greenspan would present his analysis and the monetary policy option he preferred. This option would be consistent with what had just been described by the New York Fed president as "the market expectation." It is not that the two targeted financial markets; they had their eye on an appropriate interest rate consistent with a stable economy. Their tactical maneuverings were intended to avoid large degrees of market volatility caused by disappointments in market expectations.

Sometimes, days before the Fed meeting, Greenspan would attempt to preguide the markets using various informal communications channels. His favorite reporter was John Berry, then of the *Washington Post*. The chairman's goal: to always make sure policy was in reasonable balance with what the market was expecting. Greenspan gleaned vital information from the markets, but what the market was expecting in terms of movements in short-term interest rates was usually exactly what Greenspan had leaked to the markets.

Why all this backroom maneuvering? The answer is, by now, a

familiar one: the dangerous ocean of capital. The Greenspan version of a successful monetary policy was one that did not surprise or upset the world's stock markets. Greenspan had lived through the nightmare of the 1987 stock market crash. It hit shortly after he became Fed chairman (Greenspan wisely flooded the market with liquidity even as a number of conservative economists argued publicly that the Federal Reserve should restrict credit to fight inflation and thereby support the dollar). Fearing the growing ocean of capital, his approach was always to condition the markets first through a series of subtle verbal messages. The actual event—the change in short-term rates—became from a financial market standpoint largely a point at which the positive financial market results had already occurred.

With today's larger, more volatile, and more global financial markets, such adroit maneuvering is becoming significantly more difficult. Greenspan himself admits that he served during a time when conditions were almost always on his side. In other words, he was dealt one hell of a hand. In an era of low global inflation, the series of bursting financial bubbles he faced along the way could be easily handled with quick monetary eases. Today, the options are hardly without potential nasty unintended consequences.

Even though he was ever mindful that he was always on the world stage, Greenspan occasionally made tactical decisions that misfired. For instance, the chairman regularly received two pieces of early data highly important to markets. One was the so-called Purchasing Managers Survey (now called the Institute for Supply Management, or the ISM). The other was the manufacturing component of the monthly employment report (covering less than 30 percent of the U.S. economy and shared with the Fed before its official announcement by its preparer, the Bureau of Labor Statistics, to allow the Fed to complete its job of preparing another piece of data, the Industrial Production Index). Often the chairman's speeches, reflecting his early knowledge of these two yet-to-be released reports, made it appear to the uninformed that he enjoyed special powers to see into the future. With early, but incomplete data on the economy's strength, he would, for instance, talk ominously about the economy. Within days data would appear showing weakness in manufacturing. The Cult of the Chairmanship went into overdrive. Greenspan, it appeared to those not aware, could see into the future.

At other times, however, the chairman would find his public statements to be out of whack when the final, more complete employment data was later made public by the Labor Department. The reason: While manufacturing might have been weak, to continue the example, the monthly employment report later disclosed that the services sector of the report (representing 70 to 80 percent of the economy) was unexpectedly strong. This would call into question the accuracy of the chairman's broader forecast.

These few hiccups, of course, vanish in the context of the chairman's larger track record. Despite his own admission that he failed to foresee the subprime crisis that hit world markets after he had stepped down (a regulatory blunder of historic proportions I'll describe in more detail in the final chapter), Greenspan, though committing some mistakes, was effective in the conduct of monetary policy. While in public office, he quickly grew professionally as chairman, coming to terms with the difficult, often confusing emerging revolution of integrated markets. As financial globalization became a reality, central bankers the world over found themselves increasingly forced to live by their wits.

Effective policymakers need to know when to act and when to do absolutely nothing—to do no harm. This became one of the secrets to the approach of Alan Greenspan in trying to manage an increasingly complex economy. Established monetary theories and protocol are important, but the rules, as he presciently figured out, are forever failing to work as predicted.

Yet this ability to dominate the workings of the financial system would not be long lasting. Perhaps Greenspan put it best when he said, "Global forces, combined with lower international trade barriers, have diminished the scope of national governments to affect the paths of their economies."

Sometimes Greenspan was wise enough not to step in the way of a speeding freight train. Policymakers sometimes have no choice but to operate based on their gut instincts (within the confines of some conceptual framework). One of the Bundesbank's top international specialists, Stefan Schönberg, commented that "while globalization may have weakened the short-term grip by central bankers over policy, Greenspan with the integration of financial markets actually managed to increase the Fed's influence within the global financial system."

In near-term policymaking, Greenspan was a lot less fixated on any one theory for the simple reason that many of the prevailing beliefs about data and their effect on the economy became less reliable. To establish a trend, the Fed suddenly needed several months of data. Even then, the relationships between different sets of reports often made things murkier, not clearer.

By the late 1990s, Greenspan could feel in his bones, as derived, of course, from mountains of data, that the U.S. economy was in the midst of a productivity revolution. Productivity growth was significantly above the historic norm. Greenspan sensed that the long-term productivity rate might be higher, not dramatically so, but enough to make a significant difference in the amount of wealth creation in the United States. Even a 0.5 percent sustained additional rise in productivity growth is huge in terms of its economic implications. Such a productivity improvement would make American companies more globally competitive, while at the same time keeping inflation in check.

In the end, Americans were allowed to retain trillions of dollars of wealth that would have vanished had Greenspan followed a more conventional route in the late 1990s. That route called for higher interest rates to chase after an inflationary phantom that never materialized (in principle, the higher the productivity growth, the less the inflationary pressures). Greenspan's major accomplishment was recognizing the productivity revolution and its beneficial effects on the economy. This allowed him to keep interest rates where they were (someone without his strong instincts would have raised rates), while keeping inflationary expectations in check.

The major criticism of Greenspan, which surfaced in 2006 even before he retired, was that he helped to create the dangerous housing bubble by keeping short-term interest rates too low for too long. Certainly the bubble became an ugly reality. Greenspan's critics have taken to calling him "the bubble man." What his critics often fail to mention, however, is that the chairman, at a time of serious global deflationary forces after the dot-com collapse and 9/11, successfully avoided the Japanese experience of the 1990s. As much pain as the U.S. housing bubble has produced for average Americans, it should, in fairness, be viewed in the context of the devastation of the "lost decade" of broad-based economic paralysis that gripped the Japanese economy for more than a decade.

As a precaution against that kind of devastation, Greenspan dropped short-term interest rates to an unheard-of 1 percent. The policy worked, the economy dodged a bullet; however, not without the unintended consequence of a housing bubble. Some critics argue that the U.S. central bank kept short-term rates too low for too long, but that amounts to a kind of Monday morning quarterbacking. Less than a decade before, Greenspan made the mistake of raising rates prematurely in response to a false economic rebound; the economy weakened, and the Fed was forced to do an embarrassing about-face and cut interest rates. The fact is, in the years before the subprime crisis, had the regulators done their jobs, monetary policy alone would not have created the credit crisis.

To a certain extent, Greenspan became a victim of the Cult of the Chairmanship, which had soared to a point where the chairman was referred to as "the Maestro," an all-seeing, all-knowing policymaker who controlled and directed all aspects of the financial and economic orchestra. Only on the less-than-glamorous bank regulatory matters, Greenspan took a pass. He delegated enormous regulatory authority to subordinates, including his vice chair, Roger Ferguson, in the crucial period leading up to the subprime debacle. In that position, Ferguson, lacking extensive financial market experience, was a capable administrator with extraordinary intelligence, but no match for the sophisticated market participants and their lawyers who were expert at hiding risk.

Greenspan's "maestro" status offered the entire bank regulatory community across the board a false sense of comfort that all was well despite growing evidence to the contrary. The all-seeing Maestro saw no cause for concern, so why should anyone else? The truth is the Maestro was asleep on the job, which is surprising given the risk the Chairman was assuming in keeping short-term interest rates at such a low level.

The Federal Reserve's bank regulators (as well as the Comptroller of the Currency, the Federal Deposit Insurance Corporation, and other U.S. bank regulatory agencies) failed to appreciate the toxic nature of the subprime situation. They missed the fact that mortgage lending to people who failed to even remotely qualify for a loan had spiraled out of control.

Fed officials also missed the fact that the subprime crisis represented something far more onerous—the irresponsible nature of the U.S. banking sector and the collapse in confidence and trust by global traders and investors in today's new financial architecture. In my next chapter, I will describe more fully how, in order to circumvent risk, the banks and other financial institutions set up dubious off-balance-sheet financial vehicles. This was an elaborate game of debt hide-and-seek that ended in chaos. However, before the crash of the housing market, the boom continued. It was as if the entire U.S. regulatory system, as well as the private credit rating agencies, seemed overcome by a sense of euphoria toward the new mortgage lending. Encouraged by Congress, the regulators thought the world was somehow entering a new golden age of "riskless risk." Of course, we now know that there is no such thing. And this, what I call "the mother of all regulatory failures," has brought a great deal of pain to families all over the world. Moreover, regulatory failure, and a decline of trust in today's architecture, has made today's financial world a very dangerous place that, in the long run, has destroyed the global competitiveness of the U.S. financial services sector. If Alan Greenspan had taken the regulatory part of his job more seriously, large parts of the crisis might have been avoided.

Since the beginning of globalization, the job of chairman of the Federal Reserve has become almost like central banker to the world.

That is because, while the euro has gained more usage and visibility in recent years, the Federal Reserve today still presides over what is largely a "dollarized" financial world. In other words, most developing countries still tie their currencies in one form or another to the U.S. dollar. That means the chairman must be concerned not only with events unfolding in the U.S. economy; he must appreciate the subtle complexities of many other economies across the globe.

To a certain extent, the Federal Reserve in recent years has been forced to "fly blind" without its normal statistical "radar" to conduct monetary policy. In the past, certain market indicators served as essential central banking warning signs. Not anymore. For example, whenever long-term interest rates (ten-year Treasury bond yields) dropped below the yields of the short-term interest rates (the overnight interest rate the Federal Reserve controls) and stayed in that position for some period of time, a recession was sure to follow. Credit conditions dramatically contracted. People and businesses couldn't get loans. Economists call this an inverted yield curve.

As a predictive tool, this statistical relationship now has a mixed success rate. Because so much global wealth, as a result of the expansion of the global economy after the end of the cold war, poured into long-term government bonds, the yield curve became distorted and stayed that way for some time. Greenspan called this situation "a conundrum." The conundrum developed into a situation that at times blinded Fed policymakers, as their past predictive mechanisms were rendered useless.

As odd as it sounds, the world's central bankers can't even agree on a definition of inflation. European central bankers, for example, have been driven by fears of something called headline inflation. This is a measurement of all price levels *including* the prices of food and energy. By contrast, U.S. central bankers believe headline inflation produces too many short-term distortions and prefer instead to look at something called core inflation—a measurement of the price level *without* including food and energy in the mix.

During 2007 and the first half of 2008, global energy and food prices skyrocketed. As a result, headline inflation exploded upward, causing nervous European central bankers to keep short-term interest rates high regardless of the economic weakness caused by the global credit crisis. At the same time, however, the Federal Reserve dramatically cut short-term interest rates, based on the belief that while rising inflationary expectations always remain a concern, core inflation (excluding food and energy) was surprisingly well behaved.

Which measurement is more accurate? The Europeans argued that for the average person, filling the automobile gas tank and paying the food bill are hardly trivial economic activities and thus should be included in the inflation measurement. The argument goes that food and energy price increases eventually can have a "contagion effect" on the general price level, particularly on union wage demands. U.S. officials countered that weather and geopolitical factors can temporarily cause abrupt moves in food and energy prices, thus distorting the broader price picture. Moreover, the contagion effect fear is overrated, particularly in the U.S. service-dominated economy, where union membership in recent decades has declined significantly.

In the end, the question came down to this: Were soaring food and energy prices an *inflationary* phenomenon (affecting the expectations of people and corporations about the inflation rate over the horizon) or a *contractionary* (weakening) phenomenon, as the average consumer enjoyed less after-tax discretionary income to spend, thus slowing down the economy and dampening inflationary expectations? The answer is that the European inflation concerns soon subsided. The European Central Bank slashed short-term interest rates, too.

In their conduct of business, central bankers historically have kept their eyes on one other tool—a warning sign called emerging-market risk spreads (the difference between interest rates on historically less than perfectly safe government bonds in the developing world and the ultrasafe U.S. Treasury rates). During the recent period of excess liquidity, global investors, in an effort to diversify their portfolios, placed large amounts of capital into high-yielding developing-world bond investments. As a result, the interest rates on this less than perfectly safe debt in recent years have at times reflected an incredibly rosy picture that had little in common with reality.

Brazilian bonds, for example, for quite a while were priced in such a way as to suggest that they were far safer than they actually were. This made little sense given the unpredictable political developments in the region. Venezuela's president, Hugo Chávez, is as unpredictable as was Fidel Castro. In other words, given the political risk in South America, interest rates there should have been higher. The bottom line is that today's risk spreads make it tough for central bankers to assess global risk. For the Fed chairman, understanding global risk is essential to protecting the American economy.

This is because, as we have seen, in the event of a significant global recession, these developing world markets were hit hard. Their bonds came under major pressure. The previous current risk spreads, however, failed to reflect that reality.

Today's central bank headaches seem never ending. Global imbalances grew to the point where, for some Asian economies, central bank reserves represented, incredibly, far more than half of the nation's GDP. Financial transparency in some cases was virtually nonexistent.

And these were the good times. The global protectionists, for the most part, were only complaining. They had not yet acted. And most challenging is the fact that no one is sure, when the next big financial crisis erupts, whether the central banks will be able to do much about it. Be assured, the subprime credit crisis represented a sideshow compared to the aftermath, say, of a global trade war with China and a shutdown of Asian capital flows.

Over the Greenspan years, financial markets came to believe that the Federal Reserve, in the event of a financial meltdown, functioned as the "lender of last resort." Certainly the Fed fire brigade successfully moved into action in years past. This happened during the late 1990s' Argentine and Russian debt defaults, when the U.S. stock and bond markets were affected. The Fed also moved quickly and successfully

208 · THE WORLD IS CURVED

after the collapse of the hedge fund Long-Term Capital Management, after the dot-com collapse of 2000, after the terrorist attacks of September 11, 2001, and after the breakout of the subprime crisis.

But every time the central bank intervenes and stocks rally, the question arises: Is the rally occurring because markets perceive unrealized value in those stocks? Or is the rally the result of the monetary stimulus alone, and thus vulnerable to evaporating once the central bank stops the stimulus?

Economists call this latter phenomenon moral hazard—bailing out risk-takers with taxpayer money and government policies that only encourage greater risky speculation. Central bankers in particular have an inherent fear of creating financial bubbles through their own form of moral hazard. This involves the central banks' appearing to put a floor under the stock market by allowing the market to expect aggressive interest rate cuts if stocks decline below a certain level. The fact is, however, guessing the appropriate equilibrium level for stocks (i.e., identifying a bubble and avoiding moral hazard) has become a fool's errand. In 1996, for example, Alan Greenspan, in a famous speech before the American Enterprise Institute, called the stock market "irrationally exuberant." The level of the Dow was 6,500 (compared to a much higher level today). Although that sounded like a prudent thing to say, the situation proved to be far more complex. As Obama adviser Larry Summers said in an interview in *The International Economy*, "That was a declaration of a bubble that wasn't." Several years later, Americans became irrationally exuberant about housing. That turned out to be a bubble that was.

The additional question is whether central banks can even be the complete "lender of last resort" without unintended consequences. In March of 2009, worried that the U.S. economy was not responding to the Obama administration's first stimulus and bank bailout efforts, the Bernanke Federal Reserve announced a highly unusual decision—a plan for the Fed to purchase long-term U.S. Treasury securities as a means of lowering U.S. interest rates and thawing credit markets. The U.S. ten year Treasury bond quickly rallied by 40 basis points, but within weeks lost most of this gain. Chairman Bernanke had previously initiated a number of other exotic new measures in an attempt to inject liquidity into financial markets. All of these became part of the Fed's "throw everything including the kitchen sink" at the credit crisis. But there are limits to monetary stimulus in an environment of collapsed confidence. As Greenspan himself put it, "In theory, central banks can expand their balance sheets without limit. In practice, they are constrained by the potential inflationary impact of their actions." Today's central banks remind me of a fire department with much weaker water pressure and ladders that can't reach above the first floor. When the house is on fire, the firemen still rush to the rescue. The question is how much good they can do. As I will discuss in the next chapter, it could be years before the full ramifications of the Fed's policy change are realized. Clearly, the U.S. central bank has grabbed an enormous financial tiger by the tail, loading its balance sheet with unprecedented amounts of debt with real concerns about how the Fed handles matters as the U.S. economy fully recovers.

On a broader note, I can't help but think the world's central bankers must sit up late at night and occasionally ponder this fact: that the period in the world economy from the late 1870s to 1914 bears a striking resemblance to today. That, too, was a period of trade liberalization and relatively internationalized capital markets. The amount of saving and wealth creation far exceeded the available opportunities for investment. Nominal interest rates were low worldwide. Financial panics appeared, frequently followed by market rescue efforts by the large banks. Back then, the surprise at the end of the line was the economic and financial Armageddon of the 1930s.

True, today's policymakers are far more sophisticated than they were a century ago. Plus they have the benefit of hindsight. They are far more capable of handling financial panics. However, an extended period involving a large oversupply of savings over investment is often used by economic historians to describe the events that led to the Great Depression. In the 1930s, the excess savings served as a highly contractionary (weakening) force in the global system.

So far today such a depression-like contractionary development as a result of an oversupply of global savings hardly seems in the offing. And the reason is that unlike the closed economic system the financial world had evolved into by the 1930s, today's global excess savings are still allowed to be recycled internationally. In other words, global financial capital continues to move across borders relatively freely in search of new investment opportunities. That is, at least for now.

However, the future looks troubling. There is no denying that the world of globalized trade and free-flowing financial capital is under siege. In America, both political parties are beginning to back away from the very policies that created the greatest explosion in prosperity the world has ever known. The same is true in Europe and elsewhere. The markets are starting to take notice. So too are the nervous central bankers, who know better than most that the long-term costs of a series of politically inspired policy blunders could be catastrophic.

At stake is a system of extraordinary wealth creation and poverty reduction. It is a system that produced the beginnings of a revolution in charitable giving with the potential for creating an enormous amount of good in the world. But the central banks, as they go through the process of unwinding debt in the aftermath of the subprime crisis, had better get it right. While they are at it, they had better set to work on a new global financial doctrine for the twenty-first century. The Fed desperately needs to implement targeted reforms of surgical precision and sensitivity that avoid crippling the U.S. financial sector yet restore global confidence in the system.

The current crop of central bankers, led by the Fed's Bernanke and the ECB's Trichet, may be the smartest and most intellectually gifted ever to take office. But the job of avoiding further market turbulence in coming years is not going to be easy. Today there are no simple solutions, but there are a lot of simple mistakes to be made in a world where heretofore unheard-of amounts of capital move around the globe dangerously at will, ready to bolt at the first sign of rising financial and/or geopolitical risk.

8

Class Warfare and
the Politics of Globalization

O f all the uncertainties confronting global financial markets—
from China to the fragile banking system to the shrinking of
the central banks—political change remains the most difficult to predict. Globalization and liberalized capital markets began as a
result of politics, as an answer to the economic stagnation of the 1970s.
Whether globalization survives in the twenty-first century will also
come down to whether voters are politically accepting of globalization's flaws in light of its benefits. Such acceptance increasingly seems
doubtful.

Today's global ocean of capital continually measures political risk.
Because entrepreneurial capital is highly mobile and forward-looking,
it darts across borders at the first signal of even *potential* negative
change, often leaving behind the wreckage of financial panic. These
signals of negative change include signs of class warfare (politicians
pitting one income group against another) and excessive government
intervention, including protectionism, as well as other proposed fiscal
and regulatory changes that are well intentioned but prove to be
counterproductive. Today the world is curved precisely because the

political and financial market worlds increasingly don't understand each other. This is particularly the case in the United States, where a political shift away from free trade and liberalized capital markets is under way.

What I am about to offer is a theory about the politics of globalization that may sound strange. My argument is that the last quarter-century has represented a relatively seamless, bipartisan political consensus in favor of free trade and liberalized financial markets. In the United States during this period, globalization was not a Republican or a Democratic phenomenon. Indeed, there was not much difference in economic policymaking between Democrat Bill Clinton and Republican Ronald Reagan.

The reality is that Bill Clinton as president was even more a free trader than Ronald Reagan. Clinton became the champion of globalization and liberalized financial markets. He was a lead participant in a quarter-century of prosperity and global poverty reduction. Both Reagan and Clinton grabbed on to globalization as a flawed tool to break away from the economically suffocating 1970s. The young Bill Clinton came of age in the 1970s, so he was particularly aware of the economic disillusionment of that period. Reagan was born in 1911, so he came of age during the Great Depression. In a sense, therefore, once in the White House, both recognized the urgency and opportunity of being able to ride the great globalization wave. The question today is: What happens when global financial market participants fully realize that this remarkable period of policy consensus is coming to an end?

Both political parties in America today are quickly backing away from the pro-globalization policies championed by Bill Clinton. Clearly, part of the financial market turbulence in recent times stems not only from subprime-related credit uncertainties, but also from the uncertainties about the direction of American politics. These fears have been heightened by American politicians who increasingly engage in populist attacks on capital formation, entrepreneurial initiative, and wealth creation.

Here's the problem with politicizing globalization. World financial markets had set the price of U.S. financial assets, including the price of stocks, at relatively high values. This was based on the bullish assumption that the Clinton-Reagan model of free trade, liberalized capital markets, and long-term robust growth would remain largely intact. Now a new political universe is emerging, with new rules, changing policies, and less patience for freely liberalized capital and trade. The questions of the hour are: How will markets in coming years reprice the changing nature of the political environment? And will an aggressive downward repricing of financial assets continue to happen in a further climate of panic? The threat for financial markets of unwise political change is very real. Today there is the growing belief that the financial world, politically speaking, has entered uncharted political waters.

I realize that linking Clinton and Reagan together in a global economic discussion may sound strange, but it's not as bizarre as it sounds. Over the last several decades, both were members of a large ensemble of actors on an international stage of globalized economic and financial reform. The other reformers included Narasimha Rao of India, Deng Xiaoping of China, Jacques Delors in Europe, Margaret Thatcher of the United Kingdom, Roger Douglas in New Zealand, and Fernando Henrique Cardoso in Brazil. Some analysts include former French Socialist prime minister Lionel Jospin in this august group.

All of these individuals benefited from the decline in global inflation and the emergence of new, inexpensive computing power. Facing political pressure, all turned to globalization, entrepreneurship, and global capital markets to break away from the wealth-inhibiting policies of the 1970s (and, in the case of China and India, from the heavy hand of a centrally planned economy).

Reagan and Clinton as policymakers were a kind of odd couple. The popularity of both former presidents benefitted from the economic success stemming from their support of liberalized capital and trade markets.

In the interest of full disclosure, I have to say that I did not initially see Reagan's potential for such a historic role, despite the fact that I enjoyed a front-row seat at the start of it all. Indeed, I will always remember the image of a taller-than-expected, rosy-cheeked Ronald Reagan in late 1979 barreling through the doorway of a hotel suite at the Airport Marriott in Los Angeles. Dressed in a sports jacket with bright, multicolored patches and a golf shirt that clashed in color and texture, the sixty-eight-year-old former California governor hardly resembled a man gearing up to run for the Republican presidential nomination.

Although I was originally a registered Democrat (everyone who grew up in my lower-middle-class, row-house neighborhood in the city of Baltimore was a Democrat), I was there to advise Reagan because I was an associate of Republican congressman Jack Kemp of New York. In the 1980 presidential campaign, the Buffalo-area congressman served as the Reagan campaign's chief domestic policy architect. I was Kemp's chief of staff. We were in Los Angeles to talk economics—specifically, to spend three days of nine-to-five policy discussions with Reagan, whom I had never met, and seven or eight of his closest advisers. Our goal: to devise a national recovery plan.

Despite my age at the time, twenty-six, I was seasoned enough to sense the potential importance of our meetings. Never did I imagine, though, that these three days would contribute to the globalization of the U.S. economy. They did. Nor, of course, was I aware that a Democratic president, Bill Clinton, would later ratchet up these policies to heights I never could have imagined.

The most intriguing character in attendance was Reagan's campaign mastermind, John P. Sears. He was a white-haired, chain-smoking man in his forties. Friends affectionately referred to him as John P. Satan (because of his devilish tactical cleverness against political opponents). I admired Sears for his tactical brilliance—attuned to the benefits in politics of being at times unconventional and unpredictable. He reminded me of Erwin Rommel, the World War II German general in North Africa, with his cigarette held up by three fingers looking like a minicannon aimed straight at the governor. Every time Sears spoke, there was a tension in the air. This increased in intensity when Sears was addressing Reagan (Sears was removed from the campaign several months later). Still, one of Sears's contributions turned out to be historic.

Early on during the Los Angeles meetings, he insisted the campaign push something called the "North American Accord." This was a plan to allow commerce to move freely across the borders with Mexico and Canada. Reagan loved the idea. He mentioned it in his announcement for the presidency in 1979 and in his first State of the Union. The North American Accord, of course, was the original seed that spawned the North American Free Trade Agreement, or NAFTA. NAFTA became the common thread with President Clinton, who later championed it. It established a U.S., Mexican, and Canadian free-trade zone, which became one of the major advancements of globalization.

These Reagan meetings took place at the tail end of what I call "the ugly decade"—the 1970s. Everything about the seventies—the economics, the foreign policy, the music, even the fashion—was ugly. Remember, this was just after the humiliating end of the Vietnam War. It was less than a decade after a scandal-plagued President Richard Nixon was forced out of office. The sense still lingered that the 1963 Kennedy assassination had robbed the nation of its innocence, and its promise.

One reason the world is curved is that today's median-aged voters in the United States don't remember the difficulties of this period. Today they can't imagine a less than fully employed economy with low inflation and low interest rates. Thus, they look at globalization's downsides with not enough appreciation of its upsides in helping the U.S. economy pull itself out of the 1970s period of economic heartache.

In the 1970s, a group called "the Club of Rome," which was made up of the world's leading economists, theorized that the beleaguered world economy was bumping up against limits to growth. The economy, in other words, had reached its limit in job creation.

Several years before, New York City had barely escaped bankruptcy. Apartments in the ritzy West Side residential building known as the Dakota, where John Lennon was living when he was murdered, today sell for $10 million to $20 million. Back then, they were being given away for $100,000.

Two Middle East oil cutoffs forced the United States into gas lines. A reckless Federal Reserve policy produced mortgage rates of 20 percent, double-digit inflation, and unemployment rates that topped 10 percent (compared, for instance, to 5 percent at the beginning of 2008 with mortgage rates below 6 percent).

In this post–Vietnam/Watergate era, people lost confidence in government. This is because in large part government policymakers had lost control of inflationary expectations. In 1972, the Dow Jones Industrial Average reached 1,000 but closed at the end of the decade at roughly 800. This drop amounted to not just a 20 percent loss, but negative returns year after year for many years. This represented the worst, most prolonged bear market of the last half-century.

When a stock market declines, the bond market usually rallies. By the late 1970s, incredibly both often declined simultaneously because of rising inflationary expectations. A corporate and public pension fund crisis also looked imminent. During this period, American companies were being ridiculed as dinosaurs.

In the United States, inflation, through a process of "tax bracket creep," had given middle-class families the individual tax rates once reserved for the superrich, so we urged Reagan, if he became president, to reduce those stifling tax rates immediately. He reduced all tax rates, including the top marginal rate, which had been 70 percent on personal income. Today, few Washington politicians in either party, except for the most ideologically strident, argue for returning to that top tax rate of 70 percent. It was a tax rate that was financially suffocating middle-class taxpayers. The only winners were firms that specialized in creative tax sheltering.

British historian Paul Johnson summed up the 1970s as "America's suicide attempt." What I remember is a national psyche quickly losing purpose. But as I'll demonstrate, the 1980s and 1990s produced a renaissance of American confidence and optimism about the future. All of which brings up two important questions about today's situation: Could America and the world be slowly returning to a period as economically devastating as the 1970s? And is the phrase "the seventies" even relevant to most voters today?

Of all the experts who lived through this period, Alan Greenspan enjoyed the sharpest sense of the new 1980s paradigm that began to transform the American economic system under Reagan. This was again a shift that went into hyperdrive a decade later under Clinton.

For most of two decades, from 1990 onward, my business partner Manley Johnson and I would meet Greenspan fairly regularly for breakfast in the chairman's private dining room, which had a beautiful view of Washington's Mall. Greenspan never offered any useful information about his monetary policy goals. He went to almost absurd lengths not to tip his hand. Our discussions were fascinating all the same.

In the early 1990s, at one of our breakfasts, I asked the chairman what he made of Reagan's significance as an economic policymaker. Greenspan's take reflected a unique outlook. He said the moment he knew a paradigm shift had fully occurred was when Reagan did something highly unusual and enormously risky. In 1982, he fired the air traffic control union (PATCO—Professional Air Traffic Controllers Organization) members. They had tried to shut down the nation's airports with what White House lawyers considered an illegal strike.

Almost all of the president's advisers warned Reagan of the pitfalls of firing a union. The potential for a European-style labor shutdown across the board threatened to bring all U.S. transportation systems to a halt. This would cripple the American economy, quickly throwing tens of thousands of Americans out of work. After offering a last—and unsuccessful ultimatum to go back to work, he fired the union anyway. The entire world held its breath. No economically devastating European-style shutdown occurred.

Greenspan told me he knew immediately that the episode represented a political turning point for America. Dinosaur-like American businesses would face a new climate of political and economic flexibility that would enable the restructuring necessary to compete globally. Reagan had forced a change in market expectations. The issue was not that unions were evil or lacked a role in a modern economy; the issue was whether a political consensus existed in America to allow bloated American companies to aggressively restructure. The outcome completely changed U.S. management-labor relations.

Here's the key point. Little that happened during this transition period reflected one-way partisanship. Democratic congressional efforts going back to the 1960s paved the way for Reagan's deregulation in the 1980s. It was, moreover, a Republican-appointed Federal Reserve chairman, Arthur Burns (bowing to political pressure from the Nixon administration), who initiated the early stages of the disastrous 1970s inflation. And it was a Democrat, Senator Lloyd Bentsen of Texas, as chairman of the Joint Economic Committee in the late 1970s, with Jack Albertine as staff adviser, who floated the idea throughout Washington policy circles of addressing the problem of tax bracket creep. Bentsen authored the so-called 10-5-3 tax depreciation proposal, which became a main feature in Reagan's 1981 tax plan. He later became Bill Clinton's first secretary of the Treasury.

Notice that Bentsen addressed the issue of tax bracket creep when Ronald Reagan, as the centerpiece of his economic policy, was still talking about the so-called Chicago Welfare Queen. This was a mythic figure often mentioned in Reagan's speeches throughout the 1970s who collected eighty-five separate welfare checks. Thus, she was somehow blamed for all of America's economic ills, a ridiculous assertion.

But no Democrat performed as a greater champion of globalization, entrepreneurial capitalism, and freely flowing capital markets than Bill Clinton. He thrived on free trade and rocketed the globalization argument to new heights and a highly successful economy. Clinton surrounded himself with Wall Street internationalists such as Robert Rubin, free-market economists such as Harvard's Larry Summers (who, incidentally, served on the staff of the White House Council of Economic Advisors when Reagan was president), and many other officials who fully supported the globalization model.

Indeed, Clinton surpassed Ronald Reagan as a free trader. He certainly far outperformed Reagan's successor, George H. W. Bush. Despite his free-trade credentials, Ronald Reagan, in the last years of his presidency, was bogged down with the Iran-Contra scandal. During this period, he allowed the share of U.S. imports subject to some version of restraint to jump from 12 percent to 24 percent by 1989. By contrast, in his 1997 State of the Union address, Clinton called for "the authority now to conclude new trade agreements that open markets. . . . We need not shrink from the challenge of the global economy."

Over the initial objections of the First Lady and some key advisers, Clinton pushed for adoption of NAFTA. Though some of my Clintonite friends disagree, I believe NAFTA symbolically became Clinton's air traffic control issue—a pro-globalization symbolic message to world markets. Clinton's tireless efforts to enact NAFTA telegraphed to the financial markets that the paradigm shift begun in the 1980s would both continue and deepen.

During the 2008 Democratic presidential primaries, unions and the more liberal side of the Democratic Party attacked the Clinton administration for its support of NAFTA. What these critics neglected to mention was that from NAFTA's enactment in 1993 to 2001, U.S. employment grew from 120 million to 135 million. Five years after NAFTA's enactment, the U.S. unemployment rate hit a historic low of 3.8 percent. This was a level once considered by most economists to be theoretically unachievable.

Today former Clinton officials react defensively (I believe too defensively) to criticism of their pro-globalization policies. A few have tried to rewrite history—or at least their role in that history. Instead, they should be responding that if the world rejects those policies, they will be risking nothing less than the financial health of the global economy.

In the United States, both political parties are running away from the free-trade position. The GOP in Congress, which during recent decades had joined as a significant member of the free-trade coalition, has faded into the woodwork on the trade issue. Fred Bergsten, the

Carter administration official who went on to found the Peterson Institute for International Economics, the leading think tank in the field of global economics, makes an amusing point about Republicans on trade. States Bergsten: "The greatest loss to U.S. trade policy in the past decade was the political demise of conservative House Republican firebrand Tom DeLay (R-TX). Only thanks to 'The Hammer' [DeLay's nickname] did any trade legislation get through Congress. When running the House [during the period the GOP was in charge from 1994 until January 2007], DeLay kept the rolls open; he bought votes; and he cleared the legislation by sometimes a margin of only one or two votes." Today there are no Tom DeLay tough guys on free trade left in the Republican Party. The same is true for the Democratic Party.

All of this talk of a Reagan-Clinton policy consensus, of course, begs the issue of fiscal policy. Didn't Reagan cut tax rates and Clinton raise them? The truth is not that simple. Begin with the fact that both political parties play fast and loose with Bill Clinton's fiscal policies. Many Republicans, for example, talk as if, when Bill Clinton raised the top individual tax rate from 28 to 35 percent (38 percent for super-high-income taxpayers), the economy went into recession. Just the opposite was the case.

By the same token, many Democrats have yet to acknowledge that the higher tax rates caused a distorting shift in top corporate executive compensation (under Clinton's 1993 tax bill, companies could no longer deduct executive salaries in excess of $1 million). These highly compensated executives sought to avoid paying the higher taxes through questionable use of stock options, which exploded in use. For accounting purposes during what became known as the Enron era, many top corporate executives gave themselves these options as compensation, instead of large taxable salaries, because incentive-based pay was exempt from the limitations. The entire episode is a prime example of the law of unintended consequences. What's clear is that beyond a certain tipping point in the marginal rate of taxation, the affluent deploy enormous legal efforts to avoid the additional tax.

There is one other point about Clinton's tax policy seldom mentioned. In 1997, at the start of the Internet dot-com bubble period, Bill Clinton quietly signed legislation that reduced the capital gains rate from 28 to 20 percent, a whopping 30 percent drop.

Fred Goldberg, the former IRS commissioner, makes the case that U.S. tax policy the last forty years has remained relatively seamless, and thus any abrupt change in the tax system could significantly disrupt financial markets. If this all sounds bizarre, imagine again being the Martian just landed on planet Earth not having heard the decades of partisan rhetoric to the contrary. Examining the facts, Democratic president John F. Kennedy would appear to have been the champion of capital flows. His efforts led to the cutting of the top individual tax rate from 90 to 70 percent, along with enactment of the investment tax credit for business (he also initiated the first round of multilateral trade negotiations called the Kennedy Round). Reagan eliminated the investment tax credit but reduced individual rates further. Clinton raised the top individual tax rates some but signed legislation dramatically reducing the capital gains rate (while announcing a series of new free-trade agreements that was bullish for capital markets). Goldberg's point is that it would be hard to deny that the overall trend since the 1960s has been toward tax policies that favor the flow of entrepreneurial capital. Moreover, tax policy for individuals has largely avoided the destructive politics of class warfare.

True, a lot of political observers argue that Clinton pursued his policies as a result of a cynical political strategy of "triangulation"—attempting to co-opt some of the core beliefs of the opposition party to his political advantage. But who cares about his motivation? For Clinton, the strategy worked; he became the first Democrat since Franklin Delano Roosevelt to win two full terms in the White House.

More important, if the economic policies of Bill Clinton are swept out of Washington in favor of policies anathema to entrepreneurial capital, that will represent a significant financial market event. As liberal economist Jeff Faux of the Economic Policy Institute, with a bit of hyperbole, noted just after the big Republican congressional losses of

2006: "We are at a point where the Reagan era might be finally over, *including the eight years of Bill Clinton.*" This potential political shift is a prime reason the world today is dangerously curved.

Today the U.S. political community is about to engage in a tax debate. This book is not intended as a treatise on taxation. To a certain extent, in any society voters should be encouraged to set the rates of taxation—and to live with the consequences, good or bad. But it is important that the debate reflect two realities: First, that any tax change that destroys America's entrepreneurial revolution would represent the height of idiocy. This is particularly crucial given the brutal competition the United States faces today in the global economy. And second, so too would be any discussion of taxes that fails to reflect America's fiscal challenge.

In the current debate, there is already a misperception that if only the "wealthy" in America pay more in taxes, America's fiscal nightmare will go away. This is misleading in light of the numbers. Each 1 percent increase in the top individual tax rate, as columnist David Brooks pointed out in the *New York Times*, yields only roughly $6 billion in revenue. This is a drop in the bucket in the context of the massive fiscal threat looming over the horizon. That threat can be measured in the trillions of dollars.

And what are the dimensions of that threat? Robert Samuelson of the *Washington Post* offers a useful encapsulation: From 2000 to 2030, the sixty-five-and-over U.S. population will more than double as the baby boomers continue to retire. Retirees will expand from thirty-five million to seventy-two million, or to 20 percent of the population. Spending on the big programs geared to the needs of the elderly—Social Security, Medicare, and Medicaid—today costs $1.1 trillion, or 40 percent of the federal budget (more than twice defense spending). By the year 2030, the cost of these programs will jump dramatically, consuming 75 percent of the budget, or more than $2 trillion.

Therefore, class warfare talk about soaking the superrich to solve this financial mess may make for a clever political tag line. But the rhetoric reflects the ultimate in political cynicism. The reason is that there aren't enough superrich people to foot the bill. Or put another way, a lot of Americans of both political parties who have worked hard to become affluent would be shocked to learn that Washington considers them as part of the Warren Buffett superrich class expected to carry the load in meeting the coming revenue gap.

A 2008 Morgan Stanley investment report noted that in the United States, a nation of three hundred million citizens, fewer than nineteen thousand households enjoy immediately available, investable (non–real estate, non-retirement-related) financial assets of $25 million or higher. In other words, the number of American heads of households with liquid net worth of $25 million or more could fit into New York's Madison Square Garden for an NBA basketball game. Instead, most Americans considered rich actually have accumulated relatively tiny fortunes, usually the result of successful small businesses, law partnerships, and specialized service-oriented firms. They would be stunned to be included in Warren Buffett's megarich class of people expected to easily pick up the tab for an entitlement nightmare the cost of which will run in the trillions.

In any upcoming U.S. tax legislation, tinkering with the tax code is one thing; opening the door to a new era of pitting one group of Americans against another is a very different can of worms. One thing is certain about class warfare: It is poisonous for today's highly mobile global financial markets. Once begun, class warfare is hard to stop. Indeed, avoiding class warfare was one of the remarkable feats of the Clinton era. During that period, the high-earning, jobs-producing, entrepreneurial sector was championed by Washington's political elite because of its track record in expanding employment.

As a side point, perhaps the champion of class warfare rhetoric is, ironically, the word's greatest investor, Warren Buffett. After amassing one of the world's largest fortunes, Buffett now makes the argument that he is grossly undertaxed. If he had his way, he would be paying far more to the federal government through higher marginal rates of taxation. So would other affluent Americans.

I can appreciate Buffett's concern for America's fiscal imbalances, but his policy prescriptions place him in an awkward position. There is something in the genetic makeup of highly successful risk-takers that once a certain level of success is achieved, they find themselves subconsciously trying to keep others out. Once in, they quickly feel the urge to close the door behind them. I see this in the highly competitive hedge fund world. All the big success stories have no problem with the setting up of higher governmental barriers to entering the business. This includes massive government red tape that requires prohibitively high legal fees. The red tape and legal fees keep potential newcomers out of the business.

Today, Buffett conveniently calls for massive tax hikes on capital *after* he has accumulated his own fortune. This situation reminds me of the environment in most exclusive country clubs. Those with the so-called new money often become the most snobbish and the most determined to keep others out. They don't intend to be that way; it is just something that seems to be in the genetic makeup of newly successful people.

In the case of Buffett, his actions also reflect an inconsistent approach to America's fiscal problems. Several years ago, he pledged the bulk of his fortune to the Bill & Melinda Gates Foundation, a private entity. This is a bit strange because with the U.S. government in debt, why wouldn't he have pledged his estate instead to the U.S. Department of Health and Human Services? Or to the U.S. Treasury? Or to the United Nations, a global governmental unit, as his fellow billionaire Ted Turner did a decade earlier? Buffett chose a private foundation run by Bill Gates because it is likely to be ten to twenty times more productive than a government bureaucracy. Buffett curiously chose the private route as the repository for his immense fortune at a time when the U.S. federal government and many state governments are in fiscal trouble and could have benefited from his largesse.

Today's class warfare politicians are betting that Americans have some deep-seated resentment toward those who are financially successful. The fact is Americans traditionally have admired entrepreneurial risk-takers—from Henry Ford to Bill Gates to Steve Jobs, and yes, to Warren Buffett—who build major fortunes.

What the average American resents is the perception that the system is closed to newcomers, rigged to keep things frozen in place. They have accepted the dynamic process of entrepreneurial risk and failure. But they don't understand why, for example, private equity firms receive special tax considerations when young, start-up firms pay a tax rate twice as high. They resent the perception that rich, powerful insiders can go to Washington and come away with sweet deals. But there is no denying that a majority of Americans have willingly accepted a system the last quarter-century that has handsomely rewarded extraordinarily entrepreneurial initiative at relatively low tax rates. In particular, they hardly resent the image of a young Warren Buffett, a boy of modest beginnings who grew up delivering the *Washington Post*, moved to Omaha, became the world's greatest investor, bought a large stake in that same newspaper, and now sits on its board of directors. They'd call that now immensely wealthy individual a true American hero.

Whether this political tolerance of wealth creation continues is a pivotal question. Global financial market participants wonder what's up in America. Recently a group of British parliamentarians visiting Washington stunned me with the following observation: "Something's changed. Americans for the first time seem infatuated with class warfare," one of the parliamentarians said. The rest agreed.

These parliamentarians were not imagining this seminal shift. Washington's political elite has begun to tease financial markets with the rhetoric of class war populism. It is a dangerous game, but not for the reasons many conservatives offer, which usually center on the fact that the top 10 percent of U.S. income earners account for a whopping 75 percent of federal income tax revenues; they also rake in a significant percentage of the national income produced. Instead, it is a dangerous game because class warfare policies that restrict or scare global capital can lead to the loss of entrepreneurial risk-taking—and thus bring about less job creation, and less overall economic vitality. Moreover, a climate of class warfare is highly conducive to nasty financial panics that risk seriously undermining the entire economic system.

One of the prime reasons the global investment community has overlooked America's obvious policy flaws these last decades, including its fiscal imbalances, is precisely because the United States has been a hothouse of entrepreneurial innovation. America has been the one, reliable platform where the world's creative risk-takers could strike out on their own. Some made huge fortunes, but even more important, these entrepreneurs helped to spur on strong economic growth, which translated into a record number of new American jobs.

None of this is to deny the anxiety produced by free trade and globalized financial markets. Polls show that even after years of low unemployment and robust stock markets, Americans are anxious about their economic future. This anxiety has heightened with the economic slowdown. Restructuring and downsizing are still unfortunate realities in our largest corporations. Real wages of the U.S. workforce remain stagnant. The fact that unemployment is generally lowest when trade is aggressively expanding remains a counterintuitive concept difficult for many people to comprehend.

In recent years, Americans have spent more on imports than they have paid in taxes. As a result, there is a sense that despite several decades of building enormous prosperity, Americans have lost control of their economic destiny. It is not surprising that even those most supportive of globalization are hedging their political bets.

For example, Robert Rubin is a former head of Goldman Sachs, a former Treasury secretary, the Democratic Party's intellectual leader in all things economic, and a true internationalist by profession. He surprised the Washington policymaking community as early as 2006 with a speech at the twenty-fifth anniversary of the Peterson Institute for International Economics. Rubin stunned most of the largely free-trade Democratic audience by arguing that it is naive to believe in "comparative advantage" anymore. In other words, he questioned the fundamental premise of free trade (and globalization) on which liberals and conservatives have for decades largely agreed. Afterward, many expressed hope that this comment was more a fleeting, aberrational thought, not a call to arms.

As a presidential candidate, Hillary Clinton felt forced to distance herself from many of her husband's pro-globalization positions. Reflecting changing political attitudes, she brought former House majority leader Richard Gephardt, the leader of Washington's anti-globalization forces, into her inner strategy team. But to confuse matters, she also listened to some of her husband's former pro-globalization advisers. This included Gene Sperling. Sperling adheres to his pro-globalization positions, but acknowledges that the anxieties produced by globalized markets need to be addressed. Lest this sound partisan, the leaderless Republicans on Capitol Hill are not better on globalization issues and, in some cases, may be far worse.

Clinton's Treasury secretary after Rubin, and current Obama economic adviser, Lawrence Summers, is the most interesting figure in this crowd. Like Sperling, he still retains his pro-globalization credentials, but argues, rightly so, that the "share of the pie may even be shrinking for vast segments of the middle class." After his stint at Treasury, Summers became president of Harvard University. He was subsequently bounced from the job (in part because of an artless administrative style, but also, I believe, as a kind of extreme left-wing payback for the Clinton administration's pro-globalization posture, of which Summers was a champion).

Summers was an intriguing, sometimes amusing policymaker precisely because he relied on raw intellect with little regard for the traditional social norms. In the early 1990s, for instance, years before his Treasury days, Summers served as chief economist of the World Bank. One evening, I had arranged for the visiting finance ministers of the so-called Four Tigers of the Pacific Rim (South Korea, Taiwan, Singapore, and Hong Kong) to meet with what I described as "the half-dozen most important economists in Washington." I included Summers in this exclusive club.

The dinner took place on a late summer evening at the Jefferson Hotel, four blocks due north of the White House. I had chosen a small, ornate dining room just off the lobby. We had a few quick cocktails before sitting down for the dinner discussion. As we did, I noticed an empty seat. "No Larry Summers," I mentioned to the others. I suggested that he had probably been held up by the sudden torrential rainstorm that had just blown into town. "Larry's waiting it out. These vicious Washington summer storms quickly come and go," I said as I peered out the window and watched sheets of rain coming down mercilessly.

Several minutes later, the door to the dining room slowly opened. A nervous waiter with a deeply worried look on his face appeared. I rose and moved quickly toward the door. "There is a strange man outside who says he belongs at this dinner," said the waiter, "but based on his looks I'm thinking we should turn him away." Just then, a soaking wet figure brushed past the waiter to enter the room. It was Summers who stood there, looking as if he had belly flopped into the middle of a swimming pool. He had walked through the deluge the eight blocks from the World Bank. The waiter clearly assumed he was some homeless soul in search of a hot meal. The Singapore finance minister looked particularly perplexed. Summers stood there dripping, his tan suit soaking wet. The brilliant Summers sat down for dinner seemingly unaware that a puddle was quickly forming at his feet. The rest of the room sat stunned.

Yet appearances can be deceiving. Despite an unusual personal and social style, Summers was the least partisan, most intellectually daring, and most courageous financial official I've met in more than thirty years in Washington. A diamond in the rough, only Summers, a democratically appointed Treasury secretary, took on the questionable financial leveraging practices of one of the Democratic Party's biggest sources of fund-raising cash, Fannie Mae.

For decades, the politically untouchable Fannie Mae enjoyed an implicit assumption in the markets that the U.S. Treasury guaranteed its huge portfolio of low-income mortgage loans. This allowed the firm to borrow at much lower interest rates than its competition, but created a dangerous market distortion by encouraging excessive borrowing. For Summers, partisan maneuvering was significantly less intellectually appealing than the pursuit of a policy breakthrough—or, for the lack of a better word, the old-fashioned pursuit of honest policy. In this case, a firm needed to be pulled back from the edge, just as the broader banking sector less than a decade later needed to be pulled back from its infatuation with subprime mortgages.

All of which is why the question for the Obama administration in coming years is this: Will the new class warfare protectionists take over? Or will the Clinton crowd, including people like Summers who favor liberalized markets, albeit with reforms, continue to influence the debate? Because signs show the free-trade, liberalized capital market approach of Bill Clinton is being rejected, the United States is about to experience a world that is more curved than ever imagined.

To be sure, Summers and Sperling were correct when they argued, even before the recession, that the middle class has not fully enjoyed the benefits of the global wealth machine. In today's financial system, where the wage-earning sector itself is shrinking, middle-class wages alone may never be enough to keep families from financially backsliding. This problem will remain a reality regardless of any government-sponsored programs, including hikes in the minimum wage and targeted educational benefits.

Moreover, the gap between the haves and have-nots will likely continue to grow if globalization is allowed to continue once the economy fully recovers. This is because there is an exponential aspect to wealth creation. In the 1950s, Albert Einstein was asked by a religious activist, "Do you believe in miracles?" Einstein responded: "I believe in the miracle of compound interest." Stated in global terms, wealth on a worldwide scale will resume growing exponentially if governments avoid breaking the global wealth machine.

Yet I know of no reasonable person—liberal or conservative—who believes a further increase in income disparity of any significant magnitude represents anything but a political and social house of cards. Nothing, however, about this debate fits into a neat little box. Historically, schemes in the United States for massive income redistribution (the high tax rates of the 1970s come to mind) have tended to serve as huge, abrupt disincentives to economic growth. And as a result, the entire economic system becomes poorer with fewer jobs. Moreover, schemes aimed at aggressive welfare intervention have destroyed people's dignity, robbing them of any sense of accomplishment. That is why Bill Clinton, as president, again to the consternation of some of his political allies, signed significant welfare reform legislation aimed at freeing the working poor from the indignities of being caught in a trap of welfare dependence (while maintaining a system of benefits for those truly in need).

In the end, the political tensions created by vastly unequal income distribution will likely be difficult to measure and predict, and even harder to control. Highly entrepreneurial economies create big winners and losers. The challenge comes down to how to dramatically expand society's base of winners. The best way to do that is to expand the base of the investor class. In fact, bringing more people into the economy as capital owners may in the long run be the only means politically of saving capitalism.

For the middle class, wages alone are not enough to prosper in today's new economy. Moreover, because wages generally are tied in some form to GDP growth, the United States government needs to modernize the process by which it measures the economy. Today, official GDP figures may fail to capture fully the economy's true growth and thus wages may have been for decades unfairly restrained. The service sector produces between 70 and 80 percent of private sector GDP, while manufacturing accounts for about 13 percent. The government provides an incredibly descriptive analysis of manufacturing. Yet its measurement of the service sector is bizarrely vague. That's due to the fact that for half a century, the government only had to measure manufacturing. Only in recent years has the service sector become the dominant part of the U.S. economy. As a result, it is not surprising that fifty-year-old measuring techniques may be insufficient for measuring the new economy's primary growth engine. And this is to the detriment of the wage earner.

Until the credit crisis and recession, the global economy had boomed to unprecedented levels. Mere wage earners, however, relative to those with a global stock portfolio, didn't participate in this wealth creation. They were left at a huge disadvantage by having no way to benefit from worldwide economic growth. The more affluent bought international stocks and global mutual funds and fully participated in the global productivity boom while the mere wage earner in most cases couldn't. In other words, because of financial globalization, some of the profits from stock market investments represented claims on explosive *future* growth outside the United States, which was totally out of the reach of the noninvestor. Because of the rise of globalized markets, the link therefore between national GDP and national wealth has been weakened, widening the income gap.

That is why to have benefited fully from advancements in worldwide productivity gains that resulted from globalization, working-class families needed to be invested for the long term in the global financial markets. This is true despite the market's collapse. The base of capital ownership needs to be expanded by some means of encouraging working-class families to invest based on a global strategy.

Republican candidates regularly evoke the name of Ronald Reagan as almost a mythic figure of political perfection. Yet Reagan, a former Democrat and union leader, would never have presided over an explosion in wealth creation without serious efforts to try to include all Americans in the bounty. It was in the same spirit that Reagan in the 1980s supported something called "urban enterprise zones." These zones dramatically lowered or eliminated tax rates in blighted inner-city neighborhoods to encourage small business job creation. Congressman Jack Kemp introduced this enterprise zone legislation in Congress. I was fortunate to be able to spearhead the effort at the staff level. Working with Democratic congressman Bob Garcia of the South Bronx as the cosponsor, we fashioned legislation and promoted it to the urban community and other special interest groups. At the same time, we sold the concept to Ronald Reagan. Today the enterprise zone concept has spread throughout the country, particularly at the state and local levels.

I agree with Barack Obama when he said in March 2008: "The core of our economic success is the fundamental truth that each American does better when all Americans do better; that the well-being of American business, its capital markets, and the American people are aligned."

That is why dramatically expanding the base of the so-called investor class is essential if capitalism is to survive. That is why in any future U.S. tax reform effort, I would recommend the elimination of taxes on financial market investments by low- and middle-income Americans. I would also support the proposal of former Democratic senator Bill Bradley and his tax strategist, Gina Despres, that would have the federal government give every child at birth an "American Birthright Account." The program would provide a newborn an amount of money to be invested in the financial markets for use later in life. In other words, at birth they'd receive a lump financial sum to, as Despres puts it, "allow the next generation to benefit from decades of financial compounding as much as the highly affluent do."

As they join the workforce, these new minicapitalists can add to the account and watch their earnings increase further. By way of reference, a 7.5 percent compounded return on $5,000 grows to nearly a half-million dollars in sixty-five years. For most Americans, who are not savers by nature, this financial arrangement would represent the difference between long-term financial hardship and success.

The British have just such a system to encourage newborns to become capitalists by giving them a platform for investment. Starting in 2004, British newborns receive 250 pounds ($500) each (up to 500 pounds or $1,000 for infants from low-income families) from the government. To the surprise of policymakers, even in the low-income communities, families and friends have contributed more than three times the initial government investment since the program started in 2004.

In the United States, four million babies are born each year. A program that contributed $1,000 to each of these newborns would amount to little more than a rounding error in the federal budget. For an inconsequential sum, an entire generation would participate in the dream of being a capital owner. Even more important, this would create a new generation of capitalists with a platform for future investments.

Today the future of entrepreneurial capitalism is politically unpredictable fundamentally because the base of financial capital ownership is so small. Meanwhile, the wealth gap has widened. As a result, globalization's political base of support remains tenuous at best. Here is one astonishing statistic that makes the point: Today 40 percent of Americans do not have adequate liquid savings to live at the poverty level for three months, according to New York University's Edward N. Wolff. For a family of four, living at that level for that amount of time would require $5,300 in savings.

America's low savings rate, by the way, reflects both the unequal nature of wealth distribution and a dangerous overconfidence in the sustainability of the U.S. economy. Over the last quarter-century, people had come to believe the illusion that low rates of unemployment would last forever regardless of what policymakers do—a situation that has produced waves of shock and disillusionment in today's new world of heightened financial volatility, weaker output, and less job creation.

Instead of searching for ways of bringing more people into the entrepreneurial capitalist system, however, most of our leaders play political games. Half blame globalization and the financial market itself and recommend reckless protectionist and class warfare policies that would put the international financial system at risk. Their policy recommendations, if implemented, would reduce global wealth creation and increase poverty. This use of inflammatory populist rhetoric is already destabilizing to financial markets.

The other half, however, isn't much better. They proudly propose useless tax deductions in the form of tax credits for education and worker training. But because 40 percent of Americans pay no federal income taxes (and 20 percent pay a negative income tax in that they receive a net amount from the government), these wonderful-sounding changes to the tax structure are meaningless for large segments of society.

American policymakers have no choice but to devise some creative means of dramatically expanding the financial capital ownership base.

This is a pivotal time in history when both liberals and conservatives need to think big—as when policymakers produced the Homestead Act in the nineteenth century (signed by President Lincoln in 1862, it gave each interested American free title to 160 acres of land in the American West) and the Social Security Act in the twentieth century.

Ultimately, to preserve the political base in support of the capitalist model, policymakers must concentrate on the role of human capital. One U.S. president who understood this was Abraham Lincoln. He was a great proponent of human capital. In his first State of the Union address in 1861, Lincoln said, "Labor is the superior of capital, and deserves much the higher consideration. Capital . . . could never exist if labor did not exist first."

In 1960, Theodore Schultz, who later won the Nobel Prize in economics, argued in a famous address to the American Economic Association for the central role in a modern economy of "human capital": "Our tax laws everywhere discriminate against human capital. Although the stock of such capital has become large, and even though it is obvious that human capital, like other forms of reproducible capital, depreciates, becomes obsolete, and entails maintenance, our tax laws are all but blind on these matters."

For decades in tax policy, Washington policymakers of both political parties worshipped at the tax shrine of business depreciation with generous tax incentives for machinery. The educating and, if necessary, retraining of human capital, however, was treated as almost an afterthought in the policymaking process, usually the last-minute trade-off, needed as political cover, to move the business tax provisions through Congress. My point is that for the economy to prosper in the long term, the tax code must not value and honor machinery over people. It is worth noting that because the services sector now produces 70 to 80 percent of GDP, "knowledge capital" is becoming even more important than physical and financial capital.

Notice I am not talking merely about increased spending on government retraining programs and enhanced education, as important as those goals are. American workers themselves at times seem unaware that they are participating in a global competition where continual reinvention of their own firms with new ideas is essential for success. This sense of detachment is not surprising because typical wage earners have enjoyed little of the financial profits from the new global economy. But there is another, more social or cultural phenomenon also holding many people back. Recent studies show that a skill-based educational inequality throughout society is rising such that even when funds are available for higher education, a segment of society lacks the thinking and verbal skills to step forward to take advantage of the educational opportunities offered. The skills gap results often from the different parenting approaches at various income levels, with affluent parents more encouraging of the nurturing of skills relating to thought processes and verbalization. The less affluent, because of economic considerations, often are simply away from home more, often working two jobs.

In *The New Republic*, analyst Brink Lindsey argued, however, that today's skill-based inequality should be seen not as "some populist morality play of capitalism run amok" but actually as the outgrowth of the success of the new global economy: "For a generation now, our economy has been creating more opportunities for the productive use of highly developed cognitive skills than there are people able to take advantage of them. . . . Economic development has raced ahead of cultural development; as a result, culture is now acting as a brake on upward mobility. So, instead of railing against the economic system, we need to do a better job of helping people to adapt to it and rise to its challenges. The rules of the game aren't the problem—we just need more skillful players." Put another way, our political leadership needs to better inspire society to find some means of helping families catch up in the skills department.

George Monbiot, in his book *Captive State: The Corporate Takeover of Britain*, argues that the struggle between people and corporations will be the central confrontation of the twenty-first century. While the book is directed at the United Kingdom, its lessons apply equally well to America and other parts of the world.

In Washington today, both political parties concentrate on using tax policy to help existing corporations, usually through more favorable tax treatment of the expensing of capital assets. That's fine, but not enough attention is targeted at the twin goals that are far more important— nurturing the human capital skills of the labor force and igniting an endless stream of entrepreneurial reinvention by new risk-takers.

While the U.S. Congress fixates on defending every last loophole of a tax code geared to existing businesses, what actions do they take to spur on the creation of dynamic, creative firms that don't yet exist—or are on the cusp of creation? These unborn enterprises are the future of the economy's base of employment, reinvention, and prosperity, yet they factor little into Washington's mix of policy concerns.

As is obvious by now, I still believe working-class families, if given the opportunity, want to ride the great financial wave. They want to be transformed from labor workers into capital owners. They want a real stake in the entrepreneurial capitalist system, and they are not resentful of the entrepreneurial success of others so long as the door for wealth creation and opportunity remains open for all. If policymakers fail to understand these dynamics at work, we are likely to see a whole new paradigm emerge. Policymakers worldwide will be confronted with how to manage the new politics of envy. And, once created, these nasty politics may be impossible to contain. It is the ticket to a show in which the house of cards could collapse right before our eyes.

What I hope is also clear is that the U.S. political community, in rejecting the free-trade, liberalized financial market agenda of Bill Clinton, is at risk of creating the conditions for a global financial disaster. At first, we'll see a further loss of global investor confidence in America, followed by a further shrinking of liquidity and credit availability and then a protracted period of stagnant economic growth far below potential. Weaker growth will beget even more protectionist, class warfare rhetoric and policy, which will further shrink confidence in America throughout the international system. That is why when today's politicians dare to be different on the issue of free trade and liberalized capital, they should remember that often dares can be deadly.

America in particular sits at a crucial point in its economic history. Today's politicians have experienced a quarter-century of bipartisan economic success followed by the worst financial crisis since the 1930s and an economic collapse. Now they flirt with protectionist, class warfare policies that would unravel the economy further.

None of this analysis, however, is to suggest that managing the politics of globalization will be easy. As the global economy completes the unwinding of the subprime mortgage mess and struggles to rebound, it appears there will be few heroes and more than a few villains. Indeed, as I'll show in the next chapter, only those politicians with enormous foresight and restraint will be able to resist political demagoguery about the irresponsible, even foolish, ways of the global banking sector in recent years. Indeed, the bankers placed the entire world economy in serious trouble.

9

Surviving and Prospering
in This Age of Volatility

Today the financial world is a very dangerous place and our leaders need to open their eyes. For starters, they need to devise an effective game plan for reducing today's growing global imbalances. They must delve into a discussion of the entitlement nightmare just over the horizon. They need a broad international strategy for dealing with the Chinese financial and manufacturing juggernaut and a more effective understanding of currency relationships. They must devise some means of better understanding the inherent conflicts and tensions between the need to confront the effects of climate change and maintaining the global trading system. They must fashion a credible approach geared to the opportunities and risks of sovereign wealth fund investment. And they need to stop threatening to shrink the world's financial liquidity, and risk a dollar collapse, with reckless protectionist and class warfare policies.

But there is one other problem that may trump all others. Our leadership must reform today's dangerously flawed financial architecture, including the system used to assess and allocate credit. This book began by describing the financial terror of the Great Credit Crisis. It is appropriate that it end with a discussion of the long-term consequences of that crisis. In 2007, as the subprime loans defaulted, doubts about the architecture of the financial system turned a moderately difficult problem into the worst financial panic in decades. The resulting financial wreckage has seriously undermined political support for capitalism itself and threatened the livelihoods of millions of low- and middle-class families globally. True, the financial markets eventually stabilized, yet fundamental problems remain just beneath the surface, which threaten to reappear at any time.

What I am about to describe is a subprime story with few heroes. After the crisis unfolded in August 2007, newspaper headlines blamed the inept bank regulators and their cousins—the forever-behind-the-curve credit rating agencies. Many Wall Street analysts also blamed Federal Reserve monetary policy, believing that the Fed earlier in the decade left short-term interest rates too low for too long and later, and after the crisis hit, responded too late to the difficulties. All of these complaints represent a sideshow—a serious distraction away from those who were by far the most responsible for the crisis—the bankers and investment bankers themselves. Out of sheer greed, they concocted an elaborate, legal, but risky scheme to obscure risk that nearly tanked the world economy.

If financial globalization fails, it is the large financial institutions and their regulators who will bear a large part of the blame. The ugly fact is that their actions left the international financial system dangerously vulnerable.

The conventional wisdom maintains that the subprime crisis was the result merely of the bursting of a worldwide housing bubble. Here's the drill: The prosperity created by the spread of globalization after the fall of the Berlin Wall produced greater competition in global manufacturing and services. This reduced real wages globally, which led to lower inflationary expectations and thus declining long-term interest rates. As a result of historically favorable mortgage interest rates, families in many of the industrialized countries bought houses too aggressively, producing a broad-based housing bubble. As the bubble grew larger, loan officers offered subprime mortgages to people who couldn't remotely qualify and, indeed, found themselves in deep financial trouble when long-term interest rates, and thus mortgage rates, later returned to their higher, historic levels.

Sounds like a reasonable subprime explanation, but the analysis doesn't tell the full story. Under normal conditions, the global financial system could have absorbed the bursting of the housing bubble where the initial subprime exposure in the United States was a mere $200 billion in a global economy worth several hundred trillion dollars. Financial markets for several months might have been bumpy, but things would have returned to normal relatively quickly. Clearly, something else was taking place. There was a problem more fundamental to the integrity of the financial system. That something else was a dubious dual system that the banks and investment banks had set up to hide their exposure to a lot of market risk, including mortgage risk.

What I'm about to tell, therefore, is a tale of greed, hypocrisy, and sheer folly. This is the story of the Great Credit Crisis that the bankers don't want you to know, brought on by the mother of all regulatory failures in realizing what was happening.

The story starts in 1998 after the collapse of the hedge fund Long-Term Capital Management. With great panache, the global banks responded by tightening credit controls over the hedge funds (hedge funds leverage large amounts of capital to trade, often using bank loans). But here's the irony. At the same time, the banks adopted a much looser approach to their own trading desks with weaker defined risk management standards. Not surprisingly, bank risk soared. Hoping to emulate the hedge funds and investment banks, the banks took riskier and riskier bets in search of ever-higher profits.

The financial system has safeguards to control bank risk. The Basel international bank capital adequacy standards, for example, force banks to place more capital on the sidelines as noninvested collateral if the banks want to increase their level of risk. The Basel standards are like an insurance policy to protect the integrity of the global banking system, including bank savings deposits, money market funds, and other financial instruments used by the average citizen. However, the international standards presented the banks with an unattractive choice: either opt for greater risk and larger returns but stockpile higher levels of noninvested capital in case something goes wrong, or accept lower risk and smaller returns, but have more capital that they can put to work in the markets. The banks accepted neither choice, and the results were catastrophic.

To maneuver around this Basel dilemma, the banks (joining the investment banks) set up a kind of dual market. Almost every large financial institution set up independent, off-balance-sheet financial vehicles to obscure risk. Take Citigroup, for example. The outside world, including the bank regulators and credit rating agencies, fixed their eyes on the well-known institution and the bank's visible, on-balance-sheet risk. What the world couldn't see were the less-well-known, independent financial vehicles (often called conduits or structured investment vehicles) that Citigroup set up separate from the parent institution.

Officially, the often ugly liabilities of these independent investment vehicles were not included on the books of the parent institutions. To the surprise of the parent institutions, however, in the eyes of global market traders, the off-balance-sheet vehicles and the large, well-known institutions were the same entity. They were linked by reputation. The bankers never bet on that happening, and what resulted from all this effort to obscure risk was the creation of a ticking time bomb.

But why would a bank set up a separate vehicle not under its ownership or control with the parent bank not listed on the vehicle's balance sheet as a primary beneficiary? The answer comes down to one word: greed. The banks and investment banks created their own private market—a kind of automatic, legal dumping ground with enormous profits to boot.

Here's how the system worked. Traditionally, a bank would lend a buyer the funds to purchase a home and then hold that mortgage for the duration of the loan. During the life of the loan, the bank was responsible for the risk of the mortgage. In the new economy of globalized capital, however, the banks resorted to a different system to come to terms with risk. A bank collected all its loans into a single pool and divided the collected sum into separate pieces called interest income streams. In other words, as noted earlier, the banks *securitized* the loans, selling off the repackaged individual income streams (now called mortgage-backed securities) to the global market. The banks also encouraged their independent, off-balance-sheet vehicles to buy these mortgage-backed securities, some of which held pieces of mortgages that were rated subprime. The large financial institutions made huge fees selling to their own independent investment vehicles these newly packaged mortgage-backed securities.

But then things got complicated. The independent off-balance-sheet vehicles, using the just-purchased mortgage-backed securities as collateral, went to the global credit markets and borrowed money by issuing commercial paper. Commercial paper traditionally has been considered a highly safe form of debt investment and is widely used as one of the safe backbones of money market funds.

When the global housing bubble burst in 2007, global markets suddenly became distrustful of the commercial paper market. This placed many of the off-balance-sheet vehicles immediately in deep financial trouble. Soon the parent banks and investment banks themselves were also in desperate trouble because, again, global traders made no distinction between the parent banks and the independent vehicles. Financial stocks collapsed. Global credit seized up as businesses suddenly found it far more difficult to get financing. The industrialized world economies by the beginning of 2008 began to progressively weaken, led by the U.S. economy.

What the banks did in particular was to adopt a new and dangerous business model in which, so to speak, they no longer held any skin in the game. Using the new financial instruments of securitization, the bankers faced no risk once they had sold the securitized mortgage packages to the off-the-book vehicles. As the lender who decided who would get a loan, the banks no longer had any connection to the borrower, or any need to worry about whether he or she would repay a loan. Instead of engaging in risk *management*, the traditional role of bankers, the new bankers engaged in risk *dispersion*, thinking they had discovered "riskless risk" with the added benefit of enormous profits.

As the high-wire act unfolded, the bank regulators and the credit rating agencies found themselves to be the bigger fools. As firms such as Moody's and Standard and Poor's regularly examined the banks, they marveled at the relatively good financial condition of the books of the parent banks, but they completely missed the connection to the off-balance-sheet vehicles, which in many cases were full of subprime exposure. Furthering the problem, the credit rating agencies rated the commercial paper issued by the off-balance-sheet vehicles as ultra-safe. The thinking was that because the debt was securitized (and thus diversified) and tied to real estate, it could never fail. Real estate prices, they thought, would never drop—or at least never drop nationwide.

Financially speaking, the banks thought they had achieved a state of nirvana. In the last couple of quarters before the August 2007 outbreak of the subprime crisis, some large banks were achieving rates of return on equity exceeding 30 percent, a level of financial success that is highly unusual in the banking industry. During that period, the best money managers in the world were achieving half those rates of return. Why the regulators and rating agencies never asked how the bankers could be so successful without resorting to tricks (off-balance-sheet exposure, dangerous leverage) is mind-boggling.

This new financial game is analogous to the system in America for rating colleges and universities. Every year high school seniors look to these ratings, first checking the average college Scholastic Aptitude Test (SAT) score for the university's student body as a whole, to see how they stack up. This sounds like a prudent thing to do, except for one thing. Many of these academic institutions present an incomplete picture of their test scores. Many conveniently omit the scores of certain groups—athletes, minority groups, or certain students with disadvantages. This paints a better, but misleading, picture of that school's testing results. The intention may be worthy—to tell the average, white, middle-class student what it takes to gain admission.

Nonetheless, the picture is deceptive, not to mention unfair to those institutions that play by the rules by listing accurate and complete test scores.

From this point on, the subprime story is familiar. Because of the web of linkages throughout the global system, when people in Ohio could not make their subprime mortgage payments, suddenly a bank in Germany was on its knees. The bank had no U.S. presence, except for the loads of highly rated, but ultimately questionable, U.S. commercial paper it had purchased.

European regulatory authorities, like their American counterparts, were also largely unaware that their banks had significant exposure to separate, off-balance-sheet vehicles chock-full of financial toxic waste. Suddenly money market mutual funds around the world were at risk because of their connection to American securitized debt. The money that average folks thought was ultrasafe suddenly was in question. The Great Credit Crisis was in full bloom.

What was terrifying about the subprime-related crisis is that despite efforts by the central banks to counter the situation, the industrialized world's credit markets continued to contract. Like a deteriorating asthma patient, where the airflow to the lungs continues to dissipate, the wheezing economy gradually began suffocating, desperate for oxygen.

As could be predicted, the international policy community searched desperately for quick-fix solutions. In early 2008, the U.S. Congress passed a tax stimulus package targeting the macroeconomic symptoms of the subprime mortgage mess. With the election of Barack Obama as president, the U.S. Congress quickly enacted the largest fiscal stimulus package in history. Many industrialized-world central banks aggressively reduced short-term interest rates further, with the Federal Reserve leading the way, bringing rates down to near zero percent. Washington politicians predictably marshaled their efforts at dealing only with the immediate *symptoms* of the problem that millions of Americans were at risk of losing their homes and in need of government assistance. They should have also been fixated on the fact that the entire financial system was at greater risk than at any time since the 1930s.

Therefore, despite much policy handwringing, the crisis continued, the wheezing economy having turned beet red and then deep blue from lack of oxygen. What became clear is that the fiscal and monetary remedies were unable to quickly treat a problem that was much more fundamental in nature. At the heart of the Great Credit Crisis was nothing less than a crisis of trust in financial architecture. What was at issue was something that had been brewing long before the bursting housing bubble and subprime crisis arrived on the scene. That something was a growing, widespread, worldwide distrust of the asset-backed securities market. Global financial strategist Harald Malmgren has tagged these securities, which include mortgage-backed securities, credit default swaps (a kind of insurance policy for mortgage debt), and a broad range of credit derivatives, with the clever name "trust me assets." They represent a central artery in the global economy's bloodstream for credit allocation. The subprime crisis triggered the clogging of that artery due to a lack of confidence and trust.

In chapter 2, I described how securitization was the necessary evil for assessing risk and distributing entrepreneurial capital. It is a frustratingly sophisticated financial process that both enables and threatens our productive global economy. After the outbreak of the subprime crisis, the credit markets weakened beyond anyone's expectations because the asset-backed securities market experienced essentially a buyers' strike. Global market traders became uncomfortable holding debt instruments, the value of which could not be verified except by the credit rating agencies, which had a miserable track record of success usually based on mathematical models, not direct verification of an asset's creditworthiness. This crisis in confidence instantly produced serious implications for the global economy's credit outlook. One of the economy's major windpipes for financial oxygen had all but closed.

Malmgren describes the situation in more detail: "Over the past decade, there have been a huge number of buyers of asset backed securities, including public and private pension funds, local government financial managers, insurance companies, foreign banks and asset managers, trusts and even hedge funds. . . . Yet the only available measurement of risk and value of these securities was the rating provided by rating agencies. Many buyers, particularly pension funds, were guided by regulatory constraints to follow rating agency criteria. A slow motion train wreck was set in motion in the spring of 2007 when suddenly [rating agency] downgrade after downgrade undermined initial valuations, leaving holders [of asset-backed securities] with illiquid assets."

The outgrowth of this train wreck situation was that the leadership of the large financial institutions panicked. Never did they imagine that because of a sudden lack of trust, the entire asset-backed security market, one of the main arteries of the global credit system, would become illiquid. Yet a lack of trust in these sophisticated financial instruments was expanding worldwide. And it was the financial institutions' own fault for not fully appreciating the potency of the risk with which they were dealing.

During this period, Federal Reserve officials charged to the rescue loading the Fed's own balance sheet with various debt purchases as a means of unclogging the credit system. Worried about repeating the mistake made by the Bank of Japan in the early 1990s at the beginning of Japan's "lost decade," Chairman Bernanke slashed rates faster and deeper than at any time in history. While monetary policy can stabilize the broader financial market to help buy time, however, cutting interest rates can't make investors trust financial investment instruments where the lender has no connection with the borrower. Nor can confidence be quickly restored to a system where financial risk has been offloaded to mysterious, off-balance-sheet vehicles.

By mid-March 2008, Federal Reserve officials found themselves in a panic. Bold slashes in short-term interest rates and other, more directed means of funneling capital to the banks were having only a modest effect. Worse, the investment firm Bear Stearns was teetering on the edge of bankruptcy. A collapse of a major investment bank under the current conditions, Fed officials concluded, could risk unraveling the entire global financial system and send stock markets plummeting, with the global economy not far behind. The U.S. economy was already close to recession. Then on March 16, over the St. Patrick's Day weekend, the Federal Reserve placed the investment bank Bear Stearns and potentially other so-called nonbank financial institutions under the government safety net that, until then, was an emergency device reserved exclusively for the use of Fed-regulated banks. Specifically, the Fed allowed Bear Stearns access to the Fed's Discount Window, which was established during the Great Depression to allow banks access to emergency loans regardless of the quality of their collateral. The Fed, with the backing of the U.S. Treasury, forced the sale of Bear Stearns to J. P. Morgan Chase with the U.S. central bank agreeing to lend to the troubled Wall Street investment firm in exchange for $29 billion in dubious securities.

In essence, the Federal Reserve offered a government guarantee covering the entire financial system, not just the banks, with the Fed or some other regulatory body potentially assuming a far greater regulatory role over financial markets. Given the severity of the immediate crisis, including the potential collapse of the entire financial market, it may be the Fed had no other choice. But whether a blanket government guarantee in the long run expands or restricts lending throughout the economy remains to be seen. In a government-guaranteed system, some regulatory force needs to protect the public interest. Yet the regulatory community, including the Fed, hardly enjoys a distinguished track record in the measuring of risk and the understanding of the flow of liquidity. Can a new, supersized U.S. regulatory agency, wherever located, do any better? The wizards within the financial markets have continually demonstrated an awesome ability to find legal means to skirt regulatory constraints.

Economic correspondent Greg Ip noted, "The Fed is being asked to do a job that may be beyond anyone's ability: Identify and avoid a crisis in advance." Adds Harvard's Martin Feldstein: "Supervising the very complex derivative products of the banks and of the rest of the financial system would be an enormous technical challenge. The [financial] institutions themselves—paying very high salaries and having their own survival at risk—got it wrong. Would the Fed get it right?"

The truth is, all the regulators in the subprime debacle were caught asleep at the switch, but cannot be blamed completely. A well-intentioned government bureaucrat is no match for the kind of creative and clever market wizards, and their lawyers, who begin searching for legal means around any regulatory constraint the instant the regulations are put in place. Today a senior Securities and Exchange Commission (SEC) officer earns between $143,000 and $216,000 per year. Even junior executive decision-makers at Goldman Sachs (at least before the recession set in) garnered annual compensation packages in the millions of dollars. In 2006 average Goldman employee compensation was $622,000, with some administrative assistants and secretaries earning more than $200,000.

The danger now, however, is the tendency of regulators, once caught asleep at the switch, to try to overcompensate, usually in the form of overregulation. In financial markets, overregulation can be deadly to liquidity. For the United States, the burdens of overregulation have already weakened New York as a global financial center. Regulatory mistakes could worsen an already deteriorating credit environment. An overreaction could also weaken the dollar further, as highly mobile investors can choose to move their money into less regulated markets.

The U.S. financial services industry had been the envy of the world, one of the few industries where the United States dramatically dominated relative to other countries. Indeed, the foreign financial community has no doubt enjoyed seeing the demise of the American financial sector, set in a regulatory straitjacket of passivity, having lost its edge. And the situation will worsen unless necessary reforms to achieve greater transparency and risk management are surgically precise and sensitive to avoid threatening the larger financial system as a wealth-enhancing force. Yet the bankers and investment bankers have indeed behaved badly in a system in need of careful reform. Clearly, there is need for a platform for standardizing the pricing of securitized assets. There must also be new mechanisms for increased transparency with a better understanding of the nature of market risk and excessive leveraging. Off-the-balance-sheet independent vehicles must be banned.

Some free market fundamentalists have reacted to the subprime debacle with the knee-jerk suggestion that a sober review of the financial regulatory framework would dangerously threaten to unwind the entire financial system. Yet even some of globalization's greatest champions, including scholars such as Jagdish Bhagwati and Frederic Mishkin, have from the start warned of the need for an always careful approach to our highly volatile, and sometimes destructive, global capital markets. It is important to remember that while not all investment banks are the same, two months before the Bear Stearns collapse Morgan Stanley's leverage ratio, 32.6 to 1, was almost as high as Bear Stearns's ratio of 32.8 to 1, according to the *Wall Street Journal*. Merrill Lynch and Lehman used similar proportional levels of leverage.

Yet just as extreme are those who believe the Great Credit Crisis has laid out the welcome mat for a government takeover of the financial system. These enthusiasts seem oblivious to the fact that the crisis resulted to a significant degree from the government's inability to avoid being hoodwinked by the sophisticated financial market strategists and their lawyers in institutions—the bank—that were already heavily regulated. The subprime debacle exposed the inherent weakness in government's ability to understand always-evolving markets.

The distasteful reality, moreover, is that there are no quick fixes for the global credit system's dilemma, which is why the world has become such a dangerous place with so much economic heartache. Creating confidence in today's "trust me assets" took more than a decade to accomplish. Unfortunately, re-creating trust in these sophisticated financial instruments, even after significant reform, will take time. Clearly the world's banks and investment banks need to develop a new framework of understanding of asset-backed securities, making them more transparent and thus easier to price by global market traders. But achieving a return of confidence and thus liquidity to these crucial markets will not result from some quick fix. And neither can the economy thrive without restored confidence in this new means of capital distribution.

Around the world, individual finance ministries are threatening to restrict use of these sophisticated products, including those involving securitization, to a point where the global credit market could further collapse. Meanwhile, the SEC and the Federal Bureau of Investigation (FBI) have launched investigations into whether there has been deception in the makeup and issuance of mortgage-backed securities. The New York attorney general has launched his own investigation into whether firms issuing mortgage-backed securities committed securities fraud.

The good news is that greater investigation of the financial industry will produce greater overall financial transparency. The bad news is that a financial market witch hunt would be like dumping kerosene onto an already raging fire. The global economy could worsen as financial market executives work desperately to avoid civil suits and criminal prosecution at a time when they should be focusing all of their energies on repricing their asset portfolios and returning global credit market conditions to a healthier state. U.S. policymakers are left with a particularly difficult dilemma. The U.S. financial services sector has dominated the world precisely because of its cowboy-like approach, always pushing the envelope of risk and reacting to market developments with rapid-fire decision-making. This is a system that in recent decades has contributed to an American entrepreneurial renaissance, a period of economic excitement and prosperity that has faded with today's economic collapse and crisis of confidence. The nature of this same financial system has terrorized the economic well-being of millions of middle- and low-income homeowners. The danger will intensify as today's class warfare politicians respond with continued assaults on the financial sector itself with no mention of the downside implications in terms of both job creation and economic opportunity in the event an underfunded American financial sector quietly fades into the night.

The reality is that the global credit-contraction horror show could continue for years in one form or another. The IMF estimates that the world faces more than a three-trillion-dollar credit problem, two tril-lion in the United States alone, and those numbers are based on the problems that are currently known. What is clear is that in the coming years of reduced leverage, greater bank capital set-asides, and other new, post-subprime restrictions, the profitability of the entire financial services industry is going to decline. The great unknown is whether this situation will produce a global credit contraction with lower potential GDP growth rates. Historically, dramatic restrictions in credit have had the capacity to turn economic downturns into some-thing far more serious. Here's the crux of the problem: In the wake of the subprime crisis, banks tightened credit and dramatically reduced lending, not only to their customers but to each other (driving up the so-called LIBOR interbank borrowing rate). In the process, market rates *decoupled* from the central banks' short-term interest rates. In other words, the Fed and other central banks dramatically cut their short-term interest rates, but the LIBOR rate increased, restricting credit to the economy.

None of this is to deny that the old business models need to be upgraded. In the coming years, the industrialized world's financial institutions have no choice but to pare business lines and de-leverage. Banking practices will change. Institutions with thrift and commercial deposits, with loyal customer bases, will gain in value. Money man-agers will seek equity returns at lower, but more dependable, rates of return. The great unknown, however, relates to the potential negative macroeconomic implications of this changing paradigm in the world of finance.

According to the *Wall Street Journal*, from 1996 through 2006 prof-its at financial companies rose an average of 13.8 percent a year, com-pared with 8.5 percent for nonfinancial companies, as the U.S. financial services industry was able to tap into dynamic global growth. At the peak in 2003, financial services accounted for nearly 30 percent of the U.S. stock market earnings, or 40 percent of U.S. corporate profits. True, this percentage reflects, in part, the use of excessive leverage, but even after the massive financial write-downs of 2007, financial services still accounted for 20 percent of the market's profits. That's a huge part of the American economy.

Are American policymakers, therefore, ready for the significant negative macroeconomic effects from the demise of the financial services industry? Are they ready for a subpar economic recovery? Economist Frederick Mishkin in his book *The Next Great Globalization* makes the case that a nation's financial system is key to its prosperity. The better capitalized and developed the financial industry, the greater the overall prosperity. A primary reason the world is curved stems from the unlikelihood over the long run that the financial system can be effectively regulated without seriously undermining the financing of entrepreneurial initiative. As the Pulitzer Prize–winning author Daniel Yergin recently put it, "The era of easy globalization is over. The power of the state is reasserting itself."

My fear is that in the long term, the result of the financial crisis will be a bifurcated global financial system. On the one hand, there will be the relatively slow-growing economies of the United States, Europe, and Japan, with aggressively regulated financial systems and therefore a more limited means of financing entrepreneurial risk and growth. On the other hand, there will be the fast-growing, excess-saving economies, including China and India, which will use freewheeling, "offshore" global hedge funds, private equity firms, and other investment vehicles that are increasingly politically despised in the West to help fuel ever higher expansion and control throughout the rest of the world economy. As a result, the current power shift in manufacturing away from the industrialized West to the Pacific Rim could soon include a companion shift, in which the Asian economies achieve overwhelming *financial* dominance over the West a lot sooner than we think.

This growing dominance could be enhanced by the Pacific economies' less strict approach to climate warming issues relative to the Western economies. An equally plausible scenario, however, is that the next five years could produce a longer-than-expected *global* economic slowdown as a result of credit restrictions and financial de-leveraging. In this scenario, everyone suffers.

That is why the credit market situation is too vital to be left in the hands of the regulatory police, who may not sufficiently appreciate the negative macroeconomic and market implications from less than sensitive government intervention. Clearly what is required over the next several years is a team of financial policy brain surgeons, from both the public and the private sectors, with the political backing of some powerful and sophisticated leaders in Congress. Yes, there are some sophisticated congressional leaders on both sides of the aisle. Whether in today's politically polarized environment they feel comfortable cooperating to achieve responsible solutions is another matter.

In coming to terms with these problems, Congress must avoid at all costs a "Sarbanes-Oxley II scenario"—a well-intentioned but counterproductive remedy with ugly unintended consequences. If a Sarbanes-Oxley II to deal with the banking crisis is anything like the original Sarbanes-Oxley I financial market reform legislation, the result would be the severe marginalizing of the U.S. banking sector. American companies in the future would be forced to rely largely on European, Japanese, and Chinese banks for financing. The U.S. financial services industry would go the way of the U.S. auto industry.

In the wake of the subprime disaster, when I am asked about the future of financial globalization (yes, as a Washingtonian, at dinner parties people really ask those questions), my answer always draws a look of surprise. I always say: "Ask Schumer." By "Schumer," I mean New York Democratic senator Charles Schumer. He is a U.S. senator who hardly enjoys the greatest seniority on Capitol Hill. He is not even a committee chairman. But Schumer is the prototype of a congressional leader who could provide effective oversight to keep the regulatory remedies from killing the patient. There are, of course, other central figures who will determine the future of American finance, including Democratic Congressman Barney Frank, the powerful chairman of the U.S. House Subcommittee on Financial Services. Many conservative Republicans have attacked Frank for his leadership, which has introduced greater government involvement in the decision-making of U.S. financial institutions. In a sense, however, the congressman's role should be viewed in perspective. If a majority of the Democratic members of his subcommittee had their way, the U.S. financial system would have been de facto nationalized years ago. In a sense, therefore, the chairman's role has been an essential one of fending off the radical tigers of nationalization.

Along with Schumer, Frank is one of Washington's Hedge Fund Democrats. These are smart, relatively young liberals who came into power in part thanks to the amazing prosperity of financial globalization. Today, many rake in as much hedge fund and private equity campaign contributions as the Republicans, if not more. They lived through the miserable 1970s, but came of age during the greatest quarter-century of prosperity in history. They also know from history that the last period of globalized markets concluded with a great reversal.

In my view, Schumer is a key bellwether for the U.S. political system. He, far more than most, understands what is at stake in the financial system. He is smart enough—and articulate enough—to moderate the interventionist dogs, to keep them from turning the current financial difficulties into a nightmare beyond anything imaginable. Or he could seriously undermine financial globalization as the world continues to consider reforms to the system.

One reason I think the senator is important is that he was, in a sense, part of globalization's beginning. I first met Schumer in 1988 at the height of Japan's financial power. My old Ministry of Finance friend Utsumi, the backroom Tokyo mastermind I described in chapter 5, had called with an idea. The internationally oriented Ministry of Finance bureaucrats were intent on following the rest of the industrialized world in liberalizing their financial markets. Their problem was that the *domestically* oriented bureaucrats were resisting. So were the financial institutions. Utsumi said the MoF would not be opposed to several influential American congressmen coming to Japan to serve as a human wedge. The idea was to break the policy impasse by initiating a discussion on financial liberalization. But whom should the MoF formally invite?

A then–business associate, Richard Medley, and I suggested two individuals: Republican senator Jake Garn of Utah, and from the

Democratic side of the aisle, Schumer. They could not have been more different. Garn was a staid, middle-aged, conservative Mormon. Schumer was a young, brash, liberal Jew. We made one mistake: It turned out that the men despised each other. This is why Utsumi asked if we, as a favor to him, would accompany the two legislators to Japan. We did, bringing along our wives to accompany the legislators' wives.

Almost from the moment we left, one thing became certain: Schumer would be a fun travel companion. Today, as a U.S. senator, he is recognized as the mastermind behind the 2006 Democratic takeover of the United States Senate. Back then, however, Schumer was merely another young congressman—tall, lean, with receding dark hair and a quick wit. As a House member, he was looking to make a difference. That meant serving the various Wall Street interests that had helped finance his political career.

It does not surprise me that Schumer's career took off. By the end of the first meeting with the Japanese banks and security houses, it became clear that for the American side, Schumer would carry the ball. What surprised me was his deft feel for how financial markets operate. Schumer in meeting after meeting made the case for financial global-ization long before the word *globalization* was coined. He showed little attraction to the crude, old-style trade protectionism that appealed to a significant chunk of the Democratic Party.

I remember to this day the very words of one of Schumer's state-ments. That's because he sounded at the time like conservative, free market advocate Jack Kemp: "By opening up Japan's financial system, both Japanese and U.S. financial institutions will benefit because the global financial pie will greatly expand." Schumer went on to describe, very accurately, a coming new dynamic world of financial integration. This new world would transport the global economy to new levels of prosperity.

There was one startling moment along the way. One evening, Schumer addressed the entire Japanese financial elite during a cocktail reception in our honor. The audience included the head of every financial institution and the entire senior echelons of the government at a time when Japan was at the pinnacle of its financial power. Schumer announced that he was delighted to visit Japan, hoped that the system would be opened more to foreign financial institutions (including more seats for foreign institutions on the Japanese stock exchange), and then offered a toast. Holding his glass high in the air before this powerful Japanese crowd, he referred to America proudly as the "big brother" and to Japan as "our little brother."

This was an analogy the Japanese instantly found offensive. The response, subtle as it was, came quickly: Our wives, standing together in the middle of the reception listening to the speeches, were soon asked to move to the side and rear of the room. They ended up near the entryway to the restrooms, a location deemed "more appropriate."

A minute later, Setsuya Tabuchi, known as the "senior Tabuchi," the powerful chairman of Nomura Securities, then the largest securities firm in the world and a client, tapped me on the shoulder. He had a mysterious-looking smile on his leathery, tanned face. A man in his late sixties with the look of a samurai who had fought and survived a thousand internal battles, Tabuchi always wore a double-breasted suit. He held a lit cigarette like a torpedo perched atop three fingers, like Reagan's John P. Sears.

Slowly in English without a translator, Tabuchi said, "The congressman's line about 'little brother' was your idea, right? If you insult the crowd, you break things loose. Pretty clever. People get angry, but they eventually start to negotiate." To be frank, I had no idea what the Nomura chief executive was talking about. Neither, I'm almost certain, did Schumer. What occurred as far as I can determine was simply an old-fashioned social faux pas—but it worked.

Fairly quickly, at first to a somewhat limited extent, the Japanese system began to open up to foreign investment firms. More seats became available on the stock exchange. Both little brother and big brother would prosper. (The process did not go completely smoothly because the Bank of Japan reduced interest rates. This reduced the risk that the yen would rise dramatically as a result of the increased inflows resulting from liberalization, but it led to a dangerous asset price bubble soon thereafter. The massive international pressure, including from the U.S. Treasury, on Japan to continue this policy didn't help matters.)

On that trip to Japan, Charles Schumer played a critical role in support of liberalized global financial markets. The future of financial globalization now depends on the willingness of him and other global-minded politicians and bureaucrats to provide political cover for responsible controls to restore confidence in the system.

For the Hedge Fund Democrats of the Washington power elite, however, stepping forward and defending the financial system won't be easy. One reason is the increased isolationist attitude in America and growing discomfort with all things foreign. But another stems from the fact that despite the best efforts at reform, our evolving financial architecture will likely remain less than fully adequate to handle the sophisticated products of a twenty-first-century globalized financial market. The result has already produced a scary roller-coaster ride of financial market uncertainty at times so terrifying that the public has wanted to run and hide under the bed. Financial globalization may be a highly productive means of distributing entrepreneurial capital and creating wealth, but it is a system replete with extreme volatility, where no broad series of formal or even informal understandings exists about the rules of the financial road. In times of economic weakness, it is hard as a politician not to want to demagogue against a villain. The political "tin ears" of the bailed-out bankers didn't help matters as they attempted to use taxpayer funding to pay large retention bonuses.

The congressional overseers may be timid for one other reason: It's tough to know exactly what to do with the banks. Although the greedy bankers have behaved irresponsibly and placed the global economy in serious jeopardy, the world needs the banks. If the banks fail, so too will the world economic and financial system. That is because if we destroy our means of supplying liquidity to the creative, risk-taking sector, the entire economy will suffer.

Read any of the literature on the history of economic depressions, and bank failures dominate the discussion. That is why during global financial panics, central bankers always have one immediate concern:

the potential for mass withdrawals of cash from the banking system (or of the cash being shifted out of the normal investment vehicles of a successful economy into strictly short-term government securities). In the event of mass withdrawals driven by fear of the unknown, the banking system's entire existence can be threatened by insolvency. Therefore, dealing with such an important and difficult challenge may be above the pay grade of even the smartest in Congress.

In the new global economy, controlling bank panics has become extraordinarily difficult because speed is a killer. Today money moves in an instant. Even twenty years ago, a person had to pick up a phone and call a broker or a banker to move money; today, everything happens at the push of a button on a desktop computer. Therefore, if everybody decides at once in a panic to push the button that withdraws deposits from the banking sector, the liabilities of the banks in a bank run of any endurance would be too big and too fast to contain.

In March 2008, as the investment firm Bear Stearns was on the brink of collapse and the Federal Reserve placed that institution under its bank safety net, the financial world entered uncharted waters. The sense of the unknown was heightened with the government rescues of AIG, Fannie Mae, and Freddie Mac. Central bankers walk a fine line, because too generous and broad government safety nets can throw a monkey wrench into the workings of the financial system. A government guarantee for all financial institutional investments may sound prudent, but it may not be. That's because, as we have seen in the subprime crisis, institutions get reckless when they can pass the risks off to someone else. This potentially increases the likelihood of an unending series of financial bubbles wreaking havoc on the economy. Or severe regulatory constraint could create the opposite outcome: a dramatic shrinkage in lending. If government guarantees were a panacea, then a firm such as Fannie Mae, which for years has enjoyed an implicit guarantee, would have thrived during the credit crisis. Instead, that institution and others like it became a central focus of the problem.

In this new global economy, policymakers desperately need to engage in collective forward thinking about the nature of the global financial safety net, and about risk in general. As former New York Federal Reserve president Gerald Corrigan once put it, "You can't hedge the universe." You can't eliminate all risk. The late William Seidman, a leading guru in the area of U.S. financial market regulation, put it differently: "The safety net should be operated by a divinely guided genius who hates the whole idea of government interference in the marketplace."

We are living at a time when policymakers must seize the moment if we are to save the new global economy. In the coming years, the policy world—including the central bankers, Treasury and finance officials, key government regulators, senior think tank opinion-makers, and responsible members of the political leadership—needs to reform the world's financial architecture, with "Goldilocks" guidance that is not too soft but not too strong. The stakes could not be higher. After all, if the major industrialized world regulators, including the central banks, had such a difficult time figuring out what was happening during the subprime crisis, why should we be reassured that the same parties could handle the financial implications of a terrorist strike? What about a strike targeted at the financial system itself? Clearly the policy world must engage in more effective international contingency planning—and fast.

The policy world also needs a "big-think" financial doctrine, or at least a series of informal understandings, in the anticipation of financial crises in general. This doctrine, formal or otherwise, must involve the cooperation of the private sector with the goal of greater transparency. Policymakers need to arrive at surgically precise global reforms that avoid threatening the larger financial system as a wealth-creating force. This is a task that will require extraordinary imagination, not unlike the big thinkers in economics who emerged in 1944 at the end of World War II. These individuals devised an economic and financial structure that allowed for sixty years of peace and prosperity. Policymakers today need to engage in the same kind of bold thinking and to communicate to the public that a financial doctrine to restore order is in place.

Working with the private markets, policy leaders must devise some means of better telegraphing the extent of market risk financial institutions take in the use of highly sophisticated, highly leveraged financial instruments. As financial products are bundled in the process of securitization, some way must be found to overcome the legal and tax restraints of temporarily unbundling the securitized assets to remove any discovered financial toxic waste. There must also be some new platform for providing more standardization of the pricing of securitized financial products.

On another front, policymakers need to find ways to improve the performance of the international credit rating agencies. One idea is to tie part of the financial compensation of these agencies to successful performance. Under the current system, with the exception of a blow to reputation and ego, the rating agencies pay no price for failure. Moreover, they enjoy no dramatic upside for success and accuracy. Some in Congress propose a government takeover of these agencies. This makes absolutely no sense to anyone with a modicum of understanding of global markets because government bureaucrats, even more than the specialists at the private credit rating agencies, are no match for the sophistication and complexity of today's financial market wizards. A better solution, in lieu of a government takeover, would be to disenfranchise this industry altogether and allow the market to come up with its own rating solution, a cottage industry of smaller, more creative and effective entities.

The policy world must also address the problem of the global economy's state-owned banks—whether German, Chinese, French, or Italian—which remain a major vulnerability to the global system. In Germany during the beginning stages of the subprime crisis, for instance, mid-level municipal and state-owned banks represented "political banking" at its worst. The system held back in revealing its subprime exposure until it was too late. As these institutions collapsed, they had to be taken over by the larger independent banks. The international financial system desperately needs to move these state-owned banking systems to what global banking expert Charles Dallara calls "more of a healthy, market-based footing." To be sure, market-based banks have their own problems. They have done some stupid things. But they do not exist under the direct political thumb of government politicians as do the state-run banks. Japan in the 1990s failed to recover economically precisely because its banks, under the influence of government policymakers and the political elites, were slow to clear from bank balance sheets their mountains of nonperforming loans. Such a development might not have occurred had the banks been more independent. Today, Chinese state-run banks make the Japanese banks look like amateurs in the art of hiding nonperforming loans. And the U.S. banks, under the thumb of the U.S. Treasury, risk following the Japan path themselves.

On a broader note, today's policy leaders need to be aware that even if all necessary financial reforms are in place, if financial transparency increases, and if confidence and trust in the financial architecture return, the world economy could still likely remain in jeopardy. There are, of course, the threats of terrorism, weather and climate changes, and an increasing number of financial panics despite the efforts at financial reform. But the ultimate threat to the world economic order is that financial liberalization and free trade fail to survive, with the world returning to a long-term period of economic malaise similar to the 1970s, or worse.

Some theorists suggest that globalization, particularly financial globalization and the last several decades of wealth creation, may have benefited from two developments that may never occur again: first, the absence for sixty years of a worldwide military conflict; and second, the complete breakdown of the global Marxist economic model. This breakdown unleashed perhaps a one-time-only explosion of pent-up creative energies. Therefore, globalization's success during the last several decades, the theory maintains, may be unrepeatable.

A surprising number of mainstream opinion leaders are beginning to question the very underpinnings of globalization. For instance, writing in *Foreign Affairs*, Rawi Abdelal and Adam Segal point out that "politicians and their constituents in the United States, Europe, and China have grown increasingly nervous about letting capital, goods, and people move freely across their borders. And energy—the most globalized of products—has once more become the object of intense resource nationalism." I again would add that coming disagreements over climate warming issues between Asia and the West could potentially threaten to seriously diminish support for the global trading system.

In recent years, the International Monetary Fund has become less enthusiastic about encouraging developing economies to liberalize their financial systems, allowing the free flow across borders of foreign investment capital. The reason for the reluctance is that many developing countries have financial systems with little or no transparency and little in the way of adequate regulation. Therefore, foreign investment capital is easily spooked. At the first sniff of trouble, the capital flees, leaving institutions such as the IMF with the thankless task of trying to keep the resulting crisis from spreading to the larger global financial system.

The OECD (Organisation for Economic Co-operation and Development), the Paris-based organization of the world's government economists, has also backed off its earlier support for the globalization model. The two leading international rating agencies, Moody's and Standard and Poor's, actually warn developing economies about the dangers of too rapid capital market liberalization.

If all of these international agencies won't support financial globalization, who will? The only answer, I believe, is a group of courageous, visionary policy leaders, from both the public and private sectors and including central banks and responsible members of the political leadership, that steps forward and explains the enormous negative consequences in the event the globalized model of free trade and liberalized entrepreneurial capital collapses.

Meanwhile, the signs of globalization's coming demise are everywhere. The World Trade Organization, for instance, has steadily lost effectiveness. The United States and Europe continue their hypocrisy of protecting agriculture and certain other industries while the Doha Round of international trade talks is stalled. No, the collapse of Doha would not mean global trade has come to a halt, but it would mean that the world has become even more distrustful of universal free trade, which is not a good sign for the future of globalization.

On the direct investment front, China is now reviewing all foreign applications for mergers and acquisitions, dramatically expanding the number of assets considered untouchable for "economic security" reasons or as "key industries" or as popular trademarks. This is not unlike the U.S. actions against the foreign takeover of Unocal and the effort by Dubai Ports World to take over the administration of several U.S. ports. The message of these developments to the world: free-flowing capital may not last forever.

The threat of protectionism, macroeconomic weakness, and heightened economic imbalances that contribute to greater market volatility has led some to believe the world is on the cusp of a major economic downturn, perhaps a collapse. I have a friend, Tadashi Nakamae, considered one of Japan's preeminent independent global strategists. Nakamae promotes a "Chinese Crash" scenario. He suggests that the world has entered a long-term trend of overcapacity (too many goods produced), first in the manufacturing sector, but also eventually in services. Nakamae predicts the emergence of a new "anti-Reagan Revolution" where governments, particularly in Asia, will attempt to exert even greater state control over their economies.

Nakamae believes that as emerging market economies (mostly in Asia) continue down the reckless path of adding capacity (by mass overproduction driven not by market demand but by administrative edict), the global economy will suffer from an even greater shortage of natural resources (copper, zinc, iron ore, oil, etc.). Combined with the overcapacity problem, inflation in the price of natural resources, despite some periods of price declines, will continue to accelerate. This will produce a substantial decline in the internal profitability of manufacturing.

With manufacturing hamstrung, the emerging markets, as noted earlier, will attempt to develop the services side of their economies. This is what the United States and the United Kingdom did in the

1980s and 1990s. Japan will also jump aggressively into the services sector. With India already there, the resulting oversupply will inevitably produce a ratcheting up for the first time of *both* manufacturing and service-oriented global protectionism.

For Nakamae, the most likely scenario is that while the Asian economies fall into state-initiated protectionism, Europe will muddle through while China actually "crashes." The reason is that China's level of overcapacity is the greatest. This outcome would leave the United States and other industrialized nations with the headache of having to deal with the huge stockpiles of commodities and finished goods that China, under such a scenario, would off-load onto world markets.

Meanwhile, America would also have to find a new source of domestic demand. Housing and autos, two historically enormous sectors of the American economy, have recently experienced severe weakness. In Nakamae's scenario, the United States (and Europe) would use environmental investments as the new source of demand. New standards of energy savings and environmental protection would be initiated for environmental purposes but also as a means of excluding Asian products from the American and European markets. This would be a kind of de facto protectionism, or nontariff tariff.

Says Nakamae: "This entire scenario means the rest of Asia would need to create its own internal demand. That is a very difficult job. Japan has struggled to do that [to develop an aggressive base of consumers] for three decades and still has not achieved success." The upshot will be growing Asian protectionism against American and European goods and services.

Nakamae's dire global scenario is hardly inevitable. I mention it, however, to demonstrate that a growing body of global strategists with successful predictive track records are becoming fearful that a global financial and trade collapse is a realistic possibility.

While the model in which overcapacity builds up and produces a depressive effect on wages, as occurred in the 1930s, is possible, there are other less apocalyptic scenarios. A more sanguine outcome is possible, and the likelihood of it is greatly enhanced, if global capital continues to be allowed to move freely throughout the world. Modern, free market economies over time can be highly flexible in overcoming problems. Fed chairman Alan Greenspan for years testified on Capitol Hill about the enormous flexibility of the U.S. economy. The coming decade will be a test of whether Greenspan's theory is correct—that the U.S. financial system can reform itself to achieve continued success.

Moreover, not all the news is bad. Today's central bankers are becoming wiser as they seek to understand the nature of securitized credit. It almost goes without saying that the Fed will pay more attention to the issue of credit expansion in its conduct of future monetary policy, which will help lessen the severity of financial panics. Moreover, no sensible market participant I know questions any longer the need for greater transparency, though there are differences of opinion on specifics, including, for example, how quickly complete financial exposure should be revealed to the markets. The American financial institutions revealed the ugliness of their balance sheets a lot faster than have many European institutions, which held back in hopes that the price of those subprime assets would somehow return to a higher price.

There is no denying, however, that the risks ahead for the global economy are enormous beyond the current economic weakness. There will be periods of great volatility with markets and the economy at times seeming to rebound, but then quickly retrenching. The sad fact is that the underlying sentiment of doubt toward liberalized capital markets and free trade will likely keep the economic and financial system unstable for years to come. Unstable politics beget unstable markets and troubling economic fundamentals.

During the period 1914–1945, when the last great period of globalization collapsed, cross-border trade and capital flows plummeted primarily for one reason—a crisis of ideas. Imperial ambitions and protectionist sentiment became the driving forces in an increasingly mercantilist system. Well-meaning policymakers lost sight of the idea of globalized finance and trade that had created the enormous pool of wealth in the first place. Wealth and national resources were being fought over, creating tensions that were elevated by nationalistic impulses. Between 1929 and 1932 alone, the amount of trade between countries collapsed by nearly 70 percent as international distrust sky-rocketed.

Then financial distrust set in as nations clamped on currency controls essentially to regulate the amount of capital allowed to cross borders. The global price of goods collapsed. With the collapse in prices, companies couldn't earn a profit. As a result, they couldn't meet their bank loan obligations. Many banks failed, shrinking credit further, which only suffocated more businesses, creating even more bank failures. This period, of course, was called the Great Depression.

It is amazing in the decade and a half before the Depression how little intellectual leadership there was in defending and strengthening a globalized system that had produced an impressive period of industrialization and prosperity. Instead, the people who should have been leaders were passive. Great Britain, resented by the world for its power as the United States is today, lacked the self-confidence to fight for the system. The British, still the great world power in the post–World War I period, found themselves sapped of intellectual energy. Events spun out of control in an extraordinary example of failed global leadership. As the most influential economy in the world, Britain failed to seize the moment.

Regarding this notion of poor communication and failure to recognize the role one is assumed and expected to play, let me relay the bizarre details of an awkward experience that occurred when I first started my market advisory business. I realize this story is probably misplaced, perhaps even inappropriate. On the surface, it would seem absurd to compare America's predicament with an incident early on in my own business. Nonetheless, when I think of the makeup of the policy world today, this strange tale about a European dinner party and the boorish behavior of the host keeps coming to mind.

Relatively new to foreign business travel in 1989, I was in Rome at a meeting with an important strategic Italian financial adviser. We discussed the European economy and the dollar. The individual, well known in Italian decision-making circles, ended our discussion by inviting me to a small dinner party at his home that evening. I eagerly accepted, not realizing that the evening would, in a strange way, provide a vivid example of the importance of both understanding one's role and effectively communicating in that role.

The "small" dinner party turned out to include at least two dozen people. We sipped cocktails on a veranda resting on a hillside, absorbing a spectacular three-hundred-degree view of the warm golden hues of the sun setting over the Eternal City. The only thing more breathtaking was the twinkling of the surrounding city lights after sunset. Just before going in to dinner, my host introduced me to his wife, who had just entered the veranda. I'll call her Maria—a dark-haired, strikingly beautiful woman were it not for one detail: Maria was carrying at least an extra eighty or ninety pounds. Maria smiled, and it quickly became clear she spoke no English.

My host had arranged dinner around a long rectangular table in a large but sparsely decorated dining room. Maria sat at one end and my host at the other. Those who could not speak English sat at Maria's end of the table, with the English speakers at the other.

The wine flowed. A subtly flavored pasta arrived, followed by an exceptional white fish. The entire dinner party had relaxed into a state of balmy euphoria. Then the games began. My host stood, held his wineglass in the air, and offered an elaborate toast praising the fact that America was finally taking the lead in foreign exchange matters. Others joined in as more wine flowed.

Then my host did something unusual. He stood again, announcing that it would be in poor taste were he not to congratulate his cohost for the evening, his lovely wife. Everyone came to attention. We all smiled. Maria looked straight toward us, the English speakers, at the far end of the table. Recognizing her name, she offered a wide open smile.

Our host, her husband, continued: "And now we must toast Maria, the most beautiful flower in the desert." Maria beamed more upon hearing her name, but the guest sitting next to me, an Italian investment banker, whispered, "Oh boy, here it comes," as if he had

268 · THE WORLD IS CURVED

witnessed on other occasions what was about to take place. "To Maria" (she beamed some more), the host said again as everyone raised his glass, "my wife, my rare gem. To Maria . . . THE PIG!"

At this point I felt a cold shiver run up my spine. Did he just say what I thought he said? I wondered. He must have, I concluded, because half the guests—those at Maria's end of the table—were still smiling, with the rest of us staring somberly facedown into our dessert dishes.

Our host repeated: "Let me say again, to my lovely, sweet, little bird, Maria . . . THE PIG!" Maria's smile widened again at the sound of her name. The smile gave off an impressive glow, but also a suddenly awkward sense of confusion. This was no doubt based on the obvious—those at my end of the table sat with our noses even closer to the dishes.

My host was making his approach for a third landing when the investment banking guest next to me suddenly rose. "Oops," he said, looking at his watch. "The game's over. I have an early meeting. It's been wonderful. Great fun. A lovely, lovely evening." Everyone else rose. Soon thereafter I thanked the host and Maria and rushed back to my hotel, thinking to myself, These people certainly are different.

I conclude with this bizarre, perhaps even offensive, story not to suggest that the European mind-set can be caricatured as reflecting such personal mean-spiritedness. I highlight the story of Maria because she, in my mind, is the United States—or at least she is what the United States could become if policymakers are not careful. Maria is America—overloaded with debt, self-doubt, and self-absorption—and, more important, unable to communicate its message to the world.

Today, the United States is a politically polarized nation plagued increasingly with thoughts of class warfare and unable to exert economic leadership in the world. Desperate for economic and financial leadership, the world, like Maria's despicable husband, has already become a cynical, even dangerous place, ripe for catastrophe. Nervous markets sense that American policymakers are pulling back. No one offers the big picture. Uncertainty feeds on itself as America sits there at the global dinner party of nations, unaware, with a dazed smile on its face.

The sad thing is it doesn't have to be that way. American political and policy leaders, during the rare moments when they address issues involving the international economy, play the fear card, and that needs to stop. Instead, they need to internalize the fact that only the United States is capable of mustering the leadership and courage to defend the free-trading system and the international system of freely moving capital.

This is the precise moment when the Hedge Fund Democrats, having taken the campaign funding to get into office, need to step forward and defend a flawed system that nonetheless has achieved significant success. Their message: Financial globalization is the great paradox—a flaw-ridden system producing huge, scary financial dislocations but, at the same time, the cherished goose that lays the golden eggs. And the upshot is obvious: Only a true fool would want to return to the earlier era of higher inflation, greater joblessness, and diminished wealth. Perhaps Marc Leland, the former U.S. Treasury official, put it best when he said, "Globalization is like the two institutions we know as democracy and marriage. Both institutions at times can be problematic, but the alternatives are highly unattractive."

American policymakers need to remind the world of the preglobalization period of huge inflationary and joblessness swings in a vicious business cycle of uncertainty. Political leaders need to point out that today's financial system, with effective leadership, historically has enjoyed a surprising ability to self-correct if given guidance and time. During a period of financial turbulence in the late 1980s and the early 1990s, for example, the period during the savings and loan crisis, commentators offered images of economic and financial apocalypse, just like today. We forget, but the markets back then also experienced a crisis of confidence. Yet the financial system, after the initiation of appropriate reforms, self-corrected. It cleaned up its losses (with the help of a new institution called the Resolution Trust Corporation, which helped coordinate the cleanup). Some in the markets found properties that were bargains; others who had bet wrong with their investments suffered loss and heartache. But the economic and financial system, backed by a policy game plan and new, smarter regulations, not only survived the savings and loan crisis but went on to prosper for decades.

Policymakers, therefore, need to make clear that in the coming years, we can move the global financial system toward greater transparency and trust—and thereby achieve an even more productive future. But leadership matters. Creative financial policy strategists, void of today's ugly partisanship and focused on the big picture, must step forward to work closely with the private sector. This is a unique moment in history, and they need to seize it.

Success won't come easily. Historian Paul Kennedy, in his book *The Rise and Fall of the Great Powers*, argues that today's policymakers are following a decision-making mode that brings "short term advantage but long term disadvantage." Today there are no short-term advantages commensurate with the danger of not coming up with long-term solutions to the challenges of growing fiscal imbalances, the entitlement nightmare, the Chinese juggernaut, class warfare, and the lack of trust in our financial architecture. This is the time to think big about the long term. Sadly, however, the questions remain: Are the gifted policy strategists out there listening? Is any politician thinking beyond his or her next thirty-second TV ad? Is any financial market leader looking beyond the next quarter? Do any of these people realize that nothing less than the world's financial system is at stake?

Today, like never before, a courageous body of policy leaders needs to step forward with an effective agenda to avoid disaster. With good leadership, we can rise above the current catastrophe and set a course for renewed prosperity. Without it, we risk a new era of economic heartache. A second Great Depression seems unlikely, but the thought is no longer a complete absurdity. The world is dangerously curved.

Epilogue: The Flight to New Canada

When you write a book, within months of publication people ask, "So what's your next book?" In my case, they ask something quite different: "Does the global economy have a future?"

On a number of occasions I have engaged in a bit of literary hyperbole—I respond facetiously that my new book already has a title: *New Canada: A Scenario for the World by the Year 2030.* What has been astonishing—and telling about the fundamental anxiety these days—is the number of intelligent individuals who impulsively see the scenario as plausible.

Little more than twenty years from now, I argue in this new work, the top 5 percent of American and top 1 percent of Chinese investor and innovation communities—literally tens of millions of the most affluent from these countries—will be living in Canada. By then, they will call it New Canada. It will be a kind of fortress of political, economic, and financial stability in a world gone mad. This will have been the greatest migration of elites in the history of mankind.

It turned out global warming was a far greater problem than even

Al Gore envisioned. As a result, New York in the summer sizzles worse than Macon, Georgia. Washington, D.C., has developed the insufferable summer humidity of Panama. What is left of Wall Street has moved to Toronto. Newfoundland has become the new Nantucket and Martha's Vineyard, both of which are largely underwater. The Four Seasons hotel chain has broken ground on its latest project, a presold luxury resort on the outskirts of the thawing subarctic called, no doubt, North Pole Estates.

By then, America has gone bankrupt. The U.S. debt has reached $25 trillion. The Federal Reserve tried monetizing the debt through higher inflation. Eventually, however, the government crumbled under the load and defaulted. This collapse was precipitated by the earlier breakout of the great, bloody Mexican revolution of 2012. The government there, after a valiant struggle, finally lost control to the drug cartel's coalition government. As a result, over the next fifteen years, 20 percent of the Mexican population gradually moved north to escape the new government (economically debilitated by the collapse of NAFTA), not to mention the intolerable heat and humidity from climate change.

Meanwhile, the New Canada government has just put the finishing touches on its new transcontinental wall built for one purpose—to keep out the Americans who keep trying to move north and cross the border illegally. But not all Americans. Legal immigration is possible. The ticket for entry and joint citizenship: $400,000 Canadian dollars (thank you very much) placed in a Canadian bank or other approved investment vehicle. The lines of affluent Americans and Chinese seeking citizenship seem endless.

This Sino American influx of the elite will quickly change the Canadian political and economic culture. Almost overnight, New Canada will become the world's hothouse of entrepreneurial risk, particularly in the area of new technologies, medical and drug research, and global financial services, but also in virtually any service industry that can be easily transported. The highly affluent members of the entrepreneurial sectors of Shanghai in particular, fearing for their lives because of Beijing's longstanding aggressive campaign of class warfare, have in an astonishingly short period established leadership positions within the western portion of New Canada.

And there is one other new West Coast entry: Hollywood. Most of the big movie studios have moved north to Vancouver to escape California's now prohibitive tax system. Even though the government offered massive tax credits and direct subsidies to the ailing entertainment industry, the $500,000 annual cap on actors' salaries proved intolerable.

New Canada, the world's new Saudi Arabia, has discovered major natural gas deposits. The New Canadian dollar has become the world's strongest currency. That's because New Canada, with a financial architecture offering complete online transparency, has displaced London as the world's international financial center. To no one's surprise, the world's investment capital poured into New Canadian financial investments. People have begun calling New Canada "the New Switzerland" (the real Switzerland having gone bankrupt with the collapse of the bank UBS), the one place in a world of economic and political chaos completely free from wealth confiscation.

By this point, when I tell the story, most people respond with bemused smiles of skepticism. Yet a surprising number become infatuated with the idea. One woman blurted hysterically, "Is this true? How can I join? Are you serious?" An acquaintance living in Toronto who often travels to the United States seriously responded by listing all of Canada's many problems. "I have serious doubts whether your New Canada scenario, short of serious reforms by the Canadian government, is plausible," he added.

My friend, of course, had missed the joke. The notion that Canada could somehow dominate the world is absurd. The fact that so many listeners seemed intrigued if not desperate to move north, is proof that we are truly living in what management consultant Peter Drucker decades ago called "an age of discontinuity." The only difference is that today is an age of discontinuity and fear on steroids. We are witnessing a new era of soaring financial and geopolitical unpredictability.

Devoid of global leadership, there is a sense today that the world has the potential to spin out of control. Literally anything can happen, including the crumbling of governments and institutional relationships we never thought possible. This includes the crumbling of capitalism and the open trading system. Perhaps most terrifying is that signs of a modest cyclical recovery are tempting our policymakers to ignore the fundamental systemic problems ahead that suggest a disappointing, underperforming economy.

When average folks become economically desperate, seeing the future looming darker than the past, no political outcome can be discounted. In 1910, the British intelligentsia sitting in their private London clubs could not have imagined that the United Kingdom would, within a surprisingly short period of time, stumble into an extended period of self-doubt, disillusionment, weakness, and decline. It seemed inconceivable that Germany by the 1930s, with the building of its war machine, would become the economy of relatively stable employment growth. The notion that upstart America within less than fifty years would dominate the world seemed preposterous. Yet change arrived and no one saw it coming.

Today America is in the midst of an extraordinary transition as a result of the greatest financial collapse since the 1930s. This has been the ultimate era of discontinuity. At least for the short term, the only certainty is the lack of certainty. The global economy has undergone a brutal financial deleveraging. We have seen the reappraisal of the value of virtually every asset in the world. This situation has been like an unstoppable force of nature, a swiftly downward tidal move. From August 2007 until September 2008, the United States experienced a financial crisis. After that, the world fell into a full-blown financial panic. Suddenly, nobody trusted anybody or any institution.

To be sure, our policymakers have pulled out all the stops. The Federal Reserve has slashed short-term interest rates to near 0 percent, more than doubling the debt on its balance sheet as it seeks to inject liquidity from a dozen fire hoses directly into the U.S. financial system. The central bank even took the rare move of purchasing long-term Treasury securities, which could have implications for a future of stagflation. Central banks around the world have followed the Federal Reserve's lead. The U.S. Treasury has announced new bailout packages about as frequently as officials there changed their underwear. Nevertheless, the deleveraging tidal reversal as of this writing has continued downward.

Initially, the crisis affected mostly Wall Street. Then it clobbered Main Street. The U.S. economy experienced something not seen since the Great Depression—a brutal process of demand destruction. The confidence of the American people plummeted. A new president and a Democratic Congress, and governments around the world enacted trillions of dollars of fiscal stimulus and, in the case of the United States, trillions more in spending for health care, new sources of clean, renewable energy, and education. U.S. Treasury officials, using every resource at their disposal, struggled to help the plagued American financial services industry remove mountains of toxic assets from bank balance sheets so banks could start lending again.

The economy has rebounded some as a result of the stimulus, but will this be a temporary reprieve? During the Great Depression, by the mid-1930s the economy began to show impressive signs of life. Then, in response to a series of policy blunders, everything collapsed a second time. Will that happen again to America? The answer depends on the ability of U.S. policymakers to be nimble and creative as they maneuver around the serious land mines ahead.

It is hard to be optimistic because Washington policymakers have a history of policy arrogance. Economic hubris seems to carry the day. My first introduction to policy hubris came in 1975, when I first arrived in Washington to work as a Senate staffer. I was taken aback by a comment by the economist Arthur Okun at a congressional hearing. Inflation was then gaining momentum. Okun, one of the world's most distinguished economic thinkers, bluntly admitted that we don't understand inflation—and never have.

Rarely before or since has Washington witnessed such humility in economic policy. Instead, the past five decades have been an age of economic hubris. In the 1960s, we sought to end poverty through federal spending. In the late 1970s, we thought that controlling the money supply could solve everything. In the 1980s, tax incentives were seen as capable of dramatically increasing the rate at which people saved. By the 1990s, it seemed to many that Alan Greenspan could fine-tune the business cycle out of existence by tinkering with the Federal Reserve's interest rates. Then came the various taxpayer-funded bailout schemes by a variety of George W. Bush Treasury officials. With the arrival of the Obama administration, the new hope is that massive infrastructure spending and other fiscal stimulus plans, along with targeted federal spending to revive housing, will be the magic elixir for our economic troubles. But will the latest economic remedies also turn out to be a case of economic policy hubris?

The Obama administration was correct to conclude quickly that the U.S. economy had entered an unusual period of demand destruction. Bombarding the economy with large amounts of fiscal and monetary stimulus made sense—in theory. In practice, however, things are never so simple. This fiscal stimulus may turn out to be far too small to have much of an effect. American consumers, who represent 70 percent of the U.S. economy, are undergoing long-term retrenchment. They are forgoing spending and saving more in an effort to replenish the whopping $14 trillion in collective household wealth lost in the financial crisis. Recent surveys by American Express indicate that many affluent Americans are actually enjoying pulling back in this new "be more like my neighbor" mentality.

Just several years ago, the gluttonous, overleveraged American consumer was spending more than $1.10 for every dollar earned. Not anymore. Consumption patterns appear to be returning to lower levels, perhaps to the low levels of the 1970s. In other words, instead of returning to spending 80 cents of every dollar earned, U.S. consumers could end up spending less for the foreseeable future. Instead of buying new cars, they will have old cars fixed. The same with the refrigerator that's not working properly. Why shop at Saks or Neiman Marcus at the fancy mall when the cheaper products at Walmart and Target are just up the street?

The implication of this potential consumer retrenchment is huge. Even if Washington were to double its level of government stimulus spending, which would put enormous strains on America's ability to finance its current debt, the stimulus may still be far too small to have any dramatic effect other than to produce a modest rebound. That is why, when all is said and done, whether the U.S. economy fully recovers will likely depend more than anything else on how individuals and businesses continue to respond to the Federal Reserve's unprecedentedly generous monetary policies and the question is—in light of today's massive government debt, will those monetary policies lead to a fear of higher inflation?

But there is a larger point about the dangers of economic hubris. Economies are driven by more than numbers—the size of either stimulus spending or interest rate cuts. They are driven by psychology. In recent years, psychologically speaking, Americans have seen the U.S. financial system and the larger global system as a bus racing down an icy mountain toward a village with no team of global leaders behind the wheel.

Americans are extraordinarily resourceful and, sooner or later, will arrive at the proper mix of policies that will establish a successful course toward full recovery. Let us not forget, however, that the financial crisis became apparent because the financial system experienced a sudden dramatic loss of liquidity. Liquidity, which I noted in the first chapter of this book, is nothing more than confidence. Liquidity is confidence by consumers and investors that our policymakers know what they are doing, that they are capable of thinking creatively to avoid the traditional trap of policy hubris. To restore confidence, our policymakers need to be more transparent in acknowledging the troubles plaguing our financial system. Washington, in particular, needs to be more forthright in explaining that today's difficulties are global in nature. The world is financially interconnected. Bad things that happen globally have the potential to become the tail that wags the American economic and financial dog.

Consider the financial nightmare as seen from a global perspective. The great myth is that the financial meltdown stemmed solely from a

U.S.-initiated subprime mortgage collapse and the resulting fallout. If that were the case, today's crisis would represent defaults and/or write-downs on a fraction of a $1.5 trillion mortgage market problem. It sounds big and the solution would hardly be painless. Yet the problem would be manageable by global governments and their financial markets.

The reason the financial crisis has been so resistant to policy medicine is that the markets are aware the problem is not limited to a U.S. subprime bubble. The fear is that the world financial system, in a worst case scenario, is at risk of facing not one, but perhaps nine financial bubbles in one form or another. The fear ultimately is of a perfect storm of financial failure, particularly if the global community stumbles into foolhardy policy blunders in coming years, including protectionism, crude efforts at capital controls, and currency manipulation.

Ironically, the subprime-related mortgage loan problem, at $1.5 trillion, is the world's smallest bubble. There's also the potential outstanding world credit card debt bubble at $2.5 trillion, the emerging market debt bubble at $5 trillion, the commodity derivatives bubble at $9 trillion, the corporate bond bubble at $15 trillion, the commercial real estate bubble at $25 trillion, the foreign exchange derivative bubble at as much as $40 trillion and, last but hardly least, the possible credit default swap bubble valued at as much as $50 trillion.

Global financial markets worry that these eight bubbles, representing far more than $100 trillion in worst case global financial exposure, could overwhelm the international economic and financial systems if the bubbles simultaneously burst. For example, if just ten percent of that financial value vanished, the world would face more than a $10 trillion loss. Here's the catch, and why global markets remain fundamentally so nervous: The world's GDP is barely $60 trillion.

You are probably asking, "What happened to the ninth potential financial bubble?" That's the growing bubble in government bond markets. Over the past year, other countries, also in trouble, have been following America's lead in passing major fiscal stimulus and bank bailout measures. Financial markets envision a coming global credit traffic jam as the economies of the world all line up seeking credit from the capital markets at the same time. No, interest rates globally won't rise significantly so long as the world economy remains weak. But interest rates as a result of this competition for credit will soar once our economy gives signs that a major recovery is possible.

Here's the problem. Rising interest rates could kill any chance that this recovery is both sustainable and robust. A resulting scenario of lower economic growth would limit the tax revenues that are necessary to refinance today's mountain of government debt. The danger is that America could find itself in a credit market straitjacket from which escape is extraordinarily difficult. Carrying mountains of debt doesn't mean the economy can't grow, but it is rather like trying to run a fifty-yard dash underwater. Yes, the runner is moving, but the going is strenuous—certainly not what it could or should be in a robust economic environment.

Today, America's total national debt is on course to exceed total GDP. What does that mean? It means the United States, if officials are not careful, is on course to become another Argentina—a financial system with dramatically declining credibility. To escape this potential calamity, Washington will have no choice but to resort to one of several options.

Option A could involve financing the new debt through tax increases. But because of the sheer size of the debt to be undertaken, taxes as a percent of GDP would need to move from today's 20 percent closer to Europe's 40 percent of GDP. What that means is that Americans would move closer to European-like tax rates without necessarily enjoying European-like government services. That's because much of the increase in U.S. debt is tied to bank bailouts and other measures to save the financial system. And don't forget that the current explosion in government spending does nothing to deal with the coming entitlement nightmare and the likelihood that more spending will be necessary.

Option B could have the Federal Reserve monetize, or devalue, the mountain of debt over a protracted period by letting inflation soar. The Federal Reserve is already toying with such an approach with the purchase of hundreds of millions of dollars of long-term Treasury debt. The danger of this approach, as previously noted, is that any rise in the *expectation* of future inflation would quickly produce further increases in market interest rates, smothering recovery. Be assured financial markets are watching the Federal Reserve's policy actions closely for fear that the long-term results of today's policy actions will be a 1970s-style stagflation.

Option C could have the United States rely even more on foreign capital. In other words, we could continue dealing with a banker. The choices: China, Japan, or both.

Most analysts fixate on China as America's banker because of its mountain of excess savings and recent history of massive U.S. Treasury purchases. Those Treasury purchases now exceed the purchases made by the Japanese. In the future, the United States has no choice but to cement as close a relationship as possible with the Chinese. But Beijing is sitting on a social and political bubble of its own, which appears to be about to burst. If that happens, China could be an unreliable financial partner. As noted in chapter 4, the Chinese are always at risk of being forced to draw massive amounts of its savings out of U.S. financial assets and bring them back home if only to buy off the angry mobs in the streets.

If America is forced to increase its dealings with a global banker, as seems likely, Japan should not be overlooked. Unlike China, Japan is a mature, predictable, structurally stable economy. Japan is sitting on its own mountain of savings in the form of official reserves, private savings, and public pensions, and is potentially open to a win-win deal on the issue of currencies and the purchase of America's debt.

Consider Japan's sorry predicament of the last several years. Tokyo officials have lost control over their soaring currency. The yen has risen dramatically against the dollar, despite the dollar's strengthening against most other world currencies as a result of a global flight to safety into greenbacks at a time of worldwide recession and heightened geopolitical risk. Those once-aggressive Japanese housewives mentioned in chapter 5, major purchasers of foreign bonds, have brought their savings back home as the world slashed interest rates to Japan-like levels in response to the global slowdown. When an economy experiences major capital inflows, the currency generally strengthens. This dramatic surge in the yen's strength has placed the Japanese economy in its own straitjacket. Indeed, the export-dependent Japanese economy has been in serious decline. The collapse of Japanese exports to China hasn't helped matters. To put it simply, Japan is as desperate for currency relief as U.S. officials are for credit relief.

Perhaps not now, but at some point, I predict Washington and Tokyo officials will cobble together a deal. Tokyo agrees to make ample enough additional purchases of U.S. debt and other financial assets to bring sustained downward pressure on U.S. long-term interest rates, or at least to keep rates from rising drastically. This influx of capital would give the United States some breathing room in helping to strengthen the recovery. In return, Washington agrees to a weaker yen against the dollar. Even though such a currency adjustment may seem farfetched, the truth is the yen/dollar exchange rate historically has been influenced by the markets' perception of the U.S. and Japanese governments' comfort level with the currency relationship.

Such a deal would have its complications. U.S. officials would need to prove to Tokyo officials that there are plans in place for America to get its financial house in order. Officials in both countries would have to put together a joint venture to protect American automobile companies from currency risks of their own. A case can be made, however, that a joint international effort is really the only means anyway of achieving advances such as a "next generation" environmentally friendly automobile propulsion system. Today, some of the most promising new technology is in M.I.T.-related technology firms based in the United States. Japanese and German car makers far outspend their U.S. counterparts in research and development. So a joint venture makes sense for a world automotive industry facing huge overcapacity problems.

It may turn out that an influx of both Japanese and Chinese savings to purchase U.S. Treasuries will not be enough to finance America's ballooning debt. No doubt, America's relationships with China and Japan will produce an elaborate thicket of complications. But one thing is certain: Dealing with a banker is better than protracted financial suffocation, or rampant inflation with long-term interest rates returning to high levels not seen in decades and the U.S. economy withering away.

Washington policymakers need to be careful about another form of hubris: The belief that the U.S. economy is an island unto itself where its economic solutions are largely domestically oriented. Indeed, someday historical archaeologists will sift through the rubble of this ugly financial period. They will conclude not only that our regulators were asleep at the wheel, our financial institutions deployed reckless amounts of leverage, and American consumers spent a lot more than they earned.

Historians will discover the international flip side to this morass. While Americans became dependent on leverage and overconsumption, large parts of the world, led by the emerging markets including China and Eastern Europe, became dangerously dependent on exports—either of goods and services or of high-priced oil. This emerging market export model has crashed precisely because the target for those exports, the industrialized economies, has economically deteriorated.

If the world is truly to solve the financial crisis and achieve a new path to prosperity, there needs to be a new economic model for the world economy. Building that model will first require an understanding of the fundamental elements that brought about the great credit catastrophe the world has just experienced. Even today, a mention of the financial crisis draws immediate references to the August 2007 bursting of the U.S. subprime bubble. Actually, the seeds of financial turmoil were planted much earlier—as odd as it sounds, with the 1989 fall of the Berlin Wall. Today's financial crisis began as an unintended consequence of the collapse of the state-run economic model.

Earlier in this book, I noted how emerging market economies including China, India, Eastern Europe, and the commodity producers including Russia, by the early 1990s had burst onto the global scene. All wanted to be like the capitalist industrialized world in one form or another. As they liberated their economies and financial systems, making them more efficient, the resulting new productive capacity led to the aforementioned global ocean of capital sloshing around the world. There was suddenly more money globally than there were investment opportunities.

The rest of the story is well-known—and has an ugly ending. A lot of this capital poured into the U.S. Treasury market. Emerging markets, fixing their currencies to the dollar, became giant export platforms as policymakers spent too little time enhancing the consumption bases of their domestic economies. Emerging markets became obsessed with exporting goods and recycling capital to the industrialized world. The target of choice: gluttonous, debt-ridden Americans. At one point, China had compiled a mountain of foreign exchange reserves, mostly in U.S. dollars, approaching $2 trillion.

As emerging markets recycled their capital back into the United States, Americans took a financial magic carpet ride that ended in catastrophe. This Niagara Falls of foreign capital inflows caused real U.S. interest rates to drop dramatically. This resulting abrupt financial distortion, totally unrecognized at the time by most global policymakers, is fundamentally how the stage was set for financial disaster. With such an overabundance of capital, the price of financial risk plummeted. Underqualified home owners thought they had found Nirvana. Alan Greenspan became the Maestro. Many reckoned he had conquered the business cycle. Of course, no one ever imagined the U.S. economy and financial system would, or could, collapse as it has. Nor did anyone expect overdependence on exports in emerging markets to become one of the world's fundamental Achilles' heels.

Collapsed global trade has been devastating for China. It has plunged Japan's economy into its deepest recession in decades. Europe's economy has also been in deep trouble. What began as a U.S. mortgage crisis mushroomed into a collapse of global demand and trade. The resulting crackup of the emerging market growth model has exposed the world to serious potential protectionism, currency wars, and rampant bank credit defaults.

Europe's vulnerability to this growth model crack-up is particularly significant. There is a word in German—schadenfreude—which means to experience pleasure at the misery of others. For the first year of the financial crisis, Europeans developed a case of schadenfreude toward America. Americans were the poor, reckless souls mired in a financial crisis of their own making. Some Europeans seemed delighted as they publicly scolded U.S. officials for financial wrongdoing. Not anymore. As the global economy and trade collapsed, it turned out the Europeans were in more trouble than America.

Here's the European situation in a nutshell: As the world's emerging markets continued to deteriorate, the European banks became highly vulnerable to failure. That is because the European banks are massively exposed to emerging market bank defaults, with a lot of their risk centered in the former Soviet-bloc economies of Eastern Europe. Overall, European bank exposure is at least three times U.S. bank exposure to subprime defaults. Austria's bank exposure to Eastern Europe, for example, is a whopping $290 billion; Austria's GDP is only $370 billion. As the Eastern European economies have collapsed, policymakers are resorting to protectionism and currency devaluations against the euro. In sum, European banks have been the major world financier of the emerging market growth mode. With that model cracking up, few European bankers these days are sleeping soundly.

Here's more disappointing news. The Europeans lack the financial heft to handle the problem of major bank loan defaults. Euro-zone bank assets are an incredible 330 percent of GDP. By contrast, U.S. bank assets are only 85 percent of GDP. And it is not that the Europeans can easily raise taxes to finance big bank bailouts. In Europe, taxes are already over 40 percent of GDP. In the United States, taxes have been 20 percent of GDP, but are rising in part to pay for the bailout of American banks.

And why should any of this concern Americans? The global financial system is interconnected. A major European bank collapse would wreak havoc with a U.S. financial system already on life support. Look at the catastrophic global consequences when Lehman Brothers collapsed. Growing European social unrest could also finally kill off a global trading system hanging by a thread.

It is important to remember that this emerging market export model is not something invented by policymakers. It is a model the world fell into by the force of a historic event: the fall of the Berlin Wall. The model needs to be rethought. We need a comprehensive and interactive global financial doctrine. Industrialized world leaders, continually fixated on domestic concerns, need to think more globally. They need to answer this question: Can we truly solve the financial crisis and achieve a new path to prosperity without first laying down the fundamentals of the new, global economic model? Clearly the previous model of huge imbalances, abrupt savings shifts, overconsumption, and overdependence on export expansion, is fraught with peril.

Yet market analysts still ask all the questions that would suggest that model remains intact: "Will the U.S. consumer step forward once again to serve as the world's locomotive? Will export growth in emerging markets begin to pick up?" It is like we are living the movie *Groundhog Day*. We hope that every morning the alarm clock goes off and we can once again relive the risky policies of the past. Repeating those policies would be insane, not to mention catastrophic. As it comes out of recession, America needs a long-term strategy to correct its imbalances—to consume, save, and invest with greater balance. Emerging market economies and, indeed, the rest of the world have no choice but to implement policies that promote domestic demand. A replay of the current system, if allowed to continue over the next several decades, would be the height of idiocy.

Indeed, the world has entered a new era of deglobalization. It is hardly news that the global trading system has seriously stumbled. What is striking are the growing signs that global trade could continue to shrink regardless of the strength of the world economy.

Here's one reason: The cost of shipping is about to rise dramatically. In October, 2008 the United Nations' International Maritime Organization reached an agreement that ships must cut sulfur emissions. Ships are currently allowed to burn 4.5 percent sulfur oil, but by 2020 will be forced to burn only 0.1 percent sulfur oil, a dramatic reduction.

Here's the problem. Many, if not most, of the world's refiners will likely not make the investments in scrubbers and other measures that would allow them to comply with these standards. The reason for this reluctance is that the cost to upgrade refineries would be in the hundreds of billions of dollars. Lacking the resources to make such an investment, many refiners won't be able to continue supplying fuel to the shipping industry. As a result, the cost of fuel for ships is expected to rise astronomically over the next decade. This situation is similar to the rise in diesel prices in 2008, which contributed overwhelmingly to the soaring global price of oil. The difference is that the rise in the price of oil for ships is likely to have a far larger impact on the broader oil price.

This move to limit greenhouse gas emissions is expected to lead to a dramatic reduction in shipping. Indeed, it may eventually only be profitable to move high value-to-weight items, such as laptops, by sea. The net impact is that many of the low wage jobs that moved to China and India may gradually move back to the United States and Eastern Europe, but at much higher wages. Some analysts are betting that even the furniture, clothing, and shoe industries could move back to the United States and Europe, but with these products coming at far higher prices.

There is one other development which is likely to prove complicated for policymakers over the next decade: Oil is replacing gold as a store of value. As energy expert Philip Veleger, Jr. has noted, investors in the months after the 2008 failure of the Wall Street firm Lehman Bros. began pouring large amounts of investment capital into the oil markets. This cash flow is reflected in today's increase in oil inventories, which are approaching record levels.

Borrowing at record low interest rates, various global trading companies have bought oil futures, earning returns in excess of 20 percent. Indeed, many of the large U.S. banks are in the position in which, should they desire, they can borrow from the Federal Reserve at next to nothing and purchase oil futures, betting that the oil price will go higher. The fact that the markets are aware of this potential has already produced a record increase in global oil inventories. In effect, as Verleger argues, the dramatic reductions in short-term interest rates by the global central banking community to deal with the financial crisis has "bailed out" OPEC, which had been cash-starved as a result of the global recession.

So the upshot is that global commodities (led by oil) are quickly becoming a store of value for the global financial system. This higher priced commodities scenario is unfolding at a time when global trade is potentially on course to continue either to contract or to grow at much more modest rates. And the soaring cost of shipping will accelerate this slowdown. It is difficult not to conclude, moreover, that the collapse in trade will potentially open the door for heightened geopolitical risk as nations in coming years struggle to elbow each other out of the way to gain strategic advantage.

As they confront the collapse of the U.S. economic and financial systems, Washington policymakers are about to discover the great irony of America's particular crisis. If they are wise, they will quickly undergo a transition in their economic thinking. Instead of bemoaning the reckless financial risk-taking that brought the world to the edge of Armageddon, policymakers will be forced to confront an ugly new reality: We have moved from a world of excessive financial risk-taking to a situation that may be even more dangerous—no financial risk-taking. Our innovative risk-taking sector, in particular, has largely shut down.

None of this is to suggest the American economy, as is, won't continue gradually to improve after an extended slump. What I'm talking about is the loss of the fundamental spark of creative entrepreneurial daring that keeps an economy, globally speaking, at the cutting edge—with explosive job creation.

Listening to the current economic debate, there is a strange misperception that the workings of the economy have all the precision of a giant, static machine. Increase government spending by a certain amount and a "multiplier effect" ripples through the economy (get this) not by 1.5 times the size of the spending, but by 1.6 times, the economists guarantee. Presto: out of such precision pops exactly 3.5 million new or saved jobs.

Actually, our economy is more like a highly dynamic, unpredictable, living organism. As noted in chapter 3, for decades roughly 7 million U.S. jobs have disappeared every three months while about the same amount or more were created.

There is something troubling about today's economic discussion that still seems to envision the old system in which corporations and their elite handlers work a system of controls to maintain relative stability. Over the past two decades, just the opposite has been the case. More than ever, large corporations have been threatened with permanent obsolescence by a risk-taking entrepreneurial class of individuals, who themselves, constantly face the possibility of failure. That, again, is why of the top 100 companies on the 2005 Fortune 500 List, nearly three-quarters did not appear on the list as late as 1980.

The question is whether policymakers, influenced by the new politics of envy and class warfare, continue to encourage or even tolerate an entrepreneurial class set apart from the rest of society that, frankly speaking, sometimes earns incredible sums of money. Once again, society faces a dilemma. On the one hand, we see the image of greedy Wall Street bankers using their taxpayer bailout money to distribute millions of dollars in bonuses. This is part of a broader political system that has tolerated the successful wealth-creating machine called globalization that nonetheless often distributes the wealth unequally. On the other hand, American culture celebrates the innovative pioneer, the entrepreneurial genius, who capitalizes on a bold idea, builds a company and brings that idea to market, and creates tens of thousands of exciting, new jobs. And, in the process, becomes fabulously rich. As a society, is it wise to shoot ourselves in the foot to soothe a populist impulse to punish the wealthy that does nothing to put people back to work?

There is also the question of how we finance initial entrepreneurial risk-taking. Washington policymakers seem to have not yet found a responsible fiscal formula that deals with the irresponsible bankers and crooks like Bernie Madoff—and the collapse in demand—without risking the creation of huge disincentives for society's risk-taking sector. And be assured, the demise of that sector would warm the hearts of America's competitors around the world.

Over the next several years, we will face the unintended consequences of our new economy of government guarantees and huge subsidies to those financial institutions considered too big to fail. In the financing of risk, this new financial system by definition has no choice but to favor the large, the established, and the politically connected at the expense of the small and the new. And as President Barack Obama himself has pointed out, the small and the new "are responsible for half of all private sector jobs and roughly 70 percent of all new jobs in the past decade," though the administration needs to do more to create an environment conducive to business start-ups.

Earlier in this book, I make reference to Warren Buffett. I can't help but wonder how one of the world's greatest investors views the current situation. He has spent the last several years negotiating his Berkshire Hathaway investment giant past a series of potentially lethal landmines. Like other highly rated U.S. companies, Berkshire Hathaway currently pays between 6 and 7 percent for credit, an interest rate that has actually moved higher as a result of Buffett's company having to confront enormous challenges to the broader insurance industry.

Yet Buffett and the other leaders of top-rated, well-managed corporations (whose balance sheets accurately reflect reality) must be frustrated to look around and discover that the too big to fail bankers (who lost control of any understanding of their balance sheets), can now borrow at a government subsidized interest rate of only 2.9 percent.

But Buffett can be consoled by at least one thing: the future Steve Jobses of the world—our innovators—assuming they can even get credit, are paying 12 percent for money. This is a foolhardy way to run a financial system. The talented job-creating risk-takers pay four times the rate to borrow capital than our failed but "too big to fail" politically connected bankers. In other words, the guys who were stupid and sneaky receive protection and lower, subsidized interest rates. The guys who played by the rules and succeeded honestly face tougher financial sledding. If a newspaper headline had to define the upshot of today's climate of financial bailouts and subsidies, it might read: "Silicon Valley Start-ups Lose Big to General Electric and Citigroup."

Today's high cost of, or lack of, credit is debilitating America's entrepreneurial sector. The high cost of working capital is therefore removing the sweet spot of growth in our economy. Not long ago, for a great idea potentially worth billions if brought to market, financing was readily available. That is no longer always the case. Today we reward failure while retarding the risk-takers' efforts to monetize their ideas and realize their dreams. The danger today is that an innovator can't find venture capital funding. That's because in today's system, where Washington has become the financial capital of the United States, everyone knows the innovator will never be able to complete his/her financing by launching an Initial Public Offering. So why even provide the innovator the initial funding? It sounds like a rich man's problem, but this lack of funding for business start-ups could keep the U.S. unemployment rate stubbornly high for many years.

America has traditionally been the center of the global financing of entrepreneurial risk. The world's innovators were drawn to the United States because of its ample capital markets and reliable patent system. Not anymore. The United States, in losing its status as the world's financier of innovative risk-taking (and thus explosive job creation), puts itself in a position of significant long-term economic peril.

Consider just one startling scenario: How would Americans react if one of China's sovereign wealth funds, with its mountain of excess savings, suddenly surprised the world by setting up a $25 billion special bank account to finance global entrepreneurial ventures? Of course, all participants receiving funding would be required to set up an office in Beijing or Shanghai so that China can work as a "partner" in nurturing this creative process. Americans would react, I suspect, the same way they did in the 1950s when the Soviet Union launched the Sputnik satellite. They would be both shocked and fearful about the future. This gut sense of American vulnerability to global change is why, I believe, so many in their initial responses to my New Canada story missed the joke. They recognize that the United States truly is at risk of losing its global competitive edge.

Sadly, Washington policymakers seem oblivious to the key role of entrepreneurial creativity and risk. Bill Bradley, the former Democratic Senator from New Jersey, argues that the Obama administration's recovery package should have offered more to encourage new business start-ups. He proposed that $10 billion of the funds of the president's first stimulus package (slightly more than one percent of the $800 billion plan) be used to buy 50 percent of the initial public offering of every company that filed a legitimate S-1 registration with the Securities and Exchange Commission prior to the enactment of the stimulus. The proposal received little reception.

Bradley's idea was based on the notion that the secret to achieving economic recovery entails more than injections of government money into *existing* businesses and banks. The secret is creativity, allowing new firms with new ideas to rise up, while existing firms work every day to reinvent themselves to compete on a global scale. The secret lies in the enterprises yet unborn and inventions yet untried.

As discussed in chapter 3, it is important to remember that the birth or reinvention of an enterprise involves an elusive, almost metaphysical quality that is unpredictable. Targeting and planning is difficult. You can bet that President Obama's efforts to find a source of renewable energy will not involve Exxon or any other large energy firm's research departments. Instead, some brilliant inventor, having quit her job and working in her garage, will likely discover the breakthrough.

In politics, as in war, history is written by the victors. The Clinton economy of the 1990s, therefore, has become passé. Yet one of the remarkable things about Bill Clinton was his rejection of the demagoguery of class warfare and embracing of the entrepreneurial risk-taker as authentic American hero, whether it was Henry Ford, Steve Jobs, or Bill Gates.

Over time, Barack Obama will arrive at the same place. But it would be far better were he to discover the powerful genius of the American innovative dynamic now, when it could help put the economy on a higher plane of recovery.

People secretly yearn to join the mythical New Canada because they sense that America's problems are beyond human understanding. The complexity of global financial markets and the speed of their unraveling serve as powerful reminders that Americans may have lost control of their financial destiny. Members of Congress, after virtually no hearings, have been asked to vote on bank bailout legislation worth trillions of dollars—amounts that may set America on course to longer-term economic sluggishness.

The public yearns for a transparent explanation of our financial woes, but is offered instead a vague language of fear about the need for action to avoid "systemic risk." Allowing a large bank to fail would, Washington warns, subject the entire global financial system to collapse. A mysterious web of financial paper—including the insurance product called credit default swaps—has quickly become our financial system's new master. The banks can't be restructured like failed corporate entities would because these insurance contracts are sacred. If we forced the unraveling of the web of securitized paper and other derivative products, the entire world financial system could collapse—or not, our policymakers tell us. The truth is that nobody knows for sure. We sometimes don't even know the identity of the counterparties on the other side of these insurance products that have cost American taxpayers tens of billions of dollars here, tens of billions there, in regular, middle-of-the-night emergency capital injections. What we do know is that the credit default swap market and other derivative-based financial products, some of which are owned by foreign banks, could end up bankrupting America.

Even though the market for these complex paper instruments has stabilized some, there are no guarantees about the future. We need to form a special commission chaired by a world class problem-solver who is not from Wall Street. This individual needs to pull together the best global specialists in financial engineering. The goal: to unshackle the global economy from this complex web of financial control, differentiating between financial instruments used in the legitimate course of business versus the use of these unregulated instruments in a giant speculative game for profit. The U.S. and European authorities are fixated on devising a future regulatory structure. But that exercise concentrates on prohibiting financial problems in the future. Policymakers also need to think about how to handle the trillions of dollars of existing financial paper of questionable value. That includes developing a global plan of burden sharing while the market for these paper financial instruments is reformed and made more transparent, even as the instruments considered toxic are repriced.

People yearn to be part of the mythical New Canada for one other reason: They know that as a nation, if Americans truly look inward at their cultural and ethical value structure, they won't like what they see. In March 2009, the *New York Times* reported that U.S. business schools are tripping over themselves to restore an emphasis on relevance and leadership in their curriculums—that is, they are urging their students to consider that social relevance to society is a long-term driver of prosperity. The dean of the Harvard Business School, Jay O. Light, perhaps put it best when he said: "We lived through an enormous exploding period of financial good times, and people became less focused on risks and risk management, and more focused on making money. We need to move that focus back toward the center."

If it is to remain on top, America desperately needs to rediscover the fundamental underpinnings of its value structure. The motives of our bankers in hiding dangerous off-balance-sheet risk were nearly criminal. But was it any different than a Democratic Congress passing billions in secret, middle of the night earmark spending? Or Republican congressional leaders talking of fiscal responsibility while themselves spending like drunken sailors? To a certain extent, we are all under the cloud of a Bernie Madoff mentality that has led America on a selfish detour away from a collective effort to achieve a destiny of greatness.

Our bankers are no different than our drug companies that subtly manipulate their research and product offerings for stock market gain. Nor are they different from the fiefdom of the teachers' unions that has made public education the latest, too big to fail institutional dinosaur in danger of collapsing under its own weight. How different are our bankers from Washington's army of special interest policy manipulators? These are the folks who are capable of virtually anything in their scramble to divide up the multibillion dollar pie of lobbying fees, PR contracts, high cable TV ratings and the speech income they provide. Then there are the policy sycophants capable of doing anything to achieve the intoxicating feeling of being close to power. Instead of serving as the policy center for productive change, Washington has become a fierce partisan battleground for reckless personal gain. The product of today's infighting is often about as relevant to the lives of average working Americans as a fight between the Elks Club and the Kiwanis. Yet this fruitless contest rolls on even as America's fundamental problems remain dangerously unaddressed.

In their hearts, people yearn to be citizens of the mythical New Canada based on a fear that at its core America can't be fixed. Despite all of Washington's showcasing of reform efforts, the problems are too complicated and entrenched. America's intangible spirit of greatness, goodness, openness, and integrity—the spirit of magnanimity and sacrifice that led to battlefield victory—is now lost. It may never return unless someone is willing to step forward, pull the country together, and prove the would-be citizens of New Canada wrong. But the clock is ticking.

Acknowledgments

It would be difficult not to acknowledge first my agent, Fredi Friedman. Long before the outbreak of the subprime crisis, her cunning eye caught the potential importance of this project and her guiding light has been essential. Jeffrey Krames and Adrian Zackheim of the Penguin Group's Portfolio division enjoy the same predictive abilities and offered an amazing array of astute advice. Jeffrey offered superb editorial direction, as did Nancy Cardwell.

I am grateful for—indeed humbled by—the depth of commitment of so many friends to this effort. Harry Truman was wrong when he said, "If you want a friend in Washington, get a dog." Adam Posen of the Peterson Institute for International Economics read the manuscript twice and offered invaluable suggestions for improvement. Dino Kos, formerly of the New York Federal Reserve, offered similar insights and encouragement, at one point in the midst of the subprime crisis e-mailing from Hong Kong: "Get that book out fast; the world's falling apart." Stefan Schönberg, the Bundesbank's former top international monetary specialist, offered essential nuanced advice. Columnist Robert Novak, an early enthusiast, convinced me to reveal more of myself in the manuscript. This explains the numerous personal anecdotes about my global travels.

Bob Merry, who heads up *The Congressional Quarterly*, read an early speech I gave to a college group about coming international financial dangers and recommended I write a book. John and Gina Despres, my old friends from our Bill Bradley days, provided advice, as did former U.S. Treasury officials Marc Leland, Richard Clarida, Peter Fisher, and Charles Dallara. Dallara was particularly generous with his time and provided insights in a number of key areas.

Tadashi Nakamae offered valuable suggestions for shaping the discussion on Japan. Phil Hildebrand of the Swiss central bank and financial expert Harald Malmgren both offered advice on the topic of global financial architecture. Former IRS commissioner Fred Goldberg offered cutting-edge comments on the U.S. fiscal policy discussion. And Adam Walinsky, formerly of Bobby Kennedy fame, urged me to emphasize more compellingly the economic anxiety of the 1970s.

John Mueller offered his insights on the nature of human capital. Mel Kraus provided comments about the chapter on hedge funds. Stan Druckenmiller, probably the leading financial market trader of his generation, noted several important points. And my business partner, Manley Johnson, was extraordinarily encouraging from day one, offering numerous useful insights as well.

Bill Schulz read the manuscript and offered invaluable stylistic advice, as did Matt Rees and James Freeman. Jeff Bell and Robin West early in the project offered useful encouragement. Rob Shapiro, Curtis Hoxter, Wim Kooyker, Steve Moore, John Kester, Bruce Bartlett, Mike Anderson, Gerd Haüsler, Fred Barnes, Joe Sprung, Lew Eisenberg, Pete Skirkanich, Guy Snowden, and Jeff Zimmer all read the manuscript and offered suggestions and encouragement. Early on, my brother Tim offered a useful layman's response to my approach to the subject, as did my mother, Terry, and my aunt Jane.

As every financial trader knows, nothing happens without an effective back office. Angela Wilkes, managing editor of *The International Economy*, offered both editorial and fact-checking help beyond the call.

Acknowledgments • 297

Josef Neusser lent a useful logistical hand. And last but certainly not least, Jean Holz offered a Herculean effort both in preparing a myriad of manuscript drafts while offering editorial suggestions. She approached the project with cheerful enthusiasm.

I have been blessed with an extraordinarily close family. My older son, Peter, and daughter, Sarah, both in New York, offered helpful editorial suggestions. My younger son, DJ, still at home in school, paid the price with a father temporarily preoccupied.

And, of course, there is no way to express adequately the importance of my wife, Vickie, to this effort. She inspired me to write the book, then willingly became the "author's widow," all the while offering advice and encouragement.

A Word on Sources

In writing *The World Is Curved*, I have drawn on, and been influenced by, a broad array of sources. To begin, in my more than twenty years of providing editorial direction to *The International Economy* magazine, literally hundreds of scholars, policymakers, and journalists, in presenting their views, have influenced my thinking. Articles written since 2002 are available on the magazine's Web site: http://www. international-economy.com.

Although I have drawn on a variety of publicly available sources, some of the book's discussions reflect my personal experiences and conversations on the trading floors of a number of financial institutions, and with politicians and policymakers worldwide.

In the case of chapter 6, my descriptions of the events surrounding the 1992 sterling crisis are based on personal notes I took at the time, later confirmed for the book by several former policy officials who were intimately involved in the drama.

I drew from various articles and studies, including "Is Globalization Today Really Different than Globalization a Hundred Years Ago?" by Barry Eichengreen and Michael Bordo, National Bureau of Economic

Research (1999); Federal Reserve Statistical Release on "Flow of Funds Accounts" (3rd quarter 2006, 2nd quarter 2007); BEA GNP Release (4th quarter 2006); McKinsey Global Institute Financial Stock Database (12/11/07); Leto Market Insight (12/27/06); "Good Government" by Matthew Rees, *The American* (January–February 2007); "The Payoff to America from Global Integration" by Scott C. Bradford and Gary Clyde Hufbauer, Peterson Institute for International Economics (6/7/05); "The Payoff from Globalization" by Gary Clyde Hufbauer and Paul Grieco, *Washington Post* op-ed (6/7/05); "Meeting the Challenge of Sovereign Wealth Funds" by Edwin M. Truman, *Handelsblatt* (9/18/07); "Blinder Baloney" by William T. Dickens and Stephen J. Rose, *The International Economy* (Fall 2007); "Ownership and Control in Outsourcing to China: Estimating the Property-Rights Theory of the Firm" by Robert C. Feenstra and Gordon H. Hanson, National Bureau of Economic Research (November 2003); "Can America Still Compete or Does It Need a New Trade Paradigm?" by Martin Neil Baily and Robert Z. Lawrence, Peterson Institute for International Economics (December 2006); "The New Power Brokers" by Diana Farrell and Susan Lund, *The International Economy* (Winter 2008); Congressional Budget Office Analysis (Fiscal Year 2007); Federal Reserve Board, "Flow of Funds Accounts" (1946–2004); "Revenues, Outlay, Deficits, Surplus and Debt Held by the Public 1962–2005," Congressional Budget Office; "Time Series Data of International Reserves/Foreign Currency Liquidity, for the United States (through 1/12/07)," International Monetary Fund; "Foreign Exchange: Policy, Monetary Policy and Capital Market Liberalization in Korea" by Jeffrey A. Frankel (9/3/92); Merrill Lynch "World Wealth Report, 2007"; a speech by U.S. deputy Treasury secretary Robert M. Kimmitt (2/2/07); *Where Is the Wealth of Nations?*, World Bank Conference Report, Washington, D.C. (2006); "Alternative Investments and Private Equity: Lessons from American Experience" by Malmgren Global LLC (March 1999); "Pension Reforms in America and Possible Lessons for Japan" by Malmgren Global LLC (September 1998); "China, Average Percent Change in GDP, World

Economic Outlook Database," the International Monetary Fund (October 2007); Bank of China IPO Perspectus (2007); interview with Charles Dallara, Institute for International Finance, *The International Economy* (Fall 2007); "New Investor Accounts in China," *Bloomberg* (6/13/07); "China: Toward a Consumption-Driven Growth Path" by Nicholas R. Lardy, Peterson Institute for International Economics (October 2006); "In China's Shadow: The Crisis of American Entrepreneurship" by Reed Hundt, *The American* (12/5/06); "Weak Yen Conundrum" by Tadashi Nakamae, *The International Economy* (Winter 2007); "The Asset Price Bubble and Monetary Policy: Japan's Experience in the Late 1980s and the Lessons" by Kunio Okina, Masaak Shirakawa, and Shigenori Shiratsuka, Bank of Japan (February 2001); "Household Saving Rates," OECD Economic Outlook (1990 to 2009); "Japanese Household Income" by Nakamae International Economic Research (December 2006); "Japan to the Rescue" by David Hale, *The International Economy* (July–August 1989); "Europe's Italy Problem" by Bernard Connolly, *The International Economy* (Spring 2005); "Economic Growth and Performance," OECD (2006–2007 edition); speeches by Federal Reserve chairman Alan Greenspan (12/5/96, 3/17/08); "Economic Letter," the Federal Reserve Bank of San Francisco (12/3/04); "Equity Ownership in America" by the Investment Company Institute and the Securities Industry Association (2005); 1993 and 1994 State of the Union addresses by Bill Clinton; "Recent Trends in Household Wealth in the United States: Rising Debt and the Middle-Class Squeeze" by Edward N. Wolff, Levy Economics Institute (June 2007); "Average Household Assets and Liabilities by Wealth Class, 1962–2004" by the Economic Policy Institute's *State of Working America* (2006–2007); "Poverty Thresholds 2007," U.S. Census Bureau; "Growth of HNW and UHNW Segments," a 2007 Morgan Stanley report based on McKinsey and Federal Reserve research; testimony by Federal Reserve chairman Ben S. Bernanke (9/20/07); "Global Market Commentary" by Malmgren Global LLC (2/7/08); "Has Globalization Passed Its Peak?" by Rani Abdelal and Adam Segal, *Foreign Affairs* (January–February 2007).

Bibliography

In this effort, I have quoted from, been influenced by, or reflected on a number of books and authors on the subjects of globalization, the financial markets, and monetary policy. These include:

Baldwin, Robert, and Alan Winters (eds.). *Challenges to Globalization: Analyzing the Economics.* Cambridge, Mass.: National Bureau of Economic Research Conference Report, 2004.

Bartley, Robert L. *The Seven Fat Years.* New York: Free Press, 1992.

Bhagwati, Jagdish N. *In Defense of Globalization.* New York: Oxford University Press, 2004.

Cannon, Lou. *President Reagan: The Role of a Lifetime.* New York: Public Affairs, 1991.

Clarida, Richard H. (ed.). *G7 Current Account Imbalances: Sustainability and Adjustment.* Chicago: University of Chicago Press, 2007.

Clinton, Bill. *Between Hope and History: Meeting America's Challenges for the 21st Century.* New York: Times Books, Random House, 1996.

Emmott, Bill. *20/21 Vision: Twentieth-Century Lessons for the Twenty-first Century.* New York: Farrar, Straus and Giroux, 2003.

Evans, Harold. *They Made America: From Steam Engine to the Search Engine: Two Centuries of Innovators.* New York: Little, Brown, 2004.

Fergusson, Niall. *Empire: The Rise and Demise of the British World Order and the Lessons for Global Power.* New York: Basic Books, 2003.

Friedman, Thomas L. *The World Is Flat: A Brief History of the Twenty-first Century,* New York: Farrar, Straus and Giroux, 2005.

Greenspan, Alan. *The Age of Turbulence: Adventures in a New World*. New York: Penguin Press, 2007.

Greider, William. *One World, Ready or Not*. New York: Simon & Schuster, 1997.

Hayek, F. A. *The Road to Serfdom* (50th anniversary ed.). With an introduction by Milton Friedman. Chicago: University of Chicago Press, 1994.

Hormats, Robert D. *The Price of Liberty: Paying for America's Wars from the Revolution to the War on Terror*. New York: Henry Holt, 2007.

Hufbauer, Gary, and Wendy Dobson. *World of Capital Markets: Challenge to the G-10*. Washington, D.C.: Peterson Institute for International Economics, 2001.

Huntington, Samuel P. *The Clash of Civilizations: Remaking of World Order*. New York: Simon & Schuster, 1996.

Hutton, Will. *The Writing on the Wall: Why We Must Embrace China as a Partner or Face It as an Enemy*. New York: Free Press, 2006.

Irwin, Douglas A. *Against the Tide*. Princeton, N.J.: Princeton University Press, 1996.

James, Harold. *The End of Globalization: Lessons from the Great Depression*. Cambridge, Mass.: Harvard University Press, 2001.

Keynes, John Maynard. *The General Theory of Employment, Interest and Money*. San Diego: Harcourt Brace Jovanovich, 1965.

Kindleberger, Charles P., and Robert Aliber. *Manias, Panics, and Crashes: A History of Financial Crises*. Hoboken, N.J.: Wiley Investment Classics, 2000.

Krugman, Paul R. *The Return of Depression Economics*. New York: Penguin Books, 2000.

Larsson, Tomas. *The Race to the Top: The Real Story of Globalization*. Washington, D.C.: Cato Institute, 2001.

Lawrence, Robert Z. *Blue-Collar Blues: Is Trade to Blame for Rising US Income Inequality?* Washington, D.C.: Peterson Institute for International Economics, 2008.

Lindsey, Lawrence B. *Economic Puppetmasters*. Washington, D.C.: AEI Press, 1999.

Maddison, Angus. *Contours of the World Economy 1–2030 AD: Essays in Macro-Economic History*. Paris: Organisation for Economic Co-operation & Development, 2003.

Mann, Catherine L. *Accelerating the Globalization of America: The Role for Information Technology*. Washington, D.C.: Institute for International Economics, 2006.

Mishkin, Frederic S. *The Next Great Globalization: How Disadvantaged Nations Can Harness Their Financial Systems to Get Rich*. Princeton, N.J.: Princeton University Press, 2006.

Norberg, Johan. *In Defense of Global Capitalism*. Washington, D.C.: Cato Institute, 2003.

Rajan, Raghuram G., and Luigi Zingales. *Saving Capitalism from the Capitalists: Unleashing the Power of Financial Markets to Create Wealth and Spread Opportunity*. New York: Crown Business, 2003.

Sachs, Jeffrey D. *The End of Poverty: Economic Possibilities for Our Time*. New York: Penguin Books, 2005.

Soros, George. *George Soros on Globalization*. New York: Public Affairs, 2002.

Stiglitz, Joseph E. *Globalization and Its Discontents*. New York: W. W. Norton, 2002.

———. *Making Globalization Work*. New York: W. W. Norton, 2006.

Tapscott, Don, and Anthony Williams. *Wikinomics: How Mass Collaboration Changes Everything*. New York: Portfolio, 2006.
Wolf, Martin. *Why Globalization Works*. New Haven, Conn.: Yale University Press, 2004.
Yergin, Daniel, and Joseph Stanislaw. *The Commanding Heights: The Battle Between Government & the Marketplace That Is Remaking the Modern World*. New York: Simon & Schuster, 2002.

It is virtually certain that some sources that have broadly influenced my thinking over the years have undoubtedly slipped through the cracks. For this likely omission, I extend my apologies.

Index

confidence/trust
in asset-backed securities,
245
and beginning of
globalization, 45
and benefits and
disadvantages of
globalization, 64
crisis of, 45, 245, 249–50
and Fed purchase of U.S.
Treasury securities, 210
and future of global
economy, 23
in government, 216
and liquidity, 22–23
loss of investor, 236
need for greater, 249–50,
269, 270
in 1970s, 216
in 1980s and 1990s, 217
in pre-World War II
era, 266
and protectionism, 29
and reform of global
economy, 261, 269, 270
and risk, 23
role of, 22–25
and savings and loan
crisis, 269
and securitization, 45
and stock market crash
(1987), 24–25
and subprime crisis,
245–46
in U.S. economy, 233,
274, 277
and U.S. role in global
economy, 269
and viability of global
system, 59
and vulnerability of global
economy, 29–30
Congress, U.S.
antiglobalization in, 25
and beginning of
globalization, 42, 45, 46
and confidence in global
economy, 29–30
and credit-ratings
agencies, 260
and foreign investment in
U.S., 30, 61
and future of U.S.
economy, 275, 292, 293
and politics of
globalization, 220
and reform of financial
system, 253, 257

and regulation of
mortgage lending, 204
Sarbanes-Oxley passage
by, 89
and securitization, 45, 46
and taxes, 234, 236, 244
and trade, 220
Turner testimony before,
83–84
and vulnerability of global
economy, 31–32
Congressional Summits on
the Dollar and Trade,
U.S., 8, 141
consumption
and future of U.S.
economy, 276–77,
282, 283
and reform of global
economy, 283, 285
retrenchment of, 276–77
and wealth effect, 194
See also specific nation or
continent
contagion effect, 206
conventional wisdom, 94–95
corporate bond bubble, 278
corporations
as American export
machine, 112
bloated, inefficient, 74
bonds of, 98, 278
and class warfare, 225, 236
and comparison of old
system and global
economy, 20
continuous reinvention of,
82–83, 91
executive compensation in,
87, 220, 257
and financial services
industry, 251
and future of U.S.
economy, 288
governance of, 87, 89–90
greed of, 87
management quality of, 54
in 1970s, 216
obsolescence of, 288
and politics of
globalization, 218, 234
populist discontent with, 27
productivity of, 202
profitability of, 251–52
and reform of financial
system, 253, 278, 288
restructuring and
downsizing of, 20, 226

takeovers of, 24
and taxes, 231
taxes on, 234, 236
See also specific corporation
or nation
Corrigan, Gerald, 259
Council of Economic
Advisers, White House,
197
credibility, 50, 51, 56–57, 58,
164, 165, 168, 170, 171,
179, 195–96, 279
credit
allocation of, 76
and beginning of
globalization, 46
and benefits and
disadvantages of
globalization, 17
and central banks, 249–50,
251
contraction in, 251
and Credit Crisis of
2007–2008, 12
difficulty of fixing crisis
in, 249
expansion of, 265
and Fed purchase of U.S.
Treasury securities,
208–9
and Federal Reserve, 200,
205
and future of global
economy, 22, 278–79,
282
and future of U.S.
economy, 279, 281,
288–90
importance of, 253
and liquidity concerns, 23
and need for change in
views of policymakers,
238–45
and politics of
globalization, 236
in pre-World War II
era, 266
and private equity
funds, 73
and problems of financial
services industry, 250
and regulation, 248–49
restrictions on, 250–51
and securitization, 46
and slowdown of global
economy, 253
and subprime crisis,
238–46